ISBN 978-1-334-46639-7
PIBN 10558643

1 MONTH OF
FREE
READING

at

www.ForgottenBooks.com

By purchasing this book you are eligible for one month membership to ForgottenBooks.com, giving you unlimited access to our entire collection of over 700,000 titles via our web site and mobile apps.

To claim your free month visit:

www.forgottenbooks.com/free558643

English
Français
Deutsche
Italiano
Español
Português

www.forgottenbooks.com

Mythology Photography **Fiction**
Fishing Christianity **Art** Cooking
Essays Buddhism Freemasonry
Medicine **Biology** Music **Ancient
Egypt** Evolution Carpentry Physics
Dance Geology **Mathematics** Fitness
Shakespeare **Folklore** Yoga Marketing
Confidence Immortality Biographies
Poetry **Psychology** Witchcraft
Electronics Chemistry History **Law**
Accounting **Philosophy** Anthropology
Alchemy Drama Quantum Mechanics
Atheism Sexual Health **Ancient History**
Entrepreneurship Languages Sport
Paleontology Needlework Islam
Metaphysics Investment Archaeology
Parenting Statistics Criminology
Motivational

THE LABOURER;

A

MONTHLY MAGAZINE

OF

POLITICS, LITERATURE, POETRY, &c.

E D I T E D

BY

FEARGUS O'CONNOR Esq., M.P.. & ERNEST JONES, Esq.

(BARRISTERS-AT-LAW.)

VOL. II.

LONDON:

NORTHERN STAR OFFICE, GREAT WINDMILL STREET;

MANCHESTER:

ABEL HEYWOOD, OLDHAM-STREET.

—

1847.

CONTENTS OF VOL. II.

THE LABOURER

ONWARD.

BY ERNEST JONES

Who bids us backward—laggards, stay !
As soon wave back the light of day !
We have not marched so long a way
To yield at last, like craven things,
To worn-out nobles, priests, and kings.

Go bid the eagle clip its wing !
Go bid the tempest cease to sing,
And streams to burst, and tides to spring ;
And, should they listen to your call,
We'll onward still, and face you all !

Oh ! we have battled long and true ;
While you were many, we were few,
And stronger chains we've broken through:
Think not *your* paltry silken bands
Can bind Progression's giant hands.

Go stay the earthquake in the rock,
Go quench the hot volcano's shock,
And fast the foaming cataract lock:
Ye cannot build the walls to hold
A daring heart and spirit bold.

Forbid the flowery mould to bloom,
Where years have scathed a tyrant's tomb,
And tell us slavery is our doom:
E'en as the peaceful march of time
Moulders the rampart's stony prime,
So calm Progression's steady sway
Shall sap and sweep your power away;

THE CHANGE..

Oh ! bright was her light sunny hair,
　And bright was her innocent face,
And her voice, it was melody rare,
　And her form the perfection of grace.

And pure was her young maiden heart,
　And void was her spirit of guile,
But a world of love's magical art
　Was enshrined in her beautiful smile.

It wiled you—it snared you—it won you,
　And when you were lost in its lure,
And when it had caught and undone you,
　A frown would replace it, be sure.

And thus she went, smiling and wiling,
　A light-hearted bird amid flowers,
Till one day—to Cupid's beguiling,
　Her sunshine was changed into showers

Oh ! beautiful then, in her sorrow,
　The world of her mourning made light
And thought that the sun of to-morrow
　Would banish the dew of to-night !

They know not the blossom we gather
　Awhile may its beauty retain,
But sunshine or dewdrop may never
　Restore its lost perfume again !

EDUCATION, AND THE RUSSELL CABINET.

MAN possesses by nature certain latent properties of mind, and the value of these to himself and his fellow-man depends mainly upon the power of the natural faculties and the development and application of the same. Mental and physical education resemble each other; the trained marksman makes sure of hitting his aim, his eye is educated, its natural propensities are developed; the watchmaker, from his habit of distinguishing minute objects, sees a pin-point on his board that the less accustomed eye of the ordinary observer looks for in vain; the eye of the sportsman or watchmaker differs in no particular, except that of training, from the eyes of the ploughman and labourer : the distinctness of vision is therefore mainly attributable to training.

The object of teaching should not be so much a desire to plant in as to draw out ; not to teach certain theories as true, but to so train or exercise the mental faculties to distinguish between truth and falsehood in all things, as will enable children, when arriving at maturity, to depend more upon their powers of discrimination than upon the discrimination and advice of others. Self-educated men, who have risen to an eminence in society, are distinguished for their keenness of perception and power of reflection, which properties heighten their value as thinkers, and give them a marked advantage over our men of merely school and college training. This superiority we attribute to habits of self-reliance, of free and natural exercise of the reasoning faculties; and the so-called uneducated peasant who speaks truth as by inspiration, is indeed an educated man. Some may be disposed to attribute the superiority to the force of genius, and we admit that in most cases it is a natural force of superior intellect to break through the conventionalities of habit, and to claim among men individuality and distinctness of position; but there is a training necessary before this position is acquired, and if we turn over the biographies of great men, springing from all ranks, we discover that the training of all is nearly similar; that their mental greatness is more attributable to their private and individual training than to their school or public instruction; and that their distinctness of mental vision has begot a consciousness of power which has enabled them to give manners and forms to society, to disseminate opinions, and forced the wondering many to say of them as Wordsworth hath of Milton, "Thy soul was like a star, and dwelt apart."

We think it would be advisable, on the part of teachers and parents, to endeavour to reduce the system of training practised by the self-educated great minds, into their forms of domestic and school discipline. Our public schools are lamentably deficient in their process of mental exercise. Children are taught to read and write, and in too many cases the learning by rote of a page of English grammar, or running glibly over the age of kings, is mistaken for a sound education; the pupil being disgusted by long hours and dull application, instead of a cultivation of that curiosity that made him but a few years ago desire to know all things, you have a so-called clever boy, who may perhaps tell you the names of the planets, work a question in the rule of three, and is extremely pleased when your inquiries cease. But has he been taught to reason and investigate ? to distinguish and resolve ? No, the husk has been mistaken for the kernel, and the naming of words for an exercise of thought. It is impossible to calculate the evils of such a system, affecting, as it must do, all our laws and institutions ; forcing us to grope our way through thistles and briers for life, giving error as an heirloom to our children instead of truth, and allowing ignorance and craft to usurp the place of reason and knowledge. There is no such thing as a vacuum in the material world, neither is there empty space in the world of mind. There is wisdom in the proverb of our Scotch neighbours, "Idle dogs worry sheep," and as we live but once, we must live for good or evil; hence the paramount importance of early training, and training, too, of a proper and reasoning kind.

The government plan of education is now causing considerable controversy, and the question of whether or no the government should educate the people, is warmly discussed. We submit, that society makes government, and in the present case the government measure is an effect resulting from the spread of intelligence, and general tendency of the present age for change. A few years ago the squirearchy and nobility generally declared the people knew too much, and that they were growing insolent and lazy demogogues, and objecting to obey their masters; whilst the millocracy refused to lessen the hours of toil, and spoke of their mill hands as a part of their estate. They also were too wise—they wanted to be gentlefolks, and had too much spare time already. Appearances have changed, and now dissenters and churchmen are resolved that the people shall know more than ever. Who has produced the change? The demagogues, and the public press, that great inculcator of knowledge, that powerful teacher of the nation; and the government is now discovering that the laws and institutions that suited and became the old mind of England, do not suit the growing mind of England; the swaddling clothes of infancy grace not the limbs of manhood. We have never yet heard a really valuable argument against government interference on questions of education, and, so far as the right of government is concerned, we opine that it is not only the right, but the duty of governments to do as the majority of the male adult population will they should do, and above all, that measures purporting to be for a nation's interest should be carefully constructed both for the immediate good and lasting benefit of the entire population, sound in principle, wise and efficient in execution. Neither have we any fault to find with the interested or benevolent acts of private individuals, provided such acts be not injurious to the best interests of the community, and not in opposition to laws framed by the majority for the government of all. And, under existing circumstances, we would encourage all men to aid by every laudable means the education of the people, and if the friends of voluntary education could by private subscription establish and support a school with efficient teachers in every street, our words would be, "Go on and prosper."

Much is written against government interference, and many men, who think that it is quite right to pass a new Poor Law, think it very wrong to pass a new Education Law. We think the relationship of government is parallel in both cases : Poor Laws are passed because property has ceased voluntarily to perform its duties. The right of the labourer to live is at no time denied ; but during the period that our country is' undergoing a change from a state of comparatively primitive existence, in both agricultural and commercial pursuits, a love of gold supplants a love of duty—and, as individuals cease to practise that which they know to be right, the necessity of such circumstances forces government to interfere. If a labourer working on the estate of a landlord becomes, in his master's service, old and infirm, no reasonable man denies the claim of the labourer to a maintenance, not as a deed of charity, but as a question of right—in fact, it is a debt due by the employer to the employed, and if the employer freely and voluntarily pay this debt no government interference would be necessary—no Poor Law required. No theory of "let everything alone" can absolve from duty; the non-interference doctrine will only be practicable when men know their duty and practise it. We have not yet arrived at that state of society, and, when we do so, liberty will be something more than a name, and human freedom more defined than a vacant cry of "a glorious constitution." A glorious constitution, indeed! A people poor and uneducated—working from the cradle to the grave like bond-slaves pinioned by trespass acts, game laws, handcuffed and chained by inclosure bills, trapped by acts of parliament of which they know nothing, judged by magistrates and parsons who refuse to pay their debts—mention not freedom in England, it is a mockery and an idle sound!

We affirm that the right of every child to be educated is as binding as is its right to be fed when hungry. The appetite of the youthful mind is not less keen than the appetite of the youthful man, and the good or evil services rendered to the state depend as assuredly on a well-regulated mind as they do on a healthy and well-trained body. If the low wages and inadequate means of parents be such as prevent them from educating their children, it is the duty of those parties who profit by their labour to provide the necessary education : they are debtors, and if they possess the means to pay and will not, they must be summoned, brought into court, and forced to discharge their debts, provided the claim of the creditor be fairly and truthfully established ; and this, in our case, will be an easy task. The claim of the pauper is acknowledged, and to some extent provided for ; the debt due to the mental pauper is not less just, and the necessity for payment not less urgent.

As to the deficient character of our education, both as regards quantity and quality, we have only to refer to the reports of our police courts, and the general condition of our labouring population, viewed in a mental and moral aspect. The myriads of upgrown men and women who can neither read nor write are alarming to every thoughtful observer, and filling the gin palaces and gaols follows as an inevitable result. Our every-day experience is to us all-sufficient on this question, but figures are fashionable among the opponents of national education, and perhaps the following extract from Neison's " Statistics of Crime" may be of some service to the sceptical, as well as of utility to the general reader :—

EDUCATION AND CRIME.—If the term "education" were held to signify the culture and education of the moral character, it is evident that its immediate and essential influence is to destroy crime; in fact, in this sense, education and freedom from crime must bear the relation to each other of cause and effect; and, therefore, when education is at a maximum, crime must of necessity be at a minimum; but if the term "education" be used in its ordinary acceptation, and merely implies instruction, it then becomes a fit and important question whether education in this limited sense has any influence on the development of crime. The proportion of the male population in England and Wales signing their marriage certificate with marks is 33 per cent. In eight counties, viz., Hertford, Monmouth, Bedford, Cambridge, Suffolk, Essex, Worcester, and Hants, the proportion signing with marks exceeded the general average by at least 33 per cent., and may be called the counties of least degree of education. In seven other counties—Bucks, Cumberland, Surrey, Northumberland, Westmoreland, Devon, and Durham—the proportion is at least 25 per cent. under the average, and may be termed the group of highest degree of education. On comparing the results of these two groups, it is found that where there is the least degree of education there is an excess of crime of 13 per cent.; but in the group of the highest degree of education the actual crime is 30 per cent. under the average of the whole kingdom. To this extent the influence of education is evident.

We cannot for a moment conceive that the inhabitants of Suffolk are naturally more criminal than those of Surrey. There is no divine bold enough to assert that the fall of Adam is partial in its effects, entailing on one county more misery and punishment than on another county; but there are thinking men who assert and prove that there is a graduated sliding scale, regulating knowledge and crime; and now we ask, is the rich agricultural county of Suffolk less able to educate the people than are the counties of Surrey or Northumberland,—Suffolk, proverbially famed for rich landlords and wealthy farmers, many of the latter occupying from one to two thousand acres of land, and at this time pocketing fortunes from the famine price of bread? If Surrey has done its duty, if its proprietors have discharged their debts and no more, then is Suffolk a refractory debtor, possessing the ability to pay, but defrauding the creditor; and we ask, why have courts of debtor and creditor enforcing payment of a shilling, and yet have no law to enforce the payment of thousands? But the relationship of education and crime involves a serious question—*Who are indeed the criminals?* Are they the unfortunate, who have been defrauded of their property and reared in ignorance, or are the real criminals those who possess the property, and have not fulfilled their duties,—the men who have said "honour and obey," and have not taken the necessary steps to justify their claim, or to admit of the fulfilment of their desires? But the case stops not even here. It is cruelty to exult over the lameness of the cripple. Englishmen would rise in arms against the practice of flogging the lame or goading the blind, yet she builds gaols and erects bridewells for the mentally lame and the mentally blind—nay, more, she *makes* them lame and blind, and cruelly punishes them for being creatures of her own moulding. She reads her book of laws, saying, "protect the dog, punish the man—save the horse, sink the peasant—free the black and enslave the white." Monster inconsistency, and truthfully-demonstrated national ignorance and injustice! Such hatred of cruelty is illustrated in the case of the cat that tortures the mouse previously to killing it, calmly watching its unfortunate victim, but true to the instinct of that nature which is never inconsistent with herself; there is no exclamation of "Oh, how I hate cruelty to animals!" No label mocking common sense and reason, reading, "Oh, how humane I am!"

The government scheme of education seems to us to be partial and unjust—it is no scheme of national education; the total exclusion of the Catholics shows, at first sight, the cowardice and weakness of the Russell Cabinet. If a law be enacted enforcing taxation, giving to officers the power to distrain for church-rates, or any other impost, the Catholic is not left untaxed, his money is welcome to the Exchequer, but he must not be educated. "Oh, yes," exclaim the Whigs, "but the state of parties, the Wesleyans and Quakers must be considered; they are prejudiced, and we must flatter them; by-and-by, we will make it all right." Lord Morpeth is in favour of a purely secular education, leaving religion to the private arrangements of the priests and parents; but the ignorance and fanaticism of the religious community will not admit of so thoroughly a comprehensive scheme.

Such are politics—mean trafficking to prejudice, sordid love of place—a fair specimen of genuine Whiggism. The Catholics must be insulted meantime, their faith sneered at, their privileges of citizenship denied, on purpose to be kindly treated hereafter; the Wesleyans must be deceived and hoodwinked into a belief of government distrust of Catholicism, their love of purity and Protestantism courted for ministerial advantage. The man who, in private life, would be guilty of so base and crafty a scheme of organised hypocrisy, would be denounced and mistrusted; but, in this age of strange morals, that which is private disgrace is patronised as public worth; and the solvency of the Whig ministry is proportionate to the private insolvency of its members. That which no single member can defend on its own merits and in consonance with his own opinions, all can agree to support; and the bond of union is secure relative to the sacrifice made of private principle and public integrity. The details of the government scheme indicate not only ignorance of the means of carrying their scheme of education into effect, but prove to us the inability of the Whig administration to legislate for the present and future happiness and greatness of this country. The scheme of relays of monitors and teachers will prove unworkable; good and efficient teachers are necessary for an efficient plan of National Education, but government patronage must be differently exercised, and the *modus operandi* differently arranged. It is certainly true that the government scheme of education creates no new places beyond those within its own operation; but it is also true that it gives a different direction to government patronage. Some may, like Lord Morpeth, affirm that the change is an improvement: such is not the question with us; we are no favourites in the school of thinkers, who pardon John for his crimes, because he may be less criminal than James. The question with us is not one of degree; the question is, whether the alteration be the best that could have been suggested? We love the maxim, " The labourer is worthy of his hire," but we do not love to buy brains by governmental promises and bribes, and we view the promised patronage to approved-of teachers as to some extent being an attempt, on the part of the Whig government, to buy the first minds of the rising generation for government purposes, not the laudable object of teaching the people, but the detestable one of being a custom-house police establishment.

The Whigs seem to be aware of the great truth, that early impressions form the substratum of future character, and accordingly attempt to direct the industrial pursuits and morals of the youth of England; consequently, there are sections introduced relating to workshops and trades; and we prove the incompetency of the government scheme, as an engine for

real and permanent good, by referring to the same. It is
notorious that our large cities and towns are the hotbeds of
crime and vagrancy, and it is not less true that the over-
crowded state of every kind of handicraft forces thousands
of artisans to become criminals and vagrants, swelling thereby the numbers of the community who are profitless as pro
ducers, and injurious as contaminators of the more fortunate
or virtuously-disposed portion of society; while, on the other
hand, the agricultural population are driven from their
homes to swell the masses crowding our lanes and alleys,
affording in rapid succession supplies for the prison and
brothel, the workhouse and churchyard. The wisdom of a
government would be to change this unnatural state of things;
but though bread be selling at a famine price, with millions
of acres of land profitable, if cultivated and remaining waste,
with millions more scarcely half cultivated, we have actually
a proposal to rear children to trades in our industrial schools,
situated in towns where the numbers of our artisans keep up a
constant struggle for employment, while the earth is yearning
to be cultivated, and myriads starving because the cultivation
of the soil has been neglected. Present circumstances might
have impressed the ministry with a conviction of the fatal
policy of past years, and induced the directors of the future
to exercise all the means at command to stem the tide of
national ruin and collected misery. Common sense would
have dictated that the waste lands should be cultivated, and
the surplus population of our large towns trained to cultivate
them, thereby remedying a present evil, and ensuring a
coming and permanent good.

Are we told that the squalid artisan and city-reared criminal are not prepared for rural life? we answer, come among
the people and inquire—see our Land Societies, read our
literature, and you will hear of associated families, self-sup-
porting villages, people's estates, land, air and water for man;
ay, and the people will one day impress their rulers with
the truths in which they believe. The poverty and want of
the artisan forces him to rear the children of his heart to a
trade that he hates—competition, employment of women,
forces the employment of children. The father is compelled to
rear his child to his own trade—it is of easy access, and the
little aid given is welcome—so extreme is the poverty. The
mother says, "We will apprentice him to a better business by-
and-by!" Good woman, her heart is in the right place, but
the "by-and-by" never comes. It is sometimes asked, "What
trade is better?" but the question is never answered—it can-

not be—poverty is coming to a level, and England bleeds at every pore. But open to our city mechanics the means and opportunity of benefiting their children by a good education, and rearing their little ones to an agricultural life, cultivating at the same time the mental and physical man, and see the result: our city gates will be flooded with retreating children ; the tide of migration will be reversed, and instead of the youth of our agricultural population flocking to our cities, the youth of our cities will flock to our half-peopled rural districts, distributing their race over our land and carrying with them a sea of wealth. Open the land for the people ; famine and crime will decrease. The trades yawn from surfeit ; the hungry earth cries " Come and till me ; sow and you shall reap, for I am the mother of all living." Then why not change that organization of society that shortens our lives, wastes our strength, giving up our bone and marrow to Mammon, and buying the name of national grandeur at the expense of national power ? Would it not be a wiser policy to so direct the industrial pursuits of the rising generation as to unite grandeur with power, and wealth with happiness ? The education of the people is a great and glorious theme, embracing within itself the germ of future intelligence and power, and the ministry which would give to England a truly national education, would confer on the world a blessing. The Russell Cabinet are not the men possessing the requisite knowledge and firmness for such a measure ; they are too desirous to be liberal in appearance to please the fanatics in religion, and too imbecile in action to hoist the standard of equality and right, and abide by the issue, calmly waiting the result and relying on the power of the intelligent and truly liberal—secure in the affections of the people, because of the people's confidence in their honesty of intention and boldness of action. The Whigs are not the men for the many ; they crucify progression by a conflict of opinions in the cabinet, and disturb the public mind without having the means of satisfying the people's demands ; they aim at leading the band without a knowledge of their instrument ; they blow a cracked whistle, but cannot sound a full trumpet.

Meantime the people continue to educate themselves ; knowledge progresses ; and the direction of the increasing intelligence will, at no distant day, be manifested, in forcing the rich few to contribute for the mental support of the poor many, by establishing a system of education wisely arranged in details, efficient and honest in principle, educating Jew and Gentile,

Catholic, Protestant and Freethinker, without distinction, and leaving the bubbling ocean of creeds and faiths to be quelled by increased reasoning powers, teaching all to discriminate between truth and error for themselves, having no fear, but much hope, in the result.

THE ROMANCE OF A PEOPLE.

AN HISTORICAL TALE,

OF THE NINETEENTH CENTURY.

BOOK II.—CHAPTER I.

THE INSURRECTION.

Some brief years had flown, changing the destiny of the dwellers in that lonely farm-house, and of such mighty import, that the voice of Romance must die before the words of History.

Events came hurrying on, driving the nations forward on their rapid current, till those who were gathered in the vortex had scarce leisure left to think of self. The voice of solitary complaining was drowned in their mighty march—thus the hopes of our hearts, the dearest, brightest, best, are trampled down by our fellow-men, like flowers beneath an army. And how many a noble action, how many a great lesson remains unnoticed and untold! *Time* flies away with a countless load of events,—*History*, the saving genius, throws herself in his path. He hurries on, and, as he rushes past, she snatches at his burden, and saves some of his ravished booty from the hands of the exulting robber. Yet, alas! but too often she grasps the gaudy and useless, lured by its glitter, and allows the worthiest and most sterling to pass by. Thence, doubtlessly, History is represented as a woman. Sometimes, peradventure, she will gain a glorious treasure; then she will go and exult over it in secret, keeping it to herself a long, long while, till at length she brings it forth, distorted, magnified or diminished, and laughs and chuckles at the bright phantom she has conjured from Time, whose other name is *Oblivion*.

The 29th of November was at its close—it was the evening of the insurrection; the day had been one of unusual quiet at Warsaw, and nothing betokened that a great event was on the point of taking place. The eye of tyranny seemed as watchful, and its nerves as well braced as ever; there stood the sentries —there paced the patroles—there were ranged the loaded cannon—there gleamed the lights in the barracks—there were piled the arms of the soldiery,—and there flitted the shadow-like figures of the secret police.

It was a frosty night; and at the southern extremity of Warsaw two men might be seen advancing stealthily towards an old, uninhabited building. After having ascertained that they were unobserved, they commenced striking a light, and endeavoured to fire the ruinous edifice; but the damps of winter had saturated the rotten timber, and every attempt proved fruitless. The men looked round in apprehension as the wind clattered along the houses, like the echoes of footsteps in the street; by their fear and their stealthy occupation, they might have been taken for nocturnal robbers and incendiaries—yet they were two of Poland's most gallant sons, kindling the torch that was meant to light their fatherland to liberty. Much time had been wasted in the fruitless attempt,—it was half an hour beyond the appointed period, and the conspirators had nearly exhausted their stock of combustibles. They looked round in despair at the dark sky and silent city:—should it wake? A mighty revolution hanged upon the burning of a match.

Meanwhile, many an eye watched anxiously for the signal— the appointed time was long past, and the great bulk of the conspirators slunk back to their fireside, fearing all had been discovered, or believing, at least, the insurrection was again delayed. At length a red beacon mounted in the south—the old ruin had caught fire. The leaders of the revolt kept assembling—but their followers came not. The last hues of the conflagration were fading from the sky, the signal had evidently passed unnoticed.

The most daring promoters of the movement, the forlorn hope of the coming storm, had assembled at the bridge of Sobieski, between the palace of the Belvidere and the cavalry barracks. Impenetrable darkness shrouded every object, and the insurgents, headed by Louis Nabielak, still waited in suspense for some further sound or signal. Presently a commotion was heard in the distance; lights were seen advancing down the streets in all directions, it was evident the cavalry and police had taken the alarm; the fire had warned the enemy without raising the insurgents. The little troop at the bridge stood motionless, hiding their weapons as best they might, lest they should catch the glare of the lanterns, and reveal their bearers to the Russians.

The darkness saved Poland that night. Several of the patroles passed within a few yards of Nabielak and his band, but they remained undiscovered.

Thus an hour elapsed, in anxious expectation. At length a step was heard approaching, and a well-known voice addressed

the dispirited band. It was Wysocki, the gallant superin-
tendant of the School of Ensigns, who dwelt in barracks not
far from the Belvidere. His absence had occasioned the delay,
and he was hurrying on to place himself at the head of his young
soldiers.

Louis Nabielak now divided his band into two equal parts,
and, sure of support from the military school, led them instantly
on to the attack of the palace. One detachment was destined
to guard the rear, whilst he, at the head of the other, rushed
into the court, shouting, "Death to the tyrant!"

As they burst through the outer gate, the report of firing
was heard, telling them that the ensigns were already engaged.
Animated by the sound, and by their own wild cries, the little
band rushed up the steps. No one opposed them; not a soul
was there; nothing was to be heard within, save the fall of
flying footsteps along the distant galleries. Several passages
diverged from the great landing: which was to be chosen?
While hesitating, the shadow of a man was seen moving from
behind a pillar—it was the President Lubovidzki, crouching for
concealment.

"Where is Constantine?" He answered not—but fled along
the passage towards the chambers of the duke, and with a
sudden bound, that proved the following shot told true, rolled
beneath the feet of the advancing Poles.

Door after door fell shattered beneath their blows, but Constantine was nowhere to be found; he had escaped to the pavilion
of the Princess Lowiecka, where, surrounded by women, that
man was kneeling in prayer, who had himself rejected every
supplication.

The palace was gained without a blow in its defence, though
thousands of devoted troops were within shot of its walls.
The insurgents rushed like a storm through the deserted pile,
and were proceeding down the stairs towards the pavilion of
the princess, when the tidings came that Russian cavalry were
hastening to the Belvidere! Before their arrival, however,
Nabielak made good his retreat to the bridge of Sobieski. The
ensigns were already there.

"The hour of vengeance and of victory!" exclaimed
Wysocki. "To the city! to the city!" was the answering
cry: onward they proceeded. They had not progressed far,
before they heard the cavalry closing on their rear. The
roops had mounted in haste, some in their shirt sleeves, some
with bare feet in their stirrups, but all with the assurance of
crushing the little band of the insurgents. The latter ranged
themselves in single file, their backs against a garden wall, and
a bold front turned to the enemy. Every shot told on the
advancing Russians, and then the bayonet charged their disor-
dered body, and drove them back upon the Belvidere.

A breathing time was gained, and anxiously the young
warriors looked round for the expected succour. But that succour

never appeared; the delay gave the enemy time to rally, and, indignant at being beaten by a handful of youths, their returning march was soon heard on the right, intercepting the expected retreat of the insurgents to the city.

This time Wysocki did not await their attack, but again charging with the bayonet, drove them back in confusion. Scarcely was this danger over, when two Russian regiments advanced to the aid of their discomfited comrades. A powerful and well-directed fire, sustained by rapid and repeated charges, sufficed to hold them in check, and again a lull sunk over this desperate and unequal contest.

The Poles now pushed forward until they reached the Radziwill barracks, where they expected to be joined by six companies of grenadiers, but they were again disappointed, and Wysocki directed all his efforts towards keeping the three cavalry regiments engaged, to prevent their crushing the rising in the city.

The furious struggle was prolonged, and in the intervals of the clamour the patriots listened for some sound of encouragement and succour; but in vain! nothing was heard but the eternal beating of drums, which told that the powers of the oppressor were accumulating around them. No sound of popular movement from Warsaw—it lay silent and dark; no note of approaching thousands—no cheering shout—no measured tread of Polish troops advancing to the rescue.

Thus all the progress that had been effected appeared to consist in a frantic struggle between the ensigns and the troops around the Belvidere, the number of which latter was increasing every moment; but this struggle was gradually drawing the Russian forces away from the city, and every fresh battalion gathering around this devoted band was as a weight of chains taken off the people in Warsaw.

"Hold out, brave comrades!" cried Wysocki, "they must hear the firing, if they saw not the signal; and they will be stirring soon. Every man who dies here is raising a thousand men in the city."

At that moment a fearful cry for help arose from part of his troop that had been separated from the rest by a sudden movement of the enemy, and, as a last alternative, he advanced from the Radziwill barracks, and once more headed a desperate charge. Again each of the Russian regiments was attacked in turn, again repulsed—pursued—dispersed. Wonderful as it may seem, the veterans of the Caucasus were scattered in a prolonged struggle by the charges of these daring and untried young soldiers, who were outnumbered more than tenfold by the Russian troops.

The road to the city now lay open. The enemy did not pursue, believing the force by which they had been vanquished far more numerous than it really was, and large bodies of Russians, that might have crushed the rising at a blow, stood massed about, inactive and irresolute, for want of orders and decision.

Wysocki and Nabielak now determined on leading their band into the town, and marched unimpeded down the New World Street, towards the heart of the capital. Darkness hung like a curtain before them, concealing their onward path,—not a footfall on the pavement save their own, not a light in the houses, for, at the first sound of the distant commotion, every door and window had been closed. With anxious hearts they pressed forward; no one met them in the streets—it was impossible to deny the fact—they were alone in arms against the man who reigns from Kamtschatka to the Vistula.

With foreboding ear they might have heard the cannon rolling on, and the Cossacks drawing nigh, from the heart of that vast empire; every step they took sounded a challenge to those distant armies, and yet they were alone! They halted—they listened for the report of cannon from the Radziwill barracks, which were to have been fired as alarm-guns, as soon as the Polish grenadiers should have been able to reach that point; but there came no shot booming welcome to their isolated band.

To the westward the assembling of troops could distinctly be heard, but their silence denoted that they were Russian detachments. Despair now began to weigh down the hearts of the insurgents, who escaped by but the length of a street meeting six companies of Russian infantry, sent to the assistance of the duke. Had they met it is more than probable the gallant little corps of ensigns, thinned, dispirited, and exhausted as they were, would have been overpowered, and the rising in the city prevented.

It is a strange circumstance that the bulk of the Russian forces had as yet taken no part in the events of the night. Large masses of troops kept assembling and concentrating around the Belvidere, but they still remained inactive, without orders, and apparently without leaders: it seemed as though a mysterious Providence had withheld and paralysed the enemy; while, on the other hand, the insurrection was taking an equally strange and silent course, utterly at variance with the preconcerted plans of the conspirators. The people had not moved; the Russians were under arms before the Polish troops; they were informed of the rising, yet Warsaw remained silent, and that little band of patriots had been able, after a desperate and successful encounter, to march unmolested through the deserted streets. Thus wavering and slow are the measures of cowardice and tyranny. But, when they were about to act decisively, when the Muscovite was recovering from his panic, then, at the last hour, a deep sound was heard in the heart of the city, and by the faint gleam of the flashing lamps detachments of Polish troops were seen marching from their barracks—the Polish army was pronouncing for the insurrection. They took possession of Prague, the two bridges over the Vistula, and the arsenal, while the silent and steady crowds were gathering in the old town, the hotbed of former insurrections. The hostile forces were concentrated on their respective sides, and at length the bloody issue, was at hand. Suddenly a deep, dull roar broke upon the heavy hush, red flashes mounted against the dun clouds, that hung volumed in the air, and a distant clash beneath the walls of the arsenal told that the battle of Liberty had commenced.

Steadily the Russian column advanced—a line of fire blazed forth an instant before it, a volley of musketry rolled down either front, and through the clouds was heard the simultaneous tread of either hosts, like the footfalls of two giants, as the opposing forces closed upon each other. For a moment all was veiled, and then the sharp gleam of the Polish bayonets pierced the volumed smoke, and the Russian battalions were seen sweeping back into the long lines of black streets behind them, like torrents vanishing in subterranean channels.

A. sparkling shower of shells and rockets was thrown from the artillery in their rear to cover their retreat, and as those bright and beautiful engines of destruction came arching over the house-tops, and dropping among the dense multitudes with fatal effects, like fiery garlands, cast from heaven to crown the victory, a wild cheer burst from the inspirited populace, drowning the groans of the dying, and the explosions of the deadly missives, with a sound of triumph, for the brave people were beginning to feel their strength, conspiracy had turned to war, and action was fast solving doubt, fear, and irresolution. The people, however, were still unarmed; they clamoured for arms, they were fiery and hard to restrain, while grey-haired generals shook their heads and said, "The undisciplined crowd will throw us in confusion: the mob knows how to fight!" But the Russians were again making head; they outnumbered the Polish troops, the latter were weary, the people eager and excited. "Arm the populace!" cried some of the more ardent, and thirty thousand muskets taken from the arsenal were distributed among them. The effect was electrical. Ere an hour had elapsed the city was in their power; the Russians were beaten back on the square of Saxony and avenue of Cracow, the prisons were broken open, and the long-suffering captives stood once more free among their countrymen. Many died on being brought to light; some placed themselves at the head of their friends, and led them on like spectres from the grave.

Strange as it may seem, during all this time the insurrection had no head. Every one acted and kept together from impulse; while, along the whole line taken up by the patriots, a sharp conflict was unremittingly continued, particularly in the square of Saxony, where a Polish regiment of horse-chasseurs still sided with the enemy. With but this exception the utmost unanimity prevailed in an army without a general, and a multitude without a leader.

Still the troops and people kept at their posts during the night : but when the first grey dawn stole over the spires of Warsaw, and afar were seen the Russian forces still presenting an imposing and unshaken front, and, above all, that fine regiment of Polish chasseurs engrafted on their line, a misgiving seized on all, a commotion was observable among the crowd, an irresolute welking to and fro, sadly ominous of the breaking-up of those desponding masses.

With the dawn, however, a thousand students of the university appeared before them, and these gallant youths, headed by Lach Scyrma, their professor of moral philosophy, marching through the capital, destroyed the emblazonments of Russia,. and gathering up the multitudes on their way, hurled them in one steady and unceasing tide upon the Russian line.

The enemy were borne back before this irresistible wave, their last grasp was wrenched off the capital, and their flying troops were driven tumultuously through the barriers of Mockstow. Warsaw was free !

(*To be continued.*)

"A VISIT TO O'CONNORVILLE."

READER, I have waited a day, previous to resolving on the course to be pursued in my relation to you, doubting as to the propriety of reflecting a complete picture. As an author, I am bound to instruct you, but the question, difficult to decide, is, whether should I revel free as the romping ruddy boy, smiling with the lovely girl I have just seen straw-platting by the cottage door, or, gossipping with Gipsy Bess, a true descendant of the fine Egyptian race, shall I paint to you my hospitable host, and his white-haired father, eating fruit pulled by little Fanny from the garden, seated in his own cottage, and looking on his own land? or shall I introduce old Richardson and his apple-tree, grumbling about his barley, talking of old Cobbett, and informing you that he had worked for Queen Charlotte and made pruning-knives for the nobles? Shall I introduce the holiday visitors, or describe the country swain leaning against the well? I must stop. Yes, by the black ink and old stumped pen there is something whispers ' *Labourer*'—that word puts all right; demanding St. Rollox to be serious and not stray in his favourite rambles. Well, I will describe to you O'Connorville just as it is, assuring you that my errors are of ignorance and not intention, and your duty is to scrutinize every doubtful sentiment, and admit of no conclusion which is not clearly founded on fact, and distinctly illustrated by the lights of 'perception and reason.

When I last rambled over O'Connorville, on the 17th of August, 1846, I found half-finished cottages, rugged pasture fields, a gravelly but excellent soil, and on it a vast assemblage of the men of England gathered from every corner; I then hoped for much, and as I surveyed the same fields on Sunday and Monday, June 20th and 21st of this year (1847), I was more than pleased with the changed appearance of all that I beheld; fertility surrounded me on every side; the crops look promisingly, even the very potatoes seem resolved to be healthy—no signs of the rot as yet. The change is a pleasant one, and speaks much for the flexibility of man's nature, and the unspeakable advantages of a proper application of labour on the soil. I have no fear of the result of Mr. O'Connor's small-farm system. The occupants consist of nearly every class of mechanics, including also practical gardeners and agricultural labourers. The present season is the time of trial for the allottees, many of them living in very changed circumstances compared with their past lives; but I did not meet a single one who doubted of the future, or who said that he would not prefer his present situation to a return to the workshop or factory. When I find men contented by their change of circumstances, industrious and frugal, husbanding as well as producing, I most certainly conclude that the coming years will be years of promise and profit. The change these men have undergone in their habits of life in a few months is extraordinary. To the factory worker and city artisan every Saturday night is a scene of excitement; the wages are to be taken and the Sunday's dinner provided; the club room and theatre, the tavern and concert are constant temptations to induce habits of extravagance and irregularity; the Saturday night and Sunday are the only days in which the artizan can find any change of association or pleasure, and with a frame exhausted by constant, and in many cases laborious toil, he longs for excitement; if enough of the animal spirits remain, he desires to shake off the rust of the six days' excessive toil, and spend what he calls one happy hour with his friends. The effects are too familiar to require description: the wife remains at

home cooped-up in a small room, and the children, barefooted, ragged little abortions, run about our streets learning every
vice; the wife, in many cases a self-denying, amiable creature,
bears the misery of loneliness and poverty with more than
a Spartan heroism, until death relieves her of her suffering,
whilst the neighbouring tavern affords a momentary lull to
her wretchedness. Such acts and habits slacken every
valuable link in the social condition of society, and make
men mere exotics, acting in the extreme madness of remorse
and grief, or the reverse state, of lunacy, drunken, and
unreasonable delirium.

It is not to be understood that I for a moment believe the
O'Connorville allottees are of the most degraded class of the
community—just the reverse; they are the superior men
mentally, but there is much in the associations of every-day
life that we cannot shake off in an hour, and the strongest-
minded of us have our struggles with the old habits which
we know to be evil, and the changed habits which we desire
to cultivate. I frankly confess that I have had many. A
change from one workshop to another is an obstacle in the
path of all of us, even as mere workers at the same trade.
The possessor and cultivator of two or four acres works week
after week, month after month, and receives no weekly wages;
his employment and circumstances are entirely changed,
there is no club-room, no concert-room, no theatre, no
tavern, but there is a salubrious atmosphere, a natural stimu-
lant to health and exertion—birds singing at every hour of
the day; the note of the blackbird is heard instead of the
vocal artiste; his children are weeding onions, or working
in the potato field, but Saturday night brings no particular change, no ready money, and, as the wife reminds
him that to-morrow is Sunday, he probably answers "So it is."
He too is a thoroughly industrious man, (you may see all
the families in the field by five o'clock in the morning, and
in bed by nine o'clock in the evening—I found them so);
there is no bell to ring him out of a drowsy slumber, no
overlooker to watch him at work, but he is always busy; if
he walks round his plot, to show you his crops, there is a
weed growing rank which he instantly sees, pulls it out and
leaves it to die and rot in the sun; visit him when you may
he is always prepared for you. I expect much fruit in an
intellectual and moral point of view from such a class of
men; their children will grow up trained under the immediate eye of their parents, independent, industrious and simple-minded men and women, not what the world calls

knowing men; no, unsophisticated men, but of a noble and enterprising character. Oh, I fear these sly, cunning men, the knowing ones, who call the plain country innocence ' bumpkinism.' Reader, never trust them, nor imitate them; they are educated in cunning, and refined in deceit; they possess the heart of the serpent with faces of brass, yet they may be everywhere found; nor is it to be wondered at, for

> " Society itself, which should create
> Kindness, destroys what little we had got:
> To feel for none is the true social art
> Of the world's stoics—men without a heart."

The present time is the most troublesome the new occu-pant will experience. He is short of capital, his wealth is in the ground—his live stock has yielded but little, it has been all outlay, and no income beyond a plentiful supply of vege-tables—his land has been changed from a pasture-field to a garden; it will improve every year, be easier worked and more fruitful; the pigs and poultry will increase in number, and the first harvest will provide, to some extent, for his trifling difficulties—trifling they really are compared with the fate of the aspiring emigrant to another land, or millions of men and women in the large towns and cities of England. Toil on, then, brave workmen, for much depends on you—you live not for yourselves alone, but for all.

The small-farm system, as propounded by Mr O'Connor, opens up for the industrious artizan, whose little savings cannot admit of his entering the competitive market as a capitalist, a sure investment for his savings, and a reasonable hope that, if he be blessed with good health, he shall have a security against want and the fear of want, and, relieved from the anxieties and troubles attendant on removals at rent-day, excessive work in throng-trade, and excessive want six months out of every twelve. It offers no hope which is un-realisable—it says, the first condition is " work, work, work;" the security, " eat, lodge, and live—none daring to make you afraid;" the more industrious and frugal, the surer is your reward; and when old age and its attendant frailties arrive—when withered looks and tottering steps indicate the coming day of dissolution, there will be no heartfelt anxiety, no fear of the workhouse, but a calm serenity in the natural silence of lengthened years, and security to live in returned child-hood among those whose affections and interests are linked with his own. One great evil in the past action of industrial production has been, that cheap goods nominally have been dear goods, practically they have called for extra exertion on the part of the producer, and lessened his means of consumption ; the small-farm allottee will, to some extent, reap the advantage of cheap labour, in so far as his income will be increased by the increased powers of production, and he will be entirely without the pale of monetary and commercial gambling ; the doings of the money and corn factors will in no way injure him, and the spirit of gambling and fortune-hunting, which has impregnated itself in nearly every arrangement of life, will decline in the circles in which he moves. There is no chance for the sudden rising to riches, but there is a moral certainty that he will never know want. He is subject to many contingencies and losses, his potatoes may rot—his pig die—his beans be blighted, but, if his potatoes rot, as soon as he discovers it he must act for the best, either dig them up, clear the ground, and plant or sow something else, or let them remain and make the most of them ; if his pig die, he must get another, feed it and turn his green stuff into bacon, providing at once for the winter and manure for the soil : it will be an extraordinary season indeed that injures all his crops, or even a considerable portion of them ; his losses will be natural and unavoidable, and therefore few ; but the working man of any trade thinks it an extraordinary year in which he does not endure hourly losses, whilst no year holds out a prospect of gain ; and the probability is that he every year gets poorer and more dependant. It is a common saying, "there is no weather ever pleases the farmers." A farmer desires that all the fields should be extremely profitable ; the man of trade balances the profit and loss, and is satisfied with a balance in his favour ; and the artisan has all loss and no profit ; he pays the farmer for the blight, by giving an extra price for his bread, and the tradesman suffers, for the artisan is no longer a profitable and frequent customer.

A leading feature in Mr. O'Connor's plan is, that it is well adapted to be of the greatest advantage to the most oppressed. Shoemakers, tailors, and handloom-weavers are the most oppressed and most intelligent of the operative classes, and the very men of all others best fitted to live on the land. The shoemaker and tailor can work at their trades ; the weaver also, if provided with a loom ; shoes, coats, towels, shirting, &c. must be had, and when the rain falls in spring, and during the long storms of winter, profitable, pleasant and useful employment may be found in in-door work. Well, but perhaps I am told that shoemakers and tailors are of all others least likely to be fitted for out-door labour. They certainly must undergo a change, but it is a pleasing one ; they do not become farm-servants, working out rain or dry, carrying sacks, standing in a ploughed field, over the shoe-tops in water, or driving a team of horses—they are gardeners, working for themselves, and there is but little practice necessary to learn them how to plant a cabbage or dig a potato, and the fresh air is a good exchange for the smoky shop-board or the filthy garret. I have heard much about the impossibility of men working at trades ever being able to become successful two-acre allottees. Man is a very bendable animal, fitted for nearly every change ; he strips his coat in summer, and puts on a great coat in winter, and is always ready to alter for the better.

It will be observed that I have taken no notice of those who declare that two acres of good land cannot produce sufficient of the necessaries of life to support a family ; such opponents know not what they say, many of them are mere crotchety grumblers, and scarcely know whether cheese be made from milk, or grows in the field, like turnips. The capabilities of the soil have been demonstrated ; it is no matter of doubt, but has long ago taken its place among the settled, hard and undeniable truths, which no man can gainsay, and the ignorant alone can seriously doubt ; but it seems the special province of those who never introduce any plan of their own for the investigation of the critical, to flatter a silly ambition by a constant habit of sneering at others. I have no faith in such men ; the doubts of a thinker are ever valuable and merit a serious inquiry, but the sneers of the merely disappointed grumblers are best answered by—

" Grub, little moles—grub underground,
There's sunshine in the sky."

A LEAF FROM THE ANNALS OF A
SHOE-MAKER'S GARRET.

THE INSURRECTIONS

OF

THE WORKING CLASSES.

(*Continued from Vol. I.*)

CHAPTER VI.

The Jacquerie.

The movement that had been so strangely organised, and so terribly suppressed, in Picardy, again broke forth under an altered aspect towards the close of the fourteenth century. A municipal power had now been added to the contending elements. Cities were becoming the stony cradles of liberty—and, as trade began to flourish, aristocracy began to decline. The towns of Upper Italy were the first to enforce the rights of the citizen. They had risen on the wreck of Greek and Roman empires—thrones and aristocracies had fallen away from around them, and left the young strength of industrial energy to soar upward from their ruins. Flourishing municipalities arose, gaining such force from enterprise and combination, that they were able to wage a war of one century against monarchy and priestcraft.

Germany and France followed slowly in the wake of Italy. They were more trammelled by priestly domination—for, in no country was the pontifical supremacy less honoured than in that Italy in which it was best known. The Franconian Emperors gave immunities and privileges to some of the Rhenish towns, that they might act as a check against the overgrown power of the great crown-vassals. The French kings did likewise, from a similar reason, or sold municipal grants for the sake of raising money to defray the expenses of lascivious courts and impoverishing wars. Vassals now fled to the towns, from the tyranny of the landed nobles. The fugitives were welcomed ; the rights of citizenship granted ; and protection extended even to the runaway serf, if not claimed by his master for a year and a day. Thus two distinct classes were formed—the *Burgesses* and the *Commons.* That of the former consisted partly of freeholders, partly of men of noble birth, since cities had generally been the seat of temporal or ecclesiastical princes, and thus, of a necessity, the residence of a numerous court-aristocracy ; and since many noble families left their country domains for the superior safety or luxury of the town.

The Commons consisted of artisans and working men, originally all in a state of vassalage or serfdom; but industry and the force of circumstances enabled many either to purchase or reconquer their liberty. Their number was continually recruited by the influx of serfs from the surrounding country, their wealth by the increase of trade. They now formed themselves into guilds, bore arms, assumed devices, and stood forth as an independent community by the side of their patrician masters. These latter had ruled exclusively until the middle of the thirteenth century; they had formed the councils and filled all the municipal offices : but the spirit of religious freedom that we have seen awakened in the preceding chapter, soon began to pass across the gates of cities. He who once thinks of religious, soon thinks of political freedom. The question was asked, by what right the patricians only ruled, though working men built the ramparts and defended them, raised the spikers and filled them with wealth? The question once asked could receive but one answer, and the patricians found it *expedient* to *concede*. What—not being clearly defined, the burgesses soon robbed the Commons of the little share in the government they had obtained ; the latter appealed to arms, and fierce struggles of contending parties were pent within the narrow walls of widely-scattered towns, while the landed aristocracy drew its forces to the gates, anxiously waiting the opportunity of entrance and revenge.

The Commons triumphed—the feudal lords were disappointed—the patricians reduced to submission—the municipal governments reorganised, in some towns by an admixture of the patrician and democratic elements, in most under the form of a pure democracy. Towards the latter end of the fourteenth century, the Commons were victorious throughout Germany, Italy and France.

We shall therefore not be surprised at finding this new power making head in the latter country against the combined influences of church, crown and feudalism. But the better to understand how the great outbreak that desolated France in the year 1356 originated, it will be necessary to take a glance at the state of the country during the five preceding years.

At no time did a monarch ascend the throne under more favourable circumstances for the maintenance of power than those which greeted the accession of John II. in the year 1350. A severe pestilence had prostrated the popular energy ; he was himself experienced in the art of government; a long truce with England had strengthened the hands of royalty, and ordinary prudence, integrity and wisdom might have healed the wounds of internal discord and foreign aggression. Under no reign did the miseries of a people reach a greater height, and but once have they been more fearfully avenged.

Scarce was his father dead before he was crowned at Rheims, and held his entry into Paris, with unparalleled magnificence.

There was a continuous feasting of eight days, and then a royal murder. Raoul, lord of Eu and Guines, constable of France, had been taken prisoner by the English, and, being set at liberty, returned to raise his ransom. He went to pay his homage to the king, who had him forthwith arrested, beheaded without trial, three days afterwards, and confiscated his counties of Guines and Eu, the former of which he annexed to his crown, and gave the latter to one of his dependants. No reason was assigned for this act, save that he was suspected of treasonable correspondence with the king of England. Some historians look for another reason, in his rich possessions.

The following catalogue of war and ravage impresses us with a vivid image of what must have been the sufferings of the working-classes previous to their insurrection, and affords a fair insight into the leading characteristics of the privileged orders. In 1351 the war recommenced between the French and English; the country was pillaged, towns and villages were burnt and battles fought without any definite result, when either party, being unable to agree as to the terms of peace, concluded a truce for a year, which the king employed in levying troops and raising additional taxes. Meanwhile Brittany was being ravaged by the contending factions of the countesses of Penthièvre and of Montfort, whose respective troops, when not engaged on the field of battle, showed their devotion to the cause of their fair leaders by levelling the crops and houses, and cutting down the vassals of their opponents. A Breton nobleman, Beaumanoir by name, touched with compunction at the sufferings of the poor, suggested that 30 noblemen of either party should decide the quarrel among themselves. The challenge was accepted, the encounter took place at Josselin, near Ploërmel, the champions of Penthièvre triumphed, and then the two countesses continued slaughtering and destroying as before.

In 1352, Marshal Offemont was sent into Brittany, to the assistance of Charles of Blois; further carnage ensued, the marshal was killed, and the feudal wars were prolonged. The truce was now broken by the king of England, fresh encounters occurred, and again the contention subsided into an uncertain armistice. A new agent of destruction arose in the person of Charles of Navarre, a near relative and son-in-law of the king. Gay, dissolute and reckless, this prince desired the crown of France, and, unscrupulous in his designs, thought to obtain it by plunging the country into still deeper misery. He therefore raised a claim to certain counties, which the king was forced to yield, and exchanged Angouleme for Champagne, on the plea that the former was so impoverished by having been the seat of continual war, that it *was not worth having*. What must have been the condition of the working classes, when a prince refused to take their country as a gift! The king now gave Angouleme to Charles of Spain, but Charles of Navarre, constable of France, jealous of the donation, had the former assassinated while asleep, and then, retiring to Normandy, where he enjoyed immense possessions, and issuing manifestoes to the different towns, prepared to raise the standard of revolt. War now raged again in Brittany, Picardy, Maine and Normandy, raised by the ambition of princes, maintained by the blood and treasure of peoples; private feuds desolated every province, and still fresh elements of destruction kept arising from the bosom of aristocracy. The king pacified Charles of Navarre by endowing him with immense possessions and judicial rights; but as he had murdered a royal prince and relative, some atonement was held to be necessary, and the king therefore *solicited* him to come and beg his pardon.

Charles consented, that royalty might not be humiliated in the person of King John, and after a son of the latter had been delivered up as hostage, condescended to sue for pardon at Paris. The previous ceremonies having been arranged between them, the king received Charles in open court, when the latter said he had intended no harm by killing the Lord High Constable, and was sorry it should have offended the king. John then ordered him, for form's sake, to be arrested, when, as was preconcerted, the two queens-dowager threw themselves at the feet of the monarch and sued for the pardon of the murderer, which was granted; Charles and John embraced, and thus ended a farce which must have raised royalty in the estimation of those who were told to obey the right divine, and honour the laws that were broken by the lawmaker.

Hostilities being once more about to recommence between the kings of France and England, envoys were sent from either party to Avignon, to negotiate conjointly with the papal legates for a renewal of the truce. Charles of Navarre desired the continuance of war—therefore he, too, secretly repaired to Avignon—which, being discovered, he affected to leave it publicly with a large retinue, re-entering the town by stealth the same evening. He remained there fifteen days, concealed alternately in the palaces of Cardinal Ostia, and of Cardinal Guy of Boulogne, the papal legates, who, though accredited as the Christian ministers of peace, lent their holy functions to the maintenance of bloodshed and the furtherance of court intrigues.

King John now took the field with a large force, destroying the possessions of his rebellious vassal, who retaliated on the subjects of the king. After a severe struggle peace was concluded in 1335, by John paying Charles 100,000 crowns, whereupon the latter assured his monarch he was a most loyal subject, and had the true interests of France at heart.

Scarcely had this storm subsided, before the Prince of Wales entered Gascony, devastating everything on his course to Toulouse, passing the Garonne, burning the suburbs of Carcassone, destroying the country as far as Narbonne, and returning to Bordeaux, in the month of November, with enormous booty and numerous prisoners. He was not opposed by French armies, since these were employed in the intestine dissensions of French princes and the oppression of the French people. At the same time the English king in person invaded Normandy, thus crushing either extremity of the empire, while rapine, anarchy and bloodshed were reigning in its centre. The taxation may be imagined that had been laid on the people to sustain this tumult of war; the more so, when we learn that during this period the splendours of the court and aristocracy were nothing abated, but, on the contrary, excelled in magnificence. The arms and trappings of the knights were studded with pearls and precious stones, and inlaid with gold; dames and demoiselles passed from *fête* to *fête* in sumptuous equipages—banquets and entertainments exceeded each other in rapid succession, and as taxation, luxury and war kept increasing, an uneasy movement began to be discoverable on the part of the working classes.

More money was wanted to uphold the system, but at last the king was afraid of imposing an additional tax. The government saw it had strained taxation to the utmost available limits, and now had recourse to an hitherto unprecedented step to raise additional supplies.

The development of municipal liberty, the origin and progress of which has been briefly sketched at the commencement of this chapter, had already attained considerable power in France; and the towns, by purchasing charters for surrounding themselves with fortifications and maintaining their own garrisons, had escaped some of the ravages by which the working population of the open country were ruined, and had even been enabled to accumulate some wealth amid the conflicting interests of hostile factions. They had, therefore, despite of taxation and war, risen into a position of comparative importance, and the king resolved upon obtaining their sanction and countenance in raising the requisite supplies.

To this, however, they would never consent, without having a voice in that government which they were called upon to support. Thus far already had the spirit of freedom advanced! The king, therefore, saw himself compelled to call a general assembly of the *Three Estates*. Hitherto, the king had at times convoked general assemblies of the *two* Estates, Clergy and Nobility, and Philip of Valois had on one occasion, in 1332, convoked an assembly at Orleans of the prelates, barons, and *notables*—but this was only a partial summons, partaking but little of the form of a Parliament. This time the Commons were admitted as an essential part of the deliberative council, and all the principal towns were ordered to send their delegates to the general Convention at Paris.

The delegates met accordingly, and the king made a statement of his necessities and of the sums he required. In reply, John de Craon, archbishop of Rheims, on behalf of the clergy,

Goucher de Brienne, duke of Athens, on behalf of the nobles, and Stephen Marcel, *provost of the trades*, on behalf of the Commons, replied that they were ready to raise an additional tax for levying 30,000 men, provided clergy, nobility and royalty paid in proportion, and that the Convention should reassemble in the beginning of March to concert further measures. But, when the appointed time came round, the attendance of the aristocratic envoys was very scanty, and many towns of Normandy and Picardy refused to send their delegates. Affairs had grown worse in the interval. One wail of lamentation ascended from the country—starved fugitives laid down and died before the gates of cities—famine began to be felt, while ravage continued and splendour mocked its progress, and the Commons saw the question had ceased to be one of money, it had become one of life and death. A revolt broke forth in Arras—the people rose against the aristocracy ; twenty noblemen were killed, the rest compelled to fly,—and the insurgents remained masters of the city.

At this crisis an event occurred, calculated to bring the royal family into still greater contempt. The king's eldest son, the Dauphin, entered into a conspiracy with Charles of Navarre, and the Emperor Charles the Fourth, to seize, imprison, and murder his own father. The plot was discovered : the reason assigned for its formation was, that the Dauphin had not sufficient political power, and the king was forced to reward the intended parricide by making him governor of the duchy of Normandy. King John now resolved on obtaining possession of the person of Charles of Navarre, and for this purpose engaged the Dauphin to play the further traitor, in betraying his former friends. The young prince affected the greatest possible intimacy with Charles of Navarre, and on the 5th of April, 1356, invited him and his court to a banquet in the castle of Rouen. The same day the king secretly left the village of Maineville with a hundred lances, and entered the castle unobserved in the twilight. The unsuspicious guests were seized at table, and cast into prison, without the townpeople being aware of the occurrence. Charles of Navarre was sent to Paris, but the principal among his followers, Count Harcourt, Lords Graville and Moubuc, and Olivier Doublet, were executed, their bodies suspended on scaffolds, and their heads stuck on poles in a public close near the town. On the successful termination of this attempt, the king sent Marshal Andrehen into Artois at the head of a strong force; he gained entrance into Arras by treachery, massacred the insurgents, and reduced the town to subjection.

The partisans of Charles of Navarre now took up arms throughout the kingdom, and again a horrid civil war blazed from one extremity of the country to the other, during which the king laid siege to Evreux, that was held by the troops of Charles. Its garrison burnt the city and all that was in it, thousands perished, and the troops retired to another strong-hold. The king had his revenge in other quarters, the country was given to pillage, and at this crisis the deluge of another English invasion was poured across the frontier.

(*To be continued.*)

THE LEAGUE.

So far were we from supposing that the Anti-Corn Law League had abandoned the field of agitation, that, from the passing of the measure down to the present time, we have sedulously impressed upon the popular mind the fact that the triumph of FREE TRADE is but as yet the recognition of a principle, the moulding of which, for good or for evil, must wholly and entirely depend upon the details to be determined upon for its working.

Aware of this fact, the leaders of that party will strain every nerve to insure a majority favourable to their views, and, with characteristic deception, will tack bits of extra liberality, apart from that question, to their addresses, in the hope of diverting public attention from the consideration of the MASTER-GRIEVANCE,—THE GRIEVANCE of the OWNERS OF MECHANICAL POWER REPRESENTING THE INTERESTS OF THE MANUAL LABOURER.

This should now be the all-absorbing question with all who hope to live upon their own industry, upon the proceeds of their own labour, undiminished by the clippings of protected capital and represented power. During the heat of FREE-TRADE agitation we adhered to the doctrine, that the capricious adoption of the principle, unaccompanied by PRUDENT and NECESSARY CONCESSIONS, AND FAIR ADJUSTMENT, would, firstly, pauperize the manual labourer; secondly, would make bankrupts of the small shopkeepers, who depend, for profit and existence, upon the state of the labour market; thirdly, would reduce the farming class to beggary; fourthly, would confiscate the property of the landlords to Jew jobbers, money-mongers, and mortgagees; fifthly, would convince the Free-Trade manufacturers that they had caught a

Tartar; and sixthly, would compel the government to do that, from terror of bankruptcy and revolution, which, if done in time, would have averted both, and have preserved the several classes of society in their respective positions. Our readers must do us the justice to admit that we have laboured incessantly to convince the shopkeeping class that their alliance with the free-traders resembled the union between the LAMB AND THE TIGER, THE MOUSE AND THE CAT, THE LARK AND THE KITE. We have further described the present general movement as the struggle of the DEMOCRACY of each class against the ARISTOCRACY of its own order, and our position is being daily strengthened by the increasing class feuds now promising defeat to faction, which were only smothered by the dangers threatened by famine, but which a General Election will swell to madness and rouse to fury. The destructive policy of adopting the principle of Free Trade, unaccompanied by a fair adjustment of all interests affected by the change, has rendered the stability of governments a mere problem, contingent upon the chapter of accidents, and henceforth, as now, tenure will be regulated by the BAROMETER—a glance of sunshine elevating, a cloud depressing, ministerial hope. Is this a position worthy the GREATEST NATION in the world?

Here we introduce the address of Mr. Cobden for the purpose of arousing the industrious to renewed energy and opposition, and to illustrate from it the prospects of the realisation of those very predictions which Mr. Cobden was wont to treat as chimerical, but which now haunt his Free-Trade dreams as fearful realities, only to be dispelled by a strengthening of the party, whose measures have been the cause of the admitted result, which Mr. Cobden deplores.

TO THE ELECTORS OF STOCKPORT.

Gentlemen,

Should a dissolution occur before I can have the pleasure of meeting you in person, I beg to be allowed to take this mode of again soliciting the honour of being one of your representatives in Parliament.

I deeply regret that you will be called upon to exercise the elective franchise at a time of great manufacturing depression. It is no consolation to generous minds to know that their sufferings are shared by others; but, unhappily, almost the whole of Europe is mourning over deficient harvests, amidst privations, which for severity and extent have no parallel in the present century. It is possible that to some of my friends, who rejoiced in the brighter prospects afforded by our recent commercial reforms, the existing distress may have brought feelings of doubt and discouragement. Free trade cannot avert a sudden and calamitous visitation of Providence; it can only alleviate its pressure. But the present crisis has at least this consolation,—that it has brought, from all quarters, proofs of the soundness and beneficence of our principles; for we have seen the governments of the continent, with hardly an exception, abolish their multiform regulations of the corn trade, at the moment when, if their interference be ever efficacious, it was the most needed; and we see them now relying upon the energies of emancipated commerce alone for saving their people from the horrors of famine.

It must, however, be acknowledged that we enter upon the new commercial era under unfortunate circumstances. I do not allude merely to the present scarcity of food, which in all human probability will be of short duration, but also to the possibility of a sudden reaction in the opposite direction, which may protract for a time the transition from the restrictive system to the more squabble state of freedom. The present exorbitant prices will cause, as in former times in England, a greatly increased production of corn. At the same time the agriculture of the whole civilized world is under the stimulus of famine prices; and should we be blessed with a succession of good harvests, we may anticipate a glut of corn, not as the result of free trade, but of the present scarcity. A similar process, to be followed possibly with like results, is going on with another important interest. The present enormous cost of freights, by which not a few of the shipowners of the Mediterranean will clear the value of their vessels in this year, is everywhere causing large investments of capital in shipbuilding. Judging from former experience, it is not therefore improbable that these two interests, which have been the least favourable to free trade, may be ere long simultaneously exposed to the effects of a reaction from their present excitement. If there be any force in these views, they furnish the strongest motives to the friends of free trade for sending to the next Parliament—during the existence of which the process I have described will in all probability be passed through—representatives of tried convictions, who will guard with firmness the great measures of last year from the dangers to which they may be exposed in their transition state. Should you honour me with your confidence, I shall hope to be found with renewed health at my post, prepared to show that the present state of trade is no fair experiment of our principles, and that the consequent reaction will be only an exception to the ordinary operation of free trade, which, when fairly tested by time, will, I fervently believe, promote the prosperity and harmony of the whole community; and I shall return to England confirmed in my opinion by the sympathy expressed for our principles by the best and wisest men in other countries, that if we continue with firmness to offer to the world a good example, it will be eventually followed by all other civilized nations.

Gentlemen, if at this distance I do not attempt to enter upon the discussion of other matters, it is not because I am insensible of the importance of the questions which must, at the earliest possible moment, engage the attention of the Legislature, foremost amongst which is the state of Ireland. I will only add, that in every question brought before Parliament, I shall, to the best of my humble ability, act upon the principle of doing equal justice to my fellow-countrymen in every part of the United Kingdom.

I have the honour to remain, Gentlemen,

With sentiments of respect and gratitude,

Your faithful servant,

RICHARD COBDEN.

Venice, June 15.

The reader who has followed us in our ANTI-FREE TRADE career for the last fourteen years, will, doubtless, smile at the admissions made by the acknowledged leader of the FREE-TRADE party; but we doubt that the mysterious consolation offered by the prophet will have a sufficiently instantaneous effect in dispelling the disappointment so generally felt by the enthusiastic GAPERS, who felt confident in the promised magical abundance to secure the desired hearty co-operation, for the further problematical results, for which they are now invited to contend.

We shall now consider the enigmatical and very problematical results, for which those friends of Mr. Cobden, " who rejoiced in the brighter prospects afforded by our recent commercial reforms," are sought to be enlisted as the "REPRESENTATIVES OF TRIED CONVICTIONS."

We can well believe in the disappointment experienced by Mr. Cobden's followers, and feel convinced that they are possessed of FEELINGS OF DOUBT AND DISCOURAGEMENT; but we shall select passages of the candidate's address for comment, which are apologetic for the past, or encouraging for the future. Mr. Cobden says, " Free Trade cannot arrest a sudden and calamitous visitation of Providence—it can only alleviate its pressure."

We had hoped that the blasphemous charge against Divine Providence had been abandoned; but it appears that the League, as the Church, must have its STALKING-HORSE. We, too, were aware that " Free Trade could not arrest a sudden calamity;" but we were not prepared to find those, for whose especial and sóle benefit the battle was fought, the only sufferers from the calamity ; we were not prepared to find the HIGH WAGES, CHEAP BREAD, AND PLENTY TO DO, transformed, as if by magic, into LOW WAGES, NO BREAD, AND NOTHING OR LITTLE TO DO. We were not prepared for a reduction of wages, upon the pretence of declining markets, and Free Trade opposition to a reduction in the hours of labour, upon the pretext that the IDLE POOR WOULD BE THE GREATEST SUFFERERS. We were not prepared for the brutal exercise of power, which enabled the master, with his ready-made fortune, to pass undamaged through that season of hesitation, of doubt, and confusion, which Mr. Cobden is now compelled to APPREHEND, while those who made that fortune were alone to suffer from THIS DIVINE DISPENSATION. The writer goes on :—" But the present crisis has at least this consolation : 'that it has brought from all quarters proofs of the soundness and beneficence of our principles, for we have seen the governments of the continent, with hardly an exception, abolish their multiform regulations of the corn trade, at the moment when, if their interference be ever efficacious, it was the most needed."

We know not what " CONSOLATION the PRESENT CRISIS" may derive from the fears and expediency of foreign Cabinets, but we do know the starving poor derive but little consolation from the ' LIVE HORSE AND YOU'LL-GET-GRASS' anticipations of FREE-TRADERS. Does not Mr. Cobden understand that the relaxation of the rigid rules of foreign monopolists was a tribute to FEARFUL APPREHENSIONS, rather than to the SOUNDNESS AND BENEFICENCE OF OUR PRINCIPLES ; and that his Free-Trade disciples abroad consist principally of CORN-GROWERS, who look to DEVOURING JOHN BULL as a greedy customer of their produce, rather than to manufacturers, who still look to SOME RESTRICTIONS, as their protection ? Mr. Cobden, while dealing with FREE TRADE in wholesale terms, appears to have lost sight of the question of a NATIONAL DEBT, and of the fact that no two countries, by any process of Free Trade, who are unequally taxed, can by possibility meet upon equal terms in the UNIVERSAL PRODUCE-MART. Now, these are some of the adjustments, to which we have incessantly directed public attention, showing that all Free-Trade professors have invariably lost sight of the question of RECIPROCITY. Mr. Cobden might have concluded his last paragraph in these words : " And we see them now relying upon the chances of emancipated commerce alone for saving THEMSELVES FROM REVOLUTION."

The next passage is so full of penitence, despair and dismay, that we reprint it at full length :—" It must, however, be acknowledged that we enter upon the new commercial era under unfortunate circumstances. I do not allude merely to the present scarcity of food, which in all human probability will be of short duration, but also to the possibility of a sudden reaction in the opposite direction, which may protract for a time the transition from the restrictive system to the more equable state of freedom. The present exorbitant prices will cause, as in former times in England, a greatly increased production of corn. At the same time the agriculture of the whole civilized world is under the stimulus of famine prices; and should we be blessed with a succession of good harvests, we may anticipate a glut of corn, not as the result of free trade, but of the present scarcity." Yes, in truth, " we do enter upon the new commercial era under MOST unfortunate circumstances;" but then, what brighter prospects does Mr. Cobden anticipate from future legislation, beyond the return of REPRESENTATIVES OF TRIED CONVICTIONS ? However, as our object is to strengthen the popular cause for the next struggle, let us see in how far Mr. Cobden's present opinions coincide with our UNALTERED NOTIONS. Mr. Cobden now sees and now dreads sudden fluctuations, while the grand object of FREE TRADE was, SETTLEMENT OF EVERY-THING—AN UNERRING STANDARD, BY WHICH CAPITAL MIGHT BE SAFELY EXPENDED, SPECULATIONS SAFELY UNDERTAKEN, AND, ABOVE ALL, LABOUR PLACED UPON A SOUND FOUNDATION. Now what were, and still are, our opinions, repeated to surfeit ?

" The great danger to be apprehended from a capricious
" settlement of the question, without being accompanied by
" an adjustment of the several interests to be affected by the
" principle, is sudden fluctuations, alterations from cheap to
" dear, and dear to cheap ; a period of at least three years of
" casualties, changes, speculation and derangement; in which
" the unprotected poor will be the first and greatest sufferers
" from the measure, if not preceded by the just and necessary

" adjustments, which are indispensable to the settlement of
" interests now, in some degree, based upon the old system.
" Let the poor consumer rely upon it that he will be the first
" to suffer, and his hardship will not be mitigated by the fasci-
" nation of cheap bread, as cheap and dear are relative terms,
" and the man without a penny to purchase the cheap loaf
" will be an object of greater commiseration than the man
" who is FORCED, BUT ABLE to give a shilling for the
" dear loaf."

Now, we ask the impartial reader to say, whether
or not our predictions, in part realised, and in course of
complete fulfilment, do not at present haunt the FREE-
TRADE dreams of the TOURIST ? And further, we tell
Mr. Cobden, that uncertainty will be greater, and dependence more general, when wheat is selling in MARK-LANE
FOR FORTY SHILLINGS THE QUARTER. So long
as the price of wheat, which establishes the standard value of
gold, fluctuates, so long will the poor be at the mercy of the
rich ; and in proportion as the value of the circulating medium is operated upon by monopolists and forestallers, in
the same proportion will labour suffer and industry decay,
until at length the interests of all—and labour not the last—
must be legislated for.

The Free-Trade penitent proceeds :—

" The present exorbitant prices will cause, as in former
times in England, a greatly increased production of corn."

This is but a recent discovery of Professor Cobden, who
was in the habit of assuring us that FREE TRADE was
the ONE THING, the VERY THING, the ONLY
THING required to EQUALIZE DEMAND and
SUPPLY.

But, mark our answer. We told our readers, " that the
rich market being once opened, the cotton-growers of America, and all the agriculturists throughout the world, would
set about producing for the wealthy consumers, while the
taxed home-grower could not compete against the untaxed
foreigner, and that the consequence would be a glut of agricultural labourers, thrown upon the already overstocked artificial market; and the reader may rest assured that the
amount brought here on speculation, and not the amount
paid in foreign markets, will regulate the price of home
produce."

' The Professor proceeds :—" A similar process, to be followed possibly with like results, is going on with another
important interest. The present enormous cost of freights,

by which not a few of the shipowners of the Mediterranean will clear the value of their vessels in this year, is everywhere causing large investments of capital in ship-building. Judging from former experience, it is not therefore improbable that these two interests, which have been the least favourable to FREE TRADE, may be ere long simultaneously exposed to the effects of a reaction from their present excitement."

Here, then, are symptoms of another reaction, and one which we predicted in 1842, upon the passing of Sir Robert Peel's cattle tariff. At that time all the FREE-TRADE journals had their BEAST COMMISSIONERS, or professed to have them, taking stock of foreign cattle all over the world; and the *Chronicle* and *Sun* exultingly assured us that the home breeder would find ample protection in the high rate of freights required by shipowners for bringing competitors over from Spain, amounting, as we are told, to over four pounds upon a beast not worth more than thirteen pounds. Now, what was our answer? Why, nearly the words of Mr. Cobden. We said, "That the trade was not prepared for such a sudden demand, but that the ship-builders of the world would not fail to place themselves in a position to meet it; and that the probability was, that the shipbuilders of Liverpool and of other ports were now making the necessary arrangements to meet the increased demands." Such were our predictions with regard to one branch of trade, of which Mr. Cobden appears to have lost sight; and, presently, competition in this department will cause an outcry from the shipping interest which will lead to another Free Trade difficulty.

It is really curious to see how the Free-Trade prophets are compelled to adopt our every prediction.

We have now commented upon the New Free-Trade cry of "RETURN REPRESENTATIVES OF TRIED CONVICTIONS;" and but little remains for us, beyond the duty of preparing the working classes for the CRY.

This, then, is our solemn advice : that the Chartist party should in all cases be prepared with representatives of TRIED CONVICTIONS, who will guard the interests, not of a class but of the community, in the next Parliament.

As we predicted, the enemy has drawn the sword, and naught now remains for us but to throw away the scabbard. Cobden's presence, after a convenient absence, may give vitality to his own lifeless party, when it must be our care and study to protect the unwary against the snares set for them by the designing.

There is now but one course open to the Chartist party, and that course is, to return as many Chartists as possible, of TRIED CONVICTIONS, to the next Parliament; and, further, to secure as many Chartist delegates as they can, by a show of hands, who shall speak the public mind, and who shall meet, not in a national, but in an imperial convention, when the Free Traders next assemble in St. Stephen's. And the duty of those delegates will be to secure the signatures of their constituents to a firm, a resolute, and unequivocal demand for the PEOPLE'S CHARTER.

We say an imperial convention, because there we hope to meet O'Higgins and other honest Irish representatives of TRIED CONVICTIONS, representing A TRUE AND ENLIGHTENED IRISH MIND.

In order to effect this necessary object, we shall ere long point out the easy means by which the pecuniary resources may be supplied.

In conclusion we may observe, without vanity, that our every prediction with regard to Free Trade and Free Traders has been realised; while our readers must do us the justice to admit we had prepared the public mind to resist the infliction of so great a calamity as the return of a Free-Trade Parliament consisting of Representatives of TRIED FREE-TRADE CONVICTIONS. Cobden's re-appearance, added to his plain and simple admissions of Free-Trade failure, will go far to strengthen the hands of the Protectionists; and further to nerve the opposition of the industrious.

The shopkeepers who may construe Cobden's admissions into their bankruptcy, will surely not longer hesitate, but will join those upon whose free labour and requited industry they depend.

Let all now join in a Monster Petition to the New House, demanding the PEOPLE'S CHARTER as the only means of securing the People's Rights; and let the improved mind, thus embodied in an imperial demand, be followed by the living masses, entertaining the same principles, to the door of St. Stephen's, there to be committed to the guardianship of the People's Champion—

THOMAS SLINGSBY DUNCOMBE.

THE CONFESSIONS OF A KING.

(*Continued from Vol. I. page* 259.)

In vain I searched for the merchant among the crowd—in vain I sent many in quest of him. He must have escaped amid the tumult; but all thought of him was soon lost in the absorbing vortex of my ambition. To form a democratic government, to elect me as its president, was the first care of the people. I accepted the mighty trust with a graceful modesty that won me golden opinions; but I joyed in my fierce heart at the knowledge that my irresistible career was storming onward to the height of power. Many factions now arose among the people—parties were formed and cries were raised. I baffled them all, by always propounding plans more democratic than themselves; I knew they would oppose me—I knew that through their opposition my measures would not be carried—and I thus gained the double advantage of checking liberty, while I won all the glory of its advocacy. Tyrants! take this lesson from my life! " Progression" and " Democracy," these are your 'cards to play ! I obtained another and still subtler object in addition. By my reckless advocacy of freedom, I roused the fears of surrounding monarchs. They might possibly have pardoned my usurpation of power, they could not pardon my speaking the language of liberty ; therefore they combined against me, and war became necessary. Had they left me in peace I might have fallen a prey to internal faction. War ensured the stability of my position : it directed the excited feelings of the people to another object—it enabled me to fascinate them with military glory—that handmaiden of tyranny—it empowered me to levy an army, and, strong in the brotherhood of murder, to turn victorious troops on an admiring people. I was careful, however, to let aggression come from the foe. I even offered fair terms of peace. The more I yielded, the more truculent grew the enemy. Meanwhile, I prepared for defence ; a league of crowned heads was formed, and the allied army invaded the country. Then I rallied the people ! Then again my voice was raised for liberty, and like a thunderbolt it gathered up the elements of destruction. Indescribable enthusiasm pervaded the tumultuous host I had assembled: even my own heart caught the fire, and with a chivalrous daring I dashed on the invader. I knew my irregular force to be no match for their disciplined armies, but I seized the wild impulse of the moment, and, before it cooled, I hurled the hot avalanche of popular fury on my royal foes. They were crushed beneath the fierce tread of democracy; I swept over the battle-field like a hurricane- –there was no battle—but there *was* a carnage; the stricken eagle sued for peace. Think not I granted it! I could play the invader in my turn; I advanced the people's tricolour across the border. Fatal error of democracy! On those battle-fields I was enabled to twine the laurel of victory into the crown of a despot.

A delirium of joy pervaded the populace—one blaze of festivals filled town and land on the day I ascended the throne. It was the funeral of Liberty! Fools! they had now fastened their own manacles. There is indeed a fascination in the name of "king" that rivets the slave—an old, venerative fear. Man is more prone to worship an idol than a god. Thus he upholds "law" despite of justice—"classes" instead of equality, and "rites" instead of religion.

The name of "king" was a fortress of strength; social distinctions created ready tools—and titles purchased slaves. At first, indeed, they were military titles—since it was mainly to the army that I owed my throne. I had created that army: I had shared its dangers and its hardships; I had led it to "glory"—and these poor puppets of my ambition, that I slaughtered bv tens of thousands for the most trivial object of policy, would have died at my feet to have ramparted my life. But a titled aristocracy soon superseded this—marshals changed into dukes, and a proud nobility swarmed at my court; my new position altered my policy. It was no longer my part to strike down thrones. I recalled the scourge of my invading armies—I re-established the humbled despots in their authority, and sought the alliance of the very men I had crushed. They came, gloss-faced hypocrites—but I, too, was guilty of a fatal error—they might have forgiven me their overthrow—the hereditary kings could never forgive me my birth.

I reigned in the zenith of my power, my dominions were stretched far beyond the previous limits of the empire—I was the idolised head of a magnificent people—art, science and splendour, held their home in my palaces—but a secret void kept extending in my heart. Ambition had changed into a disease—I had climbed its utmost he ght, and I craved, like the son of Philip, for another world to conquer. Domestic affection was not to be mine. The favourite I had superseded had obtained his revenge. Ere he fell, I lost my son—whether by death, or otherwise, I knew not—but suspicion and circumstance pointed to my rival. Since then, I had the country searched—I sent emissaries into foreign lands, but they brought me no tidings. And love—the balm of affliction, the fire of energy—was mine no more. It had long died in my heart—and now—strange anomaly! I loathèd my wife for the very act that had saved *my* life and our child's. Years had flown since that hour—she had been the stepping-stone of my power— and, now that power was obtained, I reasoned myself into holding her an object unworthy to share my throne. Tyrant as I was, popularity had been my element, and now the mildew began to steal over my laurels.

When the first struggle of false glory had subsided, men set about comparing my present with my past; the better among the people began to ask themselves whether this was the result they had intended; whether all that burning, and bloodshed and destruction, was, after all, meant to achieve nothing more, than to change a weak tyrant for a strong one. Then they began to discover all the mistakes they had committed: " Ah! had we not made him president!" " Ah! had we been as anxious for peace as for war, he never would have been able to create and attack enthusiastic armies!" " Ah! had we never given him the crown, he could never have identified with his own interests all the vast machinery of a state church and a nobility!" Then they made a second mistake. They rebelled, just when they had let me grow irresistibly strong. Hotheaded fools! They should have let my power sink into the sere of age, and their own reach the maturity of manhood. For three days the carnage lasted in the capital; on the third I triumphed. The best and bravest of my enemies made a last rally on the space where once towered the palace I had destroyed. From every side poured on them the tide of death, while I stood at a window of the castle and cried, " Slay! slay!"

This rising had emanated mainly from the middle classes; and, strange to say, the young soldier, to whom I have before alluded, took no part in the movement. " This is but the monied class against the titled class," he said. " There is no democracy in this. It is only the ᴏ unting-house trying to supplant the castle! Let them fight! People! bide your time!"

I saw this—and, as I had attached the landed and church-class to my throne, I saw I should still fail, unless I could gain the monied interest as well. I therefore created a NATIONAL DEBT. A great class of fundholders arose at once—speculation had scope for vast undertakings—my former enemies became vitally interested in the stability of my throne; and the middle classes of even foreign countries found it to their interest to sway the legislative bodies, of which they formed a powerful part, for the maintenance of my authority. Nay, so precious had my life become to the very men who had tried to destroy it, that, if my illness or defeat made the funds fall, half a world was praying for my recovery and success. The people only were now left; but I felt I could control them by the hand of force. I felt it was vain to attempt conciliating them, for I knew they could never be prosperous so long as I ground them to the dust by an aristocracy, a church-establishment, a funded interest, pension list, and court, supported by vast taxation, and upheld by a costly army and police. I, therefore, never gave myself the trouble to make the attempt; but held them down by the hard hand of power, without deigning to have recourse to the velvet glove. And I was well served, for I chose my servants well. I tried the metal before I took it. I singled a man from the crowd—raised him to power, and, in the flush of ambition, dashed over him the cold water of disappointment; or, from the gulf of despondency, I would pour on him the sudden splendour of success. If he bore either trial with unmoved temperance, I knew he was a man born to serve me. I then took care to give him a mutual interest with myself, by making him commit himself irrevocably with *my* enemies; and for the rest—I never let him have more to gain by treason than by loyalty. Edged tools are ever the easiest to handle by a practised hand.

I had little now to fear from open resistance; it was succeeded by the assassin's steel. I had scorned death—I now dreaded it—for my grave looked like a pit bubbling with the hot blood of my victims. I felt restless—memory was an agony—home a blank—action a lull from thought—and life itself but a respite from hell. In the camp I was safest from murder; for I could better guard my tent with triple walls of steel, than I could my palace from the thousand snares of plotting parasites. The planning of campaigns—the eves, the days of battles, were like draughts of oblivion. And thus I surged on from victory to victory while men admired my success or pitied my ambition, little knowing that the conqueror of nations was but a fugitive flying from himself!

(*To be continued.*)

THE POOR MAN'S LEGAL MANUAL.
No. II.

The Game Laws.

The present system of Game Laws owes its origin to the oppressive Forest Laws of William the Norman, who loved the red-deer as his own children, and much better than his own subjects. It is one of the relics of feudal barbarism and feudal tyranny, which in former times overcame the genuine spirit of Saxon liberty.

"From the Forest Laws," says Sir William Blackstone,* " has sprung the Game Law now arrived to, and wantoning in its highest vigour, both founded upon the same unreasonable notions of permanent property in wild creatures, and both productive of the same tyranny to the Commons; but with this difference, that the Forest Laws established only one mighty hunter throughout the land, the Game Laws raised a little Nimrod in every manor." This is pretty strong language for one who was a judge some sixty years ago, but not too strong for the subject.

The feudal system prevailed also in France to the period of the great revolution (1793), when it was wholly abolished, and, as a part of it, the Game Laws were expressly declared to be destroyed.

By the civil law of Rome, which is so often praised as a model to be followed by other countries, all wild animals, whether flesh, fish, or fowl, were the property of any who could take them; but no one was allowed to trespass on another man's land in pursuit of them; if he did so, he was punished as a trespasser, not as a poacher; it was for the

* Commentaries, vol. iv. p. 416.

sake of the land, and the property therein not game, that such trespass was prohibited.

In our country, however, the ruling powers have not been contented with so mild a measure, but statute after statute has been passed for the protection of game, and heavy and cumulative penalties denounced against all who are guilty of infringing their enactments. Game differs much from those things which may be said to be the subject of private property. It is admitted on all hands not to belong to any person in particular until it is reclaimed, or preserved, by and for that person; and even then, directly it wanders from his land it becomes the property of the person to whose land it comes. Other property, too, it is supposed, may be enjoyed by the owner without injury to others; but game preserved for the amusement of a few is the pest of the surrounding neighbourhood, and does infinite injury to the agriculture of the country. It has been with a view to supply this deficiency in game, *considered as property*, that so many grievous Acts of Parliament have been passed in regard to it; and it has been sought to remedy the weakness of the object by the strength of the means used to support it. The love of pursuing game, or of sport, is natural to man in a barbarous or civilised state, and to overcome this has been one of the causes of such severe laws. To show the character of these laws as they now exist, we propose to give an analysis of them, so that any may soon perceive the offences which come beneath them, and their respective punishments, and thus may not be ignorant upon a matter which deeply affects the classes to which we appeal.

By stats. 1 and 2 W. 4, c. 32, killing or taking game, or using any dog, gun, net, or other engine or instrument, for the purpose of killing and taking of game on a Sunday or Christmas-day, is punishable by a fine not exceeding £5. and costs, or three months' imprisonment and hard labour.

Killing or taking a partridge between the first day of February and the first day of September; a pheasant between the first of February and the first of October; or black game (except in Devon, Somerset or the New Forest), between the tenth of December and the twentieth of August, in the succeeding year.; and in Devon, Somerset, and the New Forest, between the tenth of December and the succeeding first of September; or grouse, commonly called red game, between tenth of December and the succeeding twelfth of August; or any bustard between the first of March and first of September; for every head of game a fine may be imposed not exceeding 20s. and costs, or imprisonment for two months and hard labour.

Buying, selling, or knowingly having in house, shop, stall, or possession or control, any bird of game after the expiration of ten days (one exclusive and the other inclusive), from the respective days in each year on which it shall become unlawful, or if a person not licensed to deal in game shall buy or sell any bird of game after ten days (one inclusive and the other exclusive) from the respective days on which it shall become unlawful as aforesaid, or shall knowingly have in his house, possession or control, any bird of game (except birds of game kept in a mew or breeding place) after the expiration of forty days from the expiration of the respective seasons; for every head of game 20s. and costs, or two months' imprisonment and hard labour. No restriction is imposed by this Act upon killing hares at any season.

This Act abolishes the old qualification to kill game, but empowers any person who may take out a game certificate to kill game, subject only to his liability in respect of any trespass committed in pursuit of it. But it is declared that nothing in that Act contained shall affect or alter (except as after-mentioned) any acts by which persons using any dog, gun, net or other engine, for the purpose of taking or killing any game whatever, or any woodcock, snipe, quail or landrail, or conies, are required to obtain and have annual game certificates; consequently all the Acts relating to certificates are unrepealed, and in addition, by this Act it is enacted, that taking or killing game, or using any dog, gun, net, or other engine or instrument for searching for, or killing game, such person not being authorised for want of a certificate, shall render him liable to a penalty not exceeding £5. and costs, or three months' imprisonment with hard labour.

And it is expressly provided, that the payment of this penalty shall not be exempt from certificate duty ; but this penalty shall be deemed a cumulative penalty.

Trespass by entering, or being in the day-time in search or pursuit of game or woodcocks, snipes, quails, landrails or conies, is punishable by a fine not exceeding 40s. and costs, or two months' imprisonment and hard labour. And if more than five persons together commit any such trespass, each is liable to a fine not exceeding £5. and costs, or three months' imprisonment and hard labour.

A trespasser may be required to tell his christian and sur-

name, and place of abode, or on refusal may be apprehended.
And a trespasser refusing to give his name, whether apprehended or not, may be fined not exceeding £5. and costs, or
be imprisoned for three months with hard labour.

When five or more persons trespassing in the day-time, if
any one being armed with a gun use threats or violence to
prevent, or endeavour to prevent, any authorised person from
requiring them to quit the land or to tell their names, &c., the
person offending by violence, and those aiding and abetting
him, shall be liable to an additional and independent penalty
of a sum not exceeding £5. and costs, or three months' imprisonment and hard labour.

N.B.—Game (but not woodcocks, snipes, quails, landrails,
or rabbits,) may be taken from trespassers under this section.

If proceedings be taken for trespass under this Act, a civil
action cannot be maintained.

By 52 Geo. 3, c. 93, it is provided that persons using
any dog, gun, net, or other engine for the purpose of taking
or killing any game whatever, or any woodcock, snipe, quail,
landrail or any conies, a certificate duty of £3 13s. 6d. is
imposed, which, by 3 Vic. c. 17, has been since increased to
£4 0s. 10d.

The exemptions from this duty are

1. Taking woodcocks and snipes with nets and springs.

2. Taking or destroying conies, by the proprietors of
warrens, on any inclosed ground whatever, or by the tenant
of lands by himself or his direction.

By 1 Geo. 3, c. 41' persons assisting, or intending to
assist, a certificated person, to take or kill game, are not
to be liable to duty.

By 2 Geo. 3, c. 93, sporting without a certificate is
punishable by a fine of £20. and £4 0s. 10d. duty, to be
levied by distress, or six months' imprisonment.

Persons using dog, gun, &c., refusing to produce
certificate, or, if no certificate produced, to declare his
christian and surname, and place of residence, and assess-
ment, or producing false certificate, or giving false name,
&c., liable to a penalty of £20., to be levied by distress,
or six months' imprisonment.

By 5 Geo. 4, c. 44, surveyors of taxes are empowered
to charge persons killing game without certificate, and without any previous information and conviction.

By 6 and 7 Will. 4, c. 65, persons sporting without
certificate may be charged with double duty, £8 1s. 8d.

By 1 and 2 Will. 4, c. 32, certificated persons may sell game to licensed dealers, except gamekeepers, who cannot, without the written authority of their masters. Licenses to game dealers granted by justices at petty sessions in July, yearly, who must take out certificate, pay yearly duty of £2. Purchasing or selling without license exposes to a fine of £20., or six months' imprisonment.

Selling, or offering for sale, game without a certificate to any person, or having a certificate, to any one, except a licensed dealer, renders liable to a fine not exceeding £2. and costs, or two months' imprisonment and hard labour.

Buying game, except from licensed dealers, a fine not exceeding £5. and costs, or three months' imprisonment and hard labour.

Licensed dealers buying of persons without a certificate, or selling contrary to Act, a fine not exceeding £10. and costs, or three months' imprisonment and hard labour.

By 5 and 6 Will. 4, c. 20, persons informing and prosecuting for game offences are indemnified against penalties they may have incurred in respect of the same transaction

By 1 and 2 Will. 4, c. 32, moiety of penalty goes to informer. Putting any poison on any ground, whether open or enclosed, where game usually resort, or in any highway, a fine not exceeding £10., or three months' imprisonment and hard labour.

Taking out of the nest, or destroying in the nest, or having in possession, the eggs of any bird of game, or of any swan, wild duck, teal, or widgeon, for every egg a fine not exceeding £5., or two months' imprisonment and hard labour.

By 7 and 8 Geo. 4, c. 29, taking or killing any hare or coney in a warren, on ground lawfully used for breeding or keeping of hares and conies, whether inclosed or not, is a misdemeanor.

The like in such place in the day-time, a fine not exceeding £5., or three months' imprisonment and hard labour.

By 9 Geo. 4, c. 69, night poaching commences at the expiration of the first hour after sunset, and concludes at the last hour before sunrise. Any person by night unlawfully taking and destroying any game or rabbits in any land, whether open or inclosed, or by night, unlawfully entering, or firing in any land, whether open or inclosed, with any gun, net, engine, or other instrument, for the purpose of taking or destroying game, shall for his first offence be committed for a term not exceeding three months, with hard labour, and at the expiration to find sureties, himself in £10., and two sureties in £5. each, or one in £10., for his not offending again for a year next following. If he does not find sureties, to be imprisoned, and kept to hard labour for the space of six months. For second offence, imprisonment, not exceeding six months, with hard labour, and at expiration to find sureties, himself in £20., two sureties of £10. each, or one in £20. for two years following. *If not find sureties, imprisonment for one year, with hard labour.* The third offence is declared a misdemeanor, and the offender may be, at the discretion of the court, *transported for seven years*, or imprisoned and kept to hard labour, not exceeding two years.

Owners, occupiers, gamekeepers, and servants, may apprehend such persons, who, if they offer violence, will be guilty of misdemeanor.

Prosecution within six months after offence.

Appeal against summary convictions to quarter sessions, giving notice of appeal within three days after conviction, and give security to pay costs awarded on appeal.

Three or more persons entering or being on any land, &c., with any gun, cross-bow, fire-arms, bludgeon, or other offensive weapon, each person is guilty of a misdemeanor, and punishable, at discretion of the court, with transportation, not exceeding fourteen years, nor less than seven years; or imprisoned with hard labour, not exceeding three years.

By 1 & 2 Will. 4, c. 32, trustees convicting summarily under the Act may direct the penalty and costs to be paid immediately, or within some appointed time, and, in default of payment at the time appointed, the convicted person may be imprisoned in the county gaol, or house of correction, with or without hard labour, for any term not exceeding two calendar months, where the amount to be paid, exclusive of costs, shall not amount to £5. 8s., for any term not exceeding three calendar months; in any other case, the imprisonment to cease, on payment of the amount of costs.

We had intended to offer some further remarks upon these laws, but find that our space will not permit them in the present number.

THE LABOURER,

THE SKETCH.

BY ERNEST JONES.

THROUGH our land—through our land—
  Wander, stranger, wander free!
With thy tablet in thy hand,
  Note me all that thou may'st see.

Sights of splendour, scenes of glory,
  Hills where breathes the breeze of health,
Modern halls and castles hoary,
  Hives of art and mines of wealth.

Verdant vallies, highlands sloping,
  Graceful villa, wooded glen;
Little pictures, framed for hoping,
  In the work-day dreams of men.

Sweetest homes, where thought may anchor,
  Floating o'er the sea of life,
In the lull of human rancour,
  Iu the truce of human strife.

Stately palace, crowded city,
  Ball-room bright and glowing court;
Thespic mime and concert-ditty;
  Course and stand, and bet and sport.

Piles of gold in steady banks,
  Piles of gold on gamblers' boards;
Grand parades of scarlet ranks,
  Drums, and trumps, and fiery hoards.

Banquets brave at regal tables,
   Foreign kings to grace the feasts;
Countless steeds in royal stables,
   Royal farms and fatted beasts.

See the wealth our land evinces,
   Pomp and splendour past compare;
Peers, ambassadors and princes,
   Bankers, bishops—everywhere!

This is England—this is England!
   Rule, Britannia, rule the waves!
Happy England—happy England!
   Britons never shall be slaves.

Through our land—through our land—
   Wander, stranger, wander free!
With thy note-book in thy hand,
   Tell me ALL that thou may'st see.

Ah! the starving population—
   Murdered body—murdered mind—
And the millions' desolation
   'Mid the plenty God designed.

Ah! the aged couple, parted
   In the Bastile's ward of hell—
Since those lingerers, broken-hearted,
   Lived too long, and worked too well.

Ah! the babe, from workhouse-mother
   Torn away with cruel hate;
Man! the nature ye would smother,
   Comes, her rights to vindicate!

That sickly babe, to strangers' care,
   A helpless, worse than orphan, cast,
May grow the nurseling of despair,
   And turn avenger at the last!

Ah! the workman groans in ashes,
   Trodden down 'neath Mammon's throne;
Peers! the blood that in him dashes
   Is more noble than your own.

Your strawberry-leaves and laurel crowns,
  Are dewed with patient Labour's tears :
Lightnings lurk in nations' frowns—
  Yield ! before the storm appears.

For, mid mighty disssolutions
  Of the bond 'twixt lord and slaves,
Onward—on to revolutions !
  O'er a murdered million's graves—

On—through freedom's triumph-arches,
  For its right and for its due,
Ireland marches—England marches—
  And the world is marching too.

Mark the tricky foes uniting—
  Coward still to coward clings :
No matter ! God and man are fighting
  Up against the league of kings.

Traitors—striving, secret, slavish,
  As the guilty dastard fights—
Would, with dirty fingers knavish,
  Soil the CHARTER of our Rights.

Here objections—there detractions—
  Whispering tongues, that dare not *speak* :
Now, confusion to their factions !
  Truth is strong, and lies are weak.

Slaves ! come forth, and face to face
  Cry, " infidel"—and cry again—
But do not cloak your lying base,
  By taking God's great name in vain.

Go, wolves ! and crouch within your lair,
  And watch the world becoming free ;
But, if ye'd measure strength—*prepare !*
  I'll hunt ye down as ye'd hunt me !

Go ! cringe to nobles, priests and kings ;
  Poor drops amid the waters vast ·
Crown, crozier, sword, are worn out things ;
  They're passing, and will soon be past.

Halifax, June, 1847.

THE INSURRECTIONS
OF
THE WORKING CLASSES.

(Continued from page 30.*)*

CHAPTER VI.
The Jacquerie.

The invading army, under the Duke of Lancaster, opened the campaign in the month of June, 1356, and the last hope of the neglected harvest was destroyed before this terrible scourge. Towns were stormed and taken, sanguinary actions fought, and a tide of blood and gold continued to pour out of the veins of this unhappy country. The main force of the English king was expected to follow in the wake of that of Lancaster, but his hands were tied at home, not only by Scotland, but by the growing discontent of his subjects, who began to complain that they were too heavily taxed for a foreign war. He was therefore crippled in his supplies, and obliged to content himself with sending the Prince of Wales, and a small force, to lay waste the country south of the Loire. Thus, while intestine struggles, and noble feuds, were devasting the heart of France, the fires of war were burning either extremity, and advancing rapidly towards the centre. So wretched was the state of the land, that even the invader complained of being led into a kingdom drained of wealth, and destitute of food; while the perishing peasants beheld the last crust of famine torn from them by the ruthless ambition of contending kings.

John of France now marched his entire power against the Prince of Wales. The latter retreated, but, desirous of signalising his campaign by some achievement, determined on storming the fortress of Remorantin, on his way. This caused a delay of some days; the place was ultimately taken by showering fire into it, until it was burnt to the ground;— but the time thus occupied enabled the king to overtake the English force, which awaited the enemy at Maupertuis, two leagues from Poitiers, in a strongly entrenched position. Two days were lost in fruitless negociations, but on Monday, the 19th of September, 1356, the famous battle of Poitiers was fought.

The English camp was surrounded by a difficult country, and the only means of access was by a deep road, guarded on either side by lofty hedges, lined with bowmen, who could thus single out their aim, amid the slow advance of an assailing force. At the end of this road stood the bulk of the English men-at-arms, with a body of archers before them, ready to receive the enemy with a shower of arrows, and when the latter should have weathered this double storm, assailing them in front and in either flank, they would find the strong lances of the English stretched like an impenetrable wall across their path, and a body of cavalry inserted in their line, ready to dash at the discomfited foe, and take advantage of his first confusion. Added to this, the road was so uneven and beset with brambles and vines, that many of the horsemen were obliged to dismount and advance on foot under the heavy discharges of the archery. The Black Prince was posted in the rear, with the reserve of his army, surrounded by vineyards and natural defences. The king of France opened the engagement by sending three hundred horsemen, cased in steel, up the road, to receive the first onslaught of the bowmen, thus to exhaust their store of arrows, and, like a wedge, to break through the living rampart at the other end of the road.

Headed by Marshals Andrehen and John of Clermont, they had scarcely entered the defile, before they had to encounter the cross-fire of the English. From either side, and from the front, the deadly salutation was poured upon them—and though they were encased in armour of proof, the arrows, discharged within a few paces of their aim, struck with a terrible force—piercing the fine mail of the French chivalry, who, thrown into irremediable disorder, were unable to retire, wedged together in the narrow channel of the defile, up which the main body of the infantry were steadily advancing. The wounded horses, maddened with pain, darted from side to side, throwing their riders and trampling on the dying and the dead; already all was confusion and dismay, when a squadron of horse was launched from the English line under John of Andely:— Marshal Andrehen was overthrown and taken prisoner, John of Clermont was crushed to death under the trampling of hoofs, and the French infantry, that still continued steadily advancing from their camp, were brought to a sudden halt by the refluent tide of horsemen, whom they in turn arrested. After a fearful pause, deepened by the meeting pressure of the march and flight, exposed to the ceaseless onslaught of the archery, the shattered mass began slowly to roll back towards the open plain, where they mingled with the divisions advancing under the Dauphin and the Duke of Orleans, threw these into disorder, originated a panic, of which six hundred English cavalry took advantage, and dashing down the hill on which they were posted, precipitated the flight of the French along the road of Chavigni.

The main body of the latter, commanded by the king in person, and outnumbering the English, still stood firm, as the advance and wings of their army were swept away on either side; and the steely river of the enemy was seen issuing through the fatal road, the site of the previous conflict, spreading as it reached the open plain, there forming into order of battle, and steadily bearing down upon the royal force.

The French laboured under the want of cavalry, soon rendered still more apparent, as the body of Germans under Counts Salbruck, Nosto, and Nydo, took to flight on the death of their leaders, thus discouraging their companions in arms, who still however maintained their ground, until the Lord High Constable was killed, the king twice wounded in the face, and with his son Philipp, a boy of fourteen, who was also wounded, taken prisoner by Denis of Morbec, a French knight who had been a refugee in England.

This battle had a signal influence on subsequent events. The French aristocracy had acted with great cowardice; they were defeated by a far inferior force, consisting, in great measure, of common yeomen; and the superstitious awe of their panoplied and scutcheoned prowess began to yield before the disgrace attaching to their arms. The king having been taken prisoner, the regency devolved on the Dauphin, Charles, Duke of Normandy, a young man of twenty;—the nobility were retiring before the English conqueror, and even the latter was being starved out of a desolated and exhausted country.

The peasantry, therefore, began to take the courage of despair; they had nothing to give, nothing to fear, and all to hope; while the citizens of towns, overburdened with taxation, and dreading ruin, assumed a decided tone and attitude, which rendered the Dauphin unwilling or unable to enact any legislative measure, without throwing the responsibility on the shoulders of the people.

Reduced to the necessity of assembling the States, he soon found that his authority must become a delegation from their own—for no sooner had the parliament met, than they began to discuss the form of government during the king's captivity. The Dauphin arrogated a prescriptive claim to the regency,—but, for the first time in France, the "right divine" of kings was forced to succumb before the right divine of peoples. The Dauphin was indeed recognised as vice-regent of the kingdom—but twelve members were chosen from each of the three estates, to form a permanent council, even after the dissolution of the Parliament. Thus, thirty-six deputies were elected by the majority, and among them were several who were personal opponents of the Regent. One of their first measures was to demand an account of the administration of the national revenues, the royal treasury being found exhausted, notwithstanding the extraordinary taxation. The result was, that the Archbishop of Rouen, Pierre de la Foret—Nicolas de Braque, Lord High Treasurer—Robert de Lorris, Lord Chamberlain—Jean de Peillevillain, Master of the Mint, and others, were impeached for mal-administration of the public monies. The States further demanded that Charles of Navarre should beset at liberty, and on these conditions undertook to raise an army of 30,000 men for the liberation of the king. They forthwith proceeded to levy troops, and employed them in a way little anticipated. Geoffery of Harcourt had long been the scourge of Lower Normandy, and, from his castle of Saint Saviour, had ravaged the country with impunity. One of the haughtiest of the feudal aristocracy, he treated the admonitions of the States with contempt, and was forthwith attacked, defeated and killed by the hardy soldiers of the senate.

Even this lesson failed, however, to check the pride of the aristocracy,—and the demand made for the liberation of Charles of Navarre, proved that still the votaries of royalty were not few among the ranks of the people. The most urgent for the release of the captive Prince were Robert de Coq, Bishop of Laon, Jean de Pequigni, Governor of Artois, and *Stephen Marcel, Provost of the Trades* of Paris. The two former were staunch adherents of Navarre; the latter may have thought to serve the popular cause by again sending forth the bitter opponent of the Regent, thus to weaken the power of the latter, which, undivided, might prove too strong to resist. Events showed that Marcel here committed an error in judgment. The people's battle should be fought by the people, and none other; it should be fought on the ground of principle, and not through the intrigues of princes. If not strong enough to stand alone, it is a proof that the day of victory is not come; and to wield unworthy arms but delays the hour of its arrival.

The Regent, dreading the liberation of so dangerous a foe, evaded the request by alleging his incompetency to deliver a captive who had been imprisoned by his father, (forgetting that he had not shown such reverence when he sought that father's life); and he prevented the punishment of his peculating ministers, by secretly securing their escape and subsequent flight. He also disembarrassed himself of the troublesome pressure of the states, by dissolving them (with a promise of a speedy re-assembly), on pretext of a voyage to Metz, there to concert measures with the Emperor, Charles the Fourth, for the liberation of his father.

He left his brother, Louis of Anjou, as his deputy, and directed him to publish an ordonnance respecting a change in the value of money—a prerogative which the states had claimed for themselves, and which the Regent thus endeavoured to annul, but feared to infringe in person. Stephen Marcel immediately proceeded to the Louvre, and demanded the instant revocation of the edict. Louis of Anjou postponed his reply until the next day, when the Provost went to the palace at the head of a vast multitude, and so intimidated the prince, that he consented to suspend the enactment until the return of his brother.

On receipt of these tidings, the Regent left Metz, where he had been awaiting the result of his measures, and entered Languedoc, hoping there to find men and money, for the purpose of punishing the capital. But the vicinage of the English in Guienne prevented his success, and every maritime province, from Gascony to Flanders, was held or ravaged by a foreign or a feudal enemy. The peasantry looked on in sullen apathy; one pervading idea seemed to have seized them: "What to us are the quarrels of kings?" He found no troops to command, and no men to enlist, and as princes are unable to fight their own battles with the sword, since he could not adopt the policy of terror, he resorted to that of dissimulation.

Returned to Paris with the Archbishop of Rouen, whose new dignity of Cardinal seemed to place him beyond the reach of a public impeachment, the Regent summoned Marcel to meet two of the royal Councillors at a house near St. Germain L'Auxerrois. The Provost came, accompanied not only by the populace, but also by a body of armed men; distinctly refused to sanction any change in the value of money, and assumed so decisive and threatening a demeanour, that the Dauphin was forced to concede. Without troops or money, Royalty stood forth a shadowy mockery, and the Regent was daily forced to fresh concessions, compelled to convoke the Diet, to place the impeached ministers, who had returned to Paris, under arrest, and to confiscate their property for the good of the state.

Meanwhile, the demand for the liberation of Charles of Navarre had raised the hopes of his adherents; they flew to arms, took the town and castle of Evreux, and Philipp of Navarre was soon in a position to second the efforts of his brother's friends in Paris.

The states having re-assembled, demanded the trial of the impeached ministers, their instant dismissal from office, the appointment of a commission consisting of one member out of each of the three orders, to investigate into the charges, and many other essential reforms in the government. The Regent was obliged to yield on every point—but the Archbishop of Sens, and Counts Tancarville and Eu, the envoys sent to treat for peace with the English, having returned after the accomplishment of their object, he was enabled to use this circumstance as a pretext for again dismissing the Diet, on the score that the proposed subsidies were now unnecessary, and therefore the object for which the Diet had assembled was no longer one of moment. The Dauphin had already learned the lesson, that a popular army, instead of being turned against the English, might be turned against himself. The states, however, refused to dissolve—they appealed to the people; they shewed them how dissolving the states was virtually placing them at the mercy of the Regent and his council, who "not being composed, in any part, of members of the working-classes, but of men whose interests lay in an opposite direction, could not be trusted to legislate for them." Great meetings were held in Paris—the Archbishop of Sens, and the Counts of Tancarville and Eu, were denounced as traitors; and so strong was the feeling against them, that they thought it prudent to quit the capital which they accordingly did, with open denunciations of vengeance on the populace. The animosity thus engendered between the latter and the nobles soon spread, and deepened as it went, and the Regent found in this a means for re-establishing his power. He saw, at a glance, that the surest way of rallying the nobility around the throne, was to place them at variance with the people,—let a Commons' war once be commenced, the feudal lords would see the necessity of suspending their private hostilities, and strengthening their union by the supremacy of the crown. Many were the bickerings that had already occurred between the Peers and the Commons, for the former had fallen into some degree of contempt, since their cowardly conduct at the battle of Poitiers. Many of the fugitive nobles had been received with insult on their flight through the various towns, and the Parisian populace, strong in numbers, treated them with marked contumely. Nevertheless, the latter thought it necessary to be on their guard after the threats of the Counts of Eu and Tancarville—and thence, for the first time, chains were stretched, and *barricades* erected, across the streets of Paris. Ditches were dug before the city walls where they were wanting, parapets erected on the ramparts, cannon and the mediæval implements of warfare still in use planted on the bastions and towers, and considerable property destroyed to ensure the safety of the town. An instance was here given of the self-denial of the people, where necessary, for the public good. In the preceding reign, a riot had broken out in Paris, because the king pulled down several streets to fortify the city against the English, who were encamped at only six leagues distance. The fact was, the people cared but little whether they were ruled by an English tyrant or a French one. Now, when liberty *really* was at stake, they voluntarily dismantled and destroyed their houses, and offered up their worldly goods to the general safety.

Paris was now fully in possession of the people, who had enrolled themselves into a national guard, and performed garrison duties by day and night. The town was safe, but the ravages committed in the country were fearful. The Navarrese garrison of Evreux extended its courses to the very walls of the capital; the provinces were filled with troops of brigands, consisting of disbanded soldiers; the companies of *Free Lances* lived in free quarters; and pillaged villages and open towns without respect of party or creed; and at length a rumour of insurrection was heard from the peasantry as well—they were beginning to manifest symptoms of revolt, and amid the vast confusion, all the wealthier inhabitants kept thronging to the cities. The consequence, and in Paris especially, was a dearth of provisions that gradually deepened into famine.

The inconstancy of the people, that has so frequently ruined the cause of freedom, now became glaringly apparent. Reduced to an extremity of suffering, they threw the blame, not upon their former rulers, but upon their present friends. They harboured the foolish thought, that the evils of centuries could be remedied by the enactment of a day—and, disappointed in their expectations, their affections turned back from their gallant leader, Stephen Marcel, to their hereditary enemy, the Regent. So great was the reaction, that, both at Paris and elsewhere, most of the old functionaries were restored to office, and the Dauphin, once more feeling his authority, sternly summoned the Deputies of the Senate to his presence, reproved them as the authors of the national calamities,—said that henceforth he intended to govern for himself, and forthwith dissolved the assembly of the states.

The Dauphin, finding Paris subservient to his will, left the capital for the provinces, glad of escaping from the long captivity in which he had been held, and desirous of raising subsidies and soldiers in the country. Many municipalities that had turned in his favor supplied him with money, thus enabling him to hire some of the companies of Free Lances, and to threaten the refractory in Paris. Stephen Marcel saw the danger, and therefore persuaded him to return to the capital, where, instead of calling together the States-General, he assembled seventy deputies from the principal towns, to consult with him as to the condition of the country. This measure was well calculated to lull the suspicions of the people, and divert their attention from the non-assembling of the States; but he was disappointed in the character of the delegates, who told him, they had not sufficient authority to levy taxes, that the Regent had no better authority than themselves, and that the Commons, being the only competent power, their convocation was a matter of necessity. As a last resource, he tried to obtain their consent for levying taxes in the seventy towns they represented; frustrated in this, he was forced to obey their injunction.

Jean de Peguigni, the Provost, and the Archbishop of Laon, the respective heads of the democratic party in the Nobles, Commons and Church, finding that the royal power was being much strengthened by the union of the nobles with the Regent, decided on liberating Charles of Navarre, well aware that a portion of the aristocracy would rally around him, while the remainder would side with the Dauphin, and thus weaken the ranks of their enemies by division. Another circumstance strengthened their resolution: not one member of the nobility, and but few of the clergy, attended the sittings of the Diet, thus marking their contempt of the popular assembly, and creating a belief that a secret combination was at work against the people.

The king of Navarre was therefore liberated by stratagem from his prison, at Arleux,* whence he proceeded to Amiens, winning the hearts of all by his agreeable manners, and by exaggerated statements of his sufferings. The Regent at once

---

* Some state him to have been confined in the castle of Crevecœur en Cambresis.

saw that in dissimulation lay his only safety—and, therefore, at the instance of numerous partisans, gave the fugitive a safe conduct to Paris. King Charles stopped at St. Denys, before entering the capital, and addressed the people from a scaffolding erected against the Abbey-walls, exciting their minds more and more against the Regent. The result was, that the latter was again obliged to concede all that was demanded ; but no sooner had the Navarrese Prince returned to his dominions, than the Dauphin began levying troops in the provinces, and his opponent, imitating his example, collected his scattered forces for the struggle.

The Regent gradually concentrated his powers around Paris —but the citizens, anticipating that his intention was more to coerce them himself, than to defend them from others, sternly refused admittance to his soldiers, and had every one who entered strictly searched, lest they should have weapons concealed about their persons. Thus the rancour of the rival princes once more gave the people an opportunity of asserting their power, and the Provost ably profited by the plan he had so wisely designed, while the king of Navarre, in his court of Rouen, gained daily more and more the good-will of the democracy, by inviting men from the humble ranks of life to his table, and affecting an affability and kindness foreign to his nature. The people were deceived—at that time, fair words were sufficient to calm them, and the glozing tongue of a terror-stricken prince possessed the power of blinding their judgment and controlling their actions.

While these events were passing at Paris and at Rouen, the intermediate country was ravaged by the troops of the rival leaders, (although still ostensibly friends,) and by countless brigands, owing allegiance to none, and by turns embracing the colours of all.

Want and misery now reached an unprecedented height. The winter of 1357 was one of great severity—and the populace began to manifest increasing symptoms of insurrection. The Provost held meetings almost daily in Paris—and at one of these, the resolution was adopted of distinguishing the friends of the people by a party-coloured cap of blue and red. Even those who were opposed to the popular cause, adopted the distinctive mark, lest they should fall victims to the general indignation. The standard of revolt being thus openly raised, the Dauphin rallied the aristocracy around him, and summoned the people to meet him in the market-place. He there endeavoured, partly by threats, and partly by promises, to pacify the tumult, and would have succeeded—such was the variability of the popular mind—had not the Provost immediately called a meeting on his side in the church of St. Jaques, where he unmasked the duplicity of the Regent—showed how the latter neglected to make peace with Navarre, in order to have a pretext for maintaining an armed force for the coercion of Paris, and proved that both the Dauphin and the king were seeking their private aggrandisement, and not the general good. The Dauphin, hearing of this counter-meeting, resolved on attending it in person, and endeavoured to refute the statements of the Provost. Here was a strange spectacle—new in the annals of history: a prince pleading his cause against a working-man before the people ! The immense audience listened in majestic silence, while that memorable trial was proceeding—faint murmurs of approbation or dissent arising at rare intervals from the crowd. The clamour gradually deepened—the angry masses parted in two opposite factions, but the overwhelming numbers of the populace swept back the royal partisans, and the discomfited Regent was forced to seek refuge in his palace.

Various attempts had been made to produce a reconciliation between the Regent and the king;—all depended on the restoration of the fortresses taken, and the payment of the sums promised by the former. This prince, however, at the instance of his nobles, refused to obviate so good a pretext for war, and accordingly the Provost demanded the fulfilment of the stipulations granted. The Dauphin evaded a promise by the general assurance that he would do all in his power, but that the commandants of the fortresses refused to evacuate them without an order from king John, his father. Meanwhile, the aristocracy, under Robert of Clermont, Marshal of France, and John of Conflans, Marshal of Champagne, were secretly plotting the destruction of the people of Paris. Men-at-arms kept gathering in the neighbourhood, and a martial chain, uncoiled in the provinces, was thus being wound around the capital.

These endeavours were brought to a close in the beginning of 1358, by the Provost suddenly entering the palace with a body of armed men, and laying Clermont and Conflans dead at the Dauphin's feet. The court fled, leaving the prince alone, who asked the Provost whether he had a design against his life. "No"—replied the popular tribune—"but to ensure its safety, you must wear my cap."

It was of more value in that hour than the crown of France. —the Dauphin obeyed, and the tumultuous cheers of the citizens ratified the act of their leader. Shortly afterwards, the Provost sent a quantity of red and blue stuffs to the palace, and the entire court was equipped in the colours of the people. In the midst of the struggle, the states had re-assembled. The attendance of nobles and prelates was but thin—the representatives of the commons came in great numbers—and the original decrees of the first session, that had been much modified by the Dauphin, were enforced in their pristine vigour. Their deliberations were disturbed by an unexpected circumstance. Suddenly, the king of Navarre appeared before the gates of Paris, with a numerous guard. The keen eye of the Provost at once foresaw the consequences—but he dared not refuse admission, for the wily king had gained the affections of the people, and had now, through their very assistance, a formidable and devoted army in the field. The Provost accordingly gave king Charles a welcome, and, seeing the necessity of at once bringing matters to an issue, requested his ratification of the execution of Marshals Clermont and Conflans. Charles, on his part, received the Provost with every mark of friendship, but afforded him nothing beyond a general answer—and the latter at once felt he had committed one of those acts that princes never pardon ; he felt that, henceforth, he must rely on the democracy alone,—and repented of the fatal circumstances that had induced him to call in the dangerous aid of Navarre. Marcel, however, was not one of those who succumb under difficulties ; he now formed the great plan (irresistible if once organised,) of uniting all the commons of France in one confederation. He therefore sent envoys to every large town, exhorting them to join the municipal League, and assume the colours of the people. Had he been obeyed, democracy must have triumphed—but that fatal apathy, so often characterising the working-classes, which bids one portion "wait and see," while the other portion is struggling single-handed against overwhelming force, here again interposed to prop up the sinking throne and the desecrated altars of France. Not a town responded to his call. "Let Paris fight it out," was their reply—"should Paris succeed, we shall then know our duty." They never reflected that their apathy would prevent Paris from succeeding—and that after liberty was crushed in the capital, it would be trampled down in the provinces.

Paris and the Provost thus stood alone against two princes and all France—and the undaunted champion of liberty now fell back upon his last resource—the dissensions of the royal rivals and the despair of a neglected people. The intention of Charles of Navarre to mount the throne, became more apparent—and, to some extent, he even assumed the royal authority. His safe-conducts were more respected than those of the Regent—his armies held a large part of the country in subjection—on one occasion he nearly took the Dauphin prisoner—and succeeded in having a slow poison administered to him, which materially injured his health, and is supposed to have shortened his life. Meanwhile, the Regent and the king appeared on terms of the most friendly intercourse—they frequently dined and hunted together—and the two great rivals who were tearing the heart of France, wore the semblance of peace, gaiety and friendship. The king of Navarre, lulled into a false security, imprudently quitted Paris with his guards. The Dauphin seized the opportunity—and two days after the departure of the former, had himself enthroned as Regent with all the forms of office—having hitherto held only a nominal authority. The people sanctioned the assumption, since he joined the Provost, Charles Roussac, Robert de Corbu and John of Lisle, in a council of Regency—and, thus thrown off their guard, they allowed him to escape from Paris to Senlis, and thence to Compiegne, where he had ordered the nobility to meet him with all the followers at their disposal. This circumstance caused a still closer union between Navarre and the Provost. The latter immediately enrolled all the inhabitants as a national guard; 4000 men laboured ceaselessly at the fortifications, and the popular flag was hoisted on the ramparts. King Charles could not allow such a manifestation to take place without claiming his share in the proceedings. He accordingly re-entered Paris, where he was declared governor of the town, and captain general of France, amid the ominous silence of a disappointed people. The royal governor, however, swore faithfully to serve the popular cause—it was too late to resist the new turn affairs were taking, but the keen eye and the strong hand of the Provost still felt able to cope with the wily policy of the dishonest prince.

The Regent had by this time surrounded himself with the principal nobility of France; and, strong in their support, convoked the States of Champagne in separate assemblies, first at Provins and then at Vertus. They were obliged to concede all he demanded, coerced in their turn by imposing forces; and having gained thus much from the local Diet, he now endeavoured to intimidate the general assembly.

The States-General had been summoned to Paris, on the 1st of May. The Regent ordered them to meet at Compiegne. At Paris, he would be in their power—at Compiegne, they would be in his. The Parisians were indignant—but the petty jealousies of the provincial towns were flattered by seeing the capital humiliated; they accordingly sent their deputies to Compiegne—and, as a matter of necessity, granted the subsidies and troops demanded by their master.

Now the Regent threw the mask aside — now he denounced vengeance against Paris, and with men, money, and artillery, bore down on the devoted city. The soldiers of Navarre retired before him—the aristocracy came rallying from all sides under the royal oriflamme of France; the heads of his columns already touched the suburbs of Paris; he storme and took Corbeil, built a bridge across the Seine, and well nigh encircled the capital, while reinforcements were speeding upwards from the extremities of the empire. The Provost proved himself as great in the camp as in the council. Gathering the men of Paris together, he placed himself at their head, and marched straight upon Corbeil. The royalist soldiers laughed as they saw the red and white caps of the townsmen swarming over the plain, but the lances of their chivalry shivered before the charge of the people—the gates of Corbeil were burst, the ramparts scaled simultaneously on every side; the town was taken, the bridge destroyed, and the communication between Paris and the country was free.

No sooner had the war been declared, than the whole of France was given up to pillage. The Free Companies already mentioned spread themselves over the land, destroying indiscriminately, without reference to party or to creed. The armies of the Regent, of Navarre, and of England, vied with each other in the office of destruction. Mutilated bodies might be seen unburied on the highways; the flames of burning villages glared horribly through the night; and over the mighty desolation the churches, the castles, and the fortified towns alone stood in gloomy and distinctive grandeur. Then, when liberty was half strangled in its stony cradle at Paris—when outraged humanity was driven beyond the brink of endurance; then, when despair took the armour of revenge, when every heart was excited to its wildest pitch, every passion inflamed beyond judgment and control—then it was that the insurrection of the *Jacquerie* burst forth.

(*To be continued.*)

THE POOR MAN'S LEGAL MANUAL.

No. III.

The Game Laws.—Part II.

IN our last Number, under this head, we gave the long black list of pains and penalties devised solely to protect amusements of the privileged order who possess the land.

Well might Captain Williams, (Inspector of Prisons) state before the Game Law Committee, that the "Game Law is generally more severe than the laws for protection of property, more so in its administration, and more so in itself."(1) Mr. Samuel March Phillips, one of the Secretaries of State, also said, "The Game Laws are the severest laws in the Statute Book."(2) And yet, severe and numerous as they are, what has been their result? In 1843, the convictions under them amounted to 4348, being upwards of one-seventh of all summary convictions;(3) from 1844 to 1846, no less than 11,392 persons were convicted in England and Wales

---

1 See Welford's Digest of the evidence given before the committee, appointed in 1843, p. 332.
2 The same, p. 356.
3 The same, p. 60. In the county of Bedford, out of 201 commitments, 143 were game cases. The same, p. 352.

under these laws ;(1) and between 1833 and 1844, there were 41 inquests held on gamekeepers.(2)

What a terrible amount of oppression, suffering, and crime lies beneath these dry figures! And let us see what is the system for which so cumbersome and destructive a machinery is required ?

How does it work in other respects ? Luckily we have the means of answering this question, so as not to leave it in any doubt, and to remove it beyond the suspicion of pre-judice or mis-statement. The evidence given before the committee appointed in 1843, by the House of Commons, was derived from classes of all kinds and degrees, from the Secretary of State and the squire to the poacher, and it is by this evidence that we shall convict the present system.

First.—That evidence establishes, that great damage is done by game-preserving to the produce of the land.

Mr. Pusey, M.P., said, "The tendency of the new system of farming is to render the crops more liable to injury from game, and also the tendency of the new system of preserving game is to render game more injurious to the farmer. I have not the least hesitation in saying, that the land of a small proprietor in the neighbourhood of a large cover might be injured to the extent of 50 per cent. at least, on the rental; indeed, it might be considered almost useless to cultivate it. One of my tenants had given up growing winter vetches altogether, in consequence of the abundance of the hares. In one place near a cover, two acres of barley, (then at 50s. a quarter) were completely cleared away by the rabbits. Hares seem to gnaw the wheat for their own amusement a good deal. They feed on crops in a state of growth. Game has become a source of serious loss and annoyance to tenants in those parts, where it is highly preserved."(3)

Lord Hatherton said, "I found to pursue the two occu-pations, a rigid preserver of hares and game generally, and an improver of my land by planting and farming, perfectly incompatible. I should have thought it perfectly idle to have invested capital in the improvement of the land, unless I had possessed the power of destroying hares."(4)

Sir Harry Verney said, "I have no hesitation in saying, it is my opinion, that the preservation of game in great

---

(1) Return to House of Commons moved for, by Mr. Collett, and printed August 1846.

(2) Return to House of Commons, printed in June 1844.

(3) Welford's Digest, p. 24—38.   4 The same, p. 54—70.

abundance operates as a serious discouragement to good farming. There are districts in Buckinghamshire in which one-fourth of the whole produce of the land is destroyed by game. If there were less' game, the land would be better cultivated, there would be more produce, and more food for man, and for animals subservient to man."(1)

Mr. Bates, a farmer, stated, that in one year, the damage done to his land by game, amounted to £118. 16s. 8d. "Hares," he said, " do an immensity of damage. If I had a farm of 300 acres, and it was to be enclosed, I would as soon keep one sheep, as I would two hares. Pheasants pick off green wheat. I believe 600 hares on the property would do damage to the amount of £300 a year."(2)

Mr. Nowlson, a farmer, also said, "The general impression is, that three hares will consume and damage more than will maintain one sheep."(3) So, Mr. Blatch and Mr. Chambers.

Mr. Nowlson had found the damage done by game to vary from £2 to £6 an acre. "The green crops," he said, "are injured by game to a very great extent. An agriculturist cannot thrive under the preservation of game."(4) Mr Hayward, a farmer, said the damage done to his farm of 200 acres, amounted in one year to £105. 10s. "I had," he says, "the winter-sown tares eaten off; I ploughed it up and sowed it again, and in the spring it was eaten off again."(5)

Mr. Hodding stated, that the damage he suffered by game was more than double the amount he paid for taxation. His father lost more than £200 a year by the game. The damage done by game on his farm in one year amounted to £416. 8s."(6) Mr. Blatch : " Game Preserving is very injurious to agriculture, very detrimental to improvement."(7) Mr. Saunders, a farmer : " I do not know anything that is so great a bar to cultivation as the present system of game preserving."(8) Mr. Chambers, an occupier of farms to the extent of 3,300 acres, said, " I considered last year I was a loser of nearly £1,000, by the damage done by game. They do not eat what they destroy; last year 2,500 hares were killed, and I consider, 2,000 of them were maintained by myself."(9)

1 Wilford's Digest, p. 80—108.   2 The same, p. 198—202.
3 The same, p. 209.   4 The same, p. 211.
5 The same, p. 216.   6 The same, p. 218.
7 The same, p. 227.   8 The same, p. 237.
9 The same, p. 239—241.

Captain Williams observed, " I have heard the farmers frequently say, that the landlord is obtaining another rent out of the soil, by selling the game which their crops are feeding."(1)

Secondly.—It was also proved that great injury is occasioned to farm-labourers and the poor generally, as regards their employment and comfort.

The Duke of Grafton said, that the preservation of game prevented the farmer from employing capital, and therefore from employing the poor.(2)

Sir Harry Verney said, that, by the abolition of the present system, Agriculture would receive a stimulus, which would be beneficial to the farmer, and to every class of the community, but to the labourer, *first and foremost, and above all.* I think," he continued, " the labouring population are very ill off, compared with what, I think, they might be made. I think they ought to be very well off, and the farmers too."(3)

Mr. Pusey said, " I think the labourers feel themselves, in a certain degree, objects of suspicion, wherever game is strictly preserved."(4) Captain Williams said, " There are no acts of the legislature which have tended more to destroy the friendly relations between the humbler and the upper classes of society."(5)

Thirdly.—It was shewn that Game Preserving, and its incidents, tend to demoralise the people.

Lord Hatherton said, " The preservation of game holds out an inducement to the labouring classes to become depredators, and initiates them into crime."(6)

The Duke of Grafton said, " It is a proverb in Suffolk, that ' poaching is the root of all evil.' I conclude that game preserving has demoralised the people. It holds out so great a temptation—it is injurious to the poor, to the farmer, and the community at large."(7)

Sir Henry Verney stated, " Great abundance of game makes men poachers. I think it is a very great temptation to a man who, perhaps, has a starving family, and who knows that, by one successful night in a neighbouring game-preserve, he may earn as much as by a whole fortnight's honest industry."(8)

1 Welford's Digest, p. 334.   2 The same, p. 84.
3 The same, p. 100.   4 The same, p. 329.
5 The same, p. 334.   6 The same, p. 62.
7 The same, p. 71.   8 The same, p. 89.

Mr. Gauntley said, " Game Preserving is a demoralising thing; it sets one man as a tiger against another, quarrelling and fighting about it."(1)

Such is the system which is endeavoured to be supported by harsh and cruel enactments. Never was there so strong and convincing a body of evidence collected on any subject, as on this by the Parliamentary Committee.

We have extracted a very small portion of it, but sufficient to prove the important propositions which we have submitted to our readers.

The Game Laws cannot long remain to disgrace our Statute-book, and to inflict such grievous injury upon the country. They are doomed, and we confidently expect to see them repealed for ever in the next session of Parliament.

We conclude this article in the characteristic language of Frederick Gowing, an experienced poacher, who was examined before the Committee of which we have spoken. He had been three or four times in Ipswich gaol; once in that of Beccles, and twice at Woodbridge. Within the last eighteen years he had paid from £200 to £250 as fines for offences against the Game Laws. " I have been a poacher the last eighteen years, " he said ; " I should not thieve the farmer's fowls or his pig, when I can go to this oak cover, or that birch wood, and earn a sovereign in the course of half an hour. After harvest, I can find a hundred poor men in my parish ready to go poaching with me. Low wages is what brings them to it."(2)

(*To be Continued.*)

THE CONFESSIONS OF A KING.

(*Concluded from page 43.*)

The tide of victory never flows for ever; I grappled with a mighty tyrant, and was defeated. An unwilling fugitive, I threw the blame not on myself, but on the climate. I had

---

1 Welford's Digest, p. 291.   2 The same, pp. 337, 341.

invaded a land of frost and snow—and two hundred thousand men perished by the season and the sword. But I knew the rigour of the country, and the difficulties of the march, before it was undertaken; I was aware of the resources of the enemy, and as I hurried over a narrow bridge, where the flying crushed themselves to death, I felt the blame rest heavy on my soul. Baffled and furious, I fled to my dominions—on my way, the pigmies I had conquered and spared, rose against me. I paused on my flight—turned, crushed them at a blow—and by slow marches reached and crossed the frontier of my empire. The mighty despot and his hosts were surging after me, like a wave; suddenly he paused in his career; he might still fear the last struggle of despair, or some after-thought of policy might sway him.

"Join with me!" said the mighty conqueror. "United, we will divide the world!"

I was my own master no longer; I belonged to the league of kings; with them I must stand or fall. I saw how the chain of conquest had riveted the bonds of obedience in my subjects. Defeat changed their tone; my ministers, for the first time, dared to reason with me; threatened on refusal, to resign, and my people presumed to petition! These were symptoms of the coming time. I stood beside the cradle of revolution; my army had lost its character of invincibility, my leadership its halo of victory; "Those who beard me in defeat," I cried, "shall live to mourn my revenge!"— and I ratified the league with my conqueror. But the conditions! I was to stifle the spirit I had raised; tread out the spark I had kindled; cast back the power of awakened liberty; still its hot throbs in a million hearts; undo the promise of my life, and wash out its glory in the blood of brethren. It was to be achieved by the sword, the prison, and the rack—by gold, title and preferment—by religion, policy and fraud. Impossible task! But it was undertaken, and the war of extermination commenced. To ratify the bond, and sole condition of my safety, I was to wed the tyrant's daughter. The monarch coveted the crown of one he thought a childless king!—alas! I, too, believed I was!—surer means of accomplishing his end, than by the uncertain result of a last appeal to arms. He longed, as well, to drag back his army from a country still infected with the breath of liberty. It might corrupt the allegiance of his slaves; and he left to me the performance of a task he thought too dangerous for himself.

I feared not, but the OBSTACLE! A frail and gentle woman stood in my way! Time had passed over her, and

mellowed her beauty with the placid twilight of life, yet
Myrrha had still that lingering loveliness, recalling youth,
with that soft shade of years, reminding you of heaven!
She was the same kind, confiding being as ever. Her melancholy voice was ever raised in reproachful supplication for
the victims of my ambition—or her pale, sorrowing face conveyed an unuttered reproof. I needed some gay companion
who could teach me to *forget*—and she ever forced me to
remember. The recollection of past innocence is a curse
of present guilt. We are cruel to those whom we fear. I
treated her harshly, yet she seemed to cling to me with unaltered love. This maddened me! I shunned her—she
sought me. I left her—she haunted my memory, till I
hated. Meanwhile she had gained the enthusiastic love of
the people, by her kindliness and beneficence, and of none
more than of the young soldier, who had first endeavoured to
thwart me on my march to power. I had retained him
near me in reluctant favour; since it was my habit, the more
dangerous I thought an enemy, to attach him the more closely
to my person, for then I knew my eye was on his every
action. Mine was not the plan to banish a suspected man to a
distant province, but to promote him to an office in my very
palace; such must be watched, not distanced.

He won the favour of the Queen. A strange sympathy
seemed to draw them to each other—prophetic of disasters.

When the offer of the despot was made known to me—
when the obstacle flashed across my mind—a subtle thought
came to the rescue of irresolution : "Impeach her, and the
way is free."

The young soldier seemed made for my plan. I reasoned
myself into the belief of imaginary facts, and strange inconsistency of human nature! I reproached Myrrha with the
very act by which she had saved my life and that of my
lost child! I now sought proofs; greedy ministers were
ready to supply them. No sooner did they know that I
desired freedom to wed the despot's child, than proofs became
abundant at their hands—and the innocence of an angel
would have melted beneath their breath.

They were alone—alone in night! It was the chamber of
the queen—he was at her feet, kneeling—and she wept, as
I burst with my satraps through the door.

For a moment he stood paralyzed; then his words came
thundering :—" *Murderer in Venice, King in*——"—
" Kill him !" I cried, and rushed against him, but he
dashed my sword out of my hand. " Who dares to follow ?"

he said, as the door of the chamber opened, and the figure of the MERCHANT stood on the threshold!

In truth, I dared not follow—and the terror on my face held back the pursuit of my slaves, till he made good his escape. He had learned the secret. Did she know it? Had she told him? Her fate was sealed—and to attach her life, I first sought a divorce at the hands of the church.

But churchmen hated me. I had taken the ecclesiastical revenues—kings could forgive me conquered provinces—priests never could forgive me pilfered gold. They had long cherished revenge in secrecy and impotense. Now, I placed myself within their pale. Their great superstition was, for once, arrayed on the side of right and liberty; the hierarchy declared the Queen untainted and innocent, and threw the shield of religion around the march of freedom. At once the country rose in revolution. Events hurried on, and brought me to the close of an eventful day.

My generals were beaten back on the capital—my scattered armies were pursued through the gates—I led the rallying fragments to the rescue: a day of carnage darkened into a silent night; but my despair delighted in the struggle. I stood a crowned outcast in the world, and at the world I struck. The city flamed beneath the ramparts of my castle; I walked the battlements with a fearful joy, and struck a lyre above my burning capital. But, as I stood, I looked beyond the city walls, and beheld in small groups, or in compact masses, thousands streaming to the gates from the country around. By the moonlight and the fires, I could distinguish their dress, and I saw they had come from the far confines of my empire; every province had poured forth its tributary stream, to fill the gulf of my destruction,—to swell the assault of the morrow.

The emissaries of the king were still in the castle. I acceded fully to their terms, and dismissed them, while yet one path of escape was kept open by my troops.

It was midnight when they left me. The allied army was within a short march of the frontier. Scarcely could I hold the castle till their arrival; wild apprehensions seized me; I sat alone, every footfall seemed that of an enemy; my hands played with feverish haste over the loaded pistols on the table before me: oh! the mighty battles of ambition had descended into an almost personal struggle for life. I started up; "Without there! A torch! I will to rest,—to rest!"

I heard no step, or I had heeded none; but suddenly the full red light of a torch fell over me.

" I am here ! " said a voice.

The deep hollow tone smote strangely on the silence. I looked up. Tall, proud, majestic, the MERCHANT stood before me, that same bitter smile upon his lip.

He walked on before me, leading the way in silence. I had no time to speak. He opened the folding-door, strode into the gallery. I followed by an involuntary impulse, and as his dark shadow swept across me, I felt a chill, like death, strike to my heart. He opened the portal of a chamber—I passed him—suddenly I awoke from my dream, and smiled at my own folly. I will question him, I said, but ere I spoke, the door closed behind me with a dreadful sound, as though it was the gate of heaven, that had been shut against me for ever.

I advanced into the room—it was still and calm. The lamp burnt with a holy light, all unlike the glare of that hideous torch; and on a couch, fair and tranquil, like a marble image with a hue of sunset over it, lay Myrrha.

The same calm sorrow, the same expression of uncomplaining woe, dwelt on the face of the slumberer. I bent over her, and, lovely, gentle, as she was, I hated her, and felt a bitter burning in my heart. My hot breath stirred the glossy ringlets on her white neck and awakened her; she started in terror at sight of me, my hand was stained with blood from that day's unhallowed conflict; she bent her soft eyes beseechingly on mine; at that moment, the bells of the cathedral began pealing for the people's victory, and a long undulating cheer swept distinctly around the palace, like a circling wave ! Satan was in my heart again. I crept close ; I raised my arm ; slowly, slowly it sank ; when I withdrew it, *she was no more !*

I remained motionless for a moment, then turned to fly, but a leaden weight hung on my steps, and I staggered heavily away. The instant I moved, I heard a strange, loud, ringing footstep behind me ; it seemed to follow me even from the couch. I tried, but in vain, to believe it was but the hollow echo of my own pace ; frantic, I rushed out of the room, while bound for bound that pursuing step came ringing through the chambers of my conscience.

I know not how the night passed, but as the grey dawn disclosed the angry masses forming for the assault, the sight restored me to myself, and my awed soul felt the inspiration of my physical daring. A cheer rang without, so deep, so inspiring, so enthusiastic, I knew some more than common event had transpired. And, truly, I beheld a gallant body of men marshalling in the front, and at their head, the people's tricolor in the hands of the young soldier.

Already the thunders began to roll around the time-sapped walls, that shook at every discharge, and when my bugles sounded to the ramparts, they sent no response. My defenders had fled, they had left me alone, even as the last prince of the ancient line had been deserted; alone, save a paltry few, whose crimes forced them to continue faithful.

Already the besiegers rushed on to the assault, when suddenly they paused and sent a herald commanding my surrender. Perchance, the young leader of my foes feared for the queen's safety in the struggle of despair, and as the thought struck me, it came, accompanied by a deep and subtle scheme.

"Surrender! Never," I thundered; but I grew calm and smiled as I said, "Grant me a six-hours' truce. *The queen died yesternight.* Let me bury her in peace! Let not her sacred ashes be defiled amid the horrors of an assault!"

I watched the young soldier reel beneath my words as with a blow; I had taken the brightness from his triumph. energy from his actions, and hope from his heart! Ah! I conquered in the midst of defeat—bitter was that hour to him! But I knew him well, my prayer was granted. I saw him no more that day, he had retired to his tent without the town; a sudden apathy seemed to steal over the besieging host—ah! they had lost the prompting spirit—I had tamed the fiery leader.

The portals of the church remained unopened, but I mounted the highest tower and looked towards the North. Had the envoys passed safely through the investing lines? Darkness and disguise must have favoured their flight through the undisciplined masses. Had they succeeded, then succour might arrive in time! Woe, unto me, should it reach too late!

Hour passed after hour: the truce was fast expiring, and I saw the multitude re-arming below, and the engines of death ready to open on the walls. The sixth hour was passing—*it passed!* Little knew the enemy of the dreadful doom preparing, as little, that I was at that moment almost utterly defenceless. But I triumphed in my very weakness, and smiled to think, that I alone thus held my fate aloof by a master-thought, and made the frail ashes of a murdered queen guard those ramparts ten-thousand warriors could scarce have held.

The clock had struck the sixth-hour of the truce, and the

assault began; but up the distant horizon, I beheld moving a cloud-like line!

The desperate resistance of the few within, was soon overpowered; but my banner still waved unruffled over the human storm.

Again the rebels bade me surrender. "Look to yonder gate," I thundered, "and kneel for mercy!"

They turned, beheld and fled, and with pealing bands, the long lines of the relieving army swept up the deserted streets.

I held a dreadful day of reckoning with my enemies. Their strength withered like a burning scroll in my hand, but their leader had escaped. The scaffolds were kept red and warm, and when the rivers of human blood had ceased to pour from the fountains of legal murder, the peace of death sunk over the land;—the only sound breaking the ominous silence was the marching and counter-marching of troops, and the loud splendours of a reckless court. But spectres crowded on my solitary grandeur. The turn of events had taken occupation from me. Conquest was to be mine no more; the cold arm of power must weigh heavily on the land; change, action, excitement were to be banished; my craving spirit had no food in strife. I was turned inward on myself, I there met retribution and despair! Wild fancies haunted me—fancies, my stronger manhood would have scorned. Strange, that even over my hardened brain they should sweep, and rack and madden. Like a child, I feared to be alone! The unquiet corpse of the murdered queen haunted me even by day. I thought she might rest within a royal grave, and I had her disinterred from the obscure tomb to which she had been consigned, and with a pomp befitting her imperial death, she was buried in the castle church, and at *noon of day!* I can still smile at the puerile fear, but I understand its retributive power.

The glare and gloom of life chace each other with alternate wings.

Again a festival blazed in the castle—again a bride, a royal bride, trod its halls, as I wedded the tyrant's daughter, and the dead heart of the empire was forced to beat with a galvanic joy at the ill-omened alliance.

Months passed, and prematurely brought the snows of age on my head, dimness on my sight, and furrows on my face. Men remarked how I withered away. My once erect figure stooped earthward, and my enemies pointed to my feeble pace with a cursed joy; they began to count the days of my life, and make preparations for meeting the event; while I gathered up the remnants of my shattered strength in the vain and peevish hope to spite them by yet living long. Alas! bitterly I felt remorse and fear, pushing me towards the gates of hell, and I cursed through my sleepless nights, as I felt the fever burning away the oil of life with fatal greediness. Then I would at times assume a jocund air, tax my poor strength to walk erect and firm, exhaust my feeble lungs to speak in round full tones, that they might not have the satisfaction of knowing how weak I was; and then I have sunk down in my lonely chamber, and cried, cried child-like, at the pitiable mockery. My authority, too, was fleeting away like my life. I could no longer appoint my ministers, nor even the officers of my household; the imperious queen threatened me with her father's power, and I bent like a poor slave beneath the feet of my merciless protectors. I feared to command, lest I should be disobeyed; I was no longer master in my own house, my menials treated me with insolence, and I dared not reprove them, lest I should expose my impotence still further. How was the mighty fallen! The dreadful conqueror was become the slave of a woman and her minions. Ah! then the thought came on me, like a river seen at distance in a desert, when the traveller has wandered from its track, too far ever to regain its banks: why did I forsake the people? the dear, brave, generous, warm-hearted people, to be a crowned mockery among abject things, more worthless, more helpless, more despised than they?

Months passed, and a son was born to the throne. They called it mine, and I laughed as I held it in my arms, and thought of my own brave boy; lost, lost, but unforgotten. Oh! Where was he then? Why could he not come to avenge me—dash down my vile tyrants at my feet, and let me die a king! Vain thought—for, were he found, his life would not be safe. I was but spared to assure the throne to the issue of my conqueror, and were such an *obstacle* to rise, it would be removed, *as I had once removed another!*

Ah! but at times the old spirit leaped within me, and I burnt with indignation to see the people tamely submit to the despotism now falsely practised in my name. I longed for them to rise, as they once had risen, were even I to be crushed by the result. My wish was realised. Again the young soldier took the field, rallied the far provinces, and advanced on the capital. I watched his every progress with breathless anxiety; Men thought I feared it—they thought I trembled: no! they erred, I hoped—I prayed for his success! Oh! how my heart beat when I heard of his victories—beat, with what appeared an unnatural joy. How it sunk, when after all his gallantry, after all his endurance, chivalry and wisdom; after the transient gleam of a god-like success, the great armies of the tyrant were put in motion against him: he was defeated, taken—fighting gallantly to the last, and led to execution on the gibbet-hill, within three miles of the capital.

Then some one came and whispered to me: "IT IS THY SON!" It was as though scales had fallen from my eyes. Then I recollected how I had yearned towards him; then I knew why that strange sympathy existed between the unknown boy and his murdered mother! All was plain, plain, plain! The proofs were given of his identity; the damning, cruel proofs! It was the hour of execution—I gave a few confused, hurried orders, that set the minions staring and doing nothing; I rushed to the castle court; a trooper was standing listless by his horse; I leaped into the saddle; the strength of boyhood boiled along my veins— away! over the drawbridge thundered the hoofs of my horse; the guard gazed after me, appalled; in the streets was a crowd; I called to them to make way; they gazed stupidly, weltered over each other and heeded not. I spurred till the maddened steed broke through them like a hurricane, and trampling his way over them, reached the open country. On, on, on! I could see the scaffold on the top of the hill! Thank heaven! there was no one on it yet, but the executioner! I was in time! With my eyes fixed on the dreadful object, I rushed through the valley, till I came on the outskirts of the great crowd. In vain I called to them to make room; I was not heeded; the victim was king for them that hour. Precious, precious time was lost. Breathless I wore my way through the masses, and reached the inner circle guarded by deep lines of halberdiers. "Pardon!" I cried. "From whom?" "The king! the king!" Whether they knew me not, or that they had received unalterable orders, they hesitated, bowed with supercilious smiles, but never obeyed. There was a commotion in the crowd, figures were mounting the platform—he was there! "It is my son, my son!" I cried, when—who gave the accursed signal?—suddenly the music burst with a crashing noise, and a gory head ascended on a lance-point, over the crowd.

I rode back to the castle, like a goodly horseman, calm, proud, impassive; men wondered as I reached the castle-court, to see me mount the stair so firmly. I reached my chamber, sunk on my couch, and for days I knew of nought that was passing around. When first I awoke to conscious-ness, I heard a whispering by my bedside. "Is he dead?" asked a woman's voice.

"I fear he is not," replied the physician, and the lady stamped her foot in petulant impatience. Then they conversed in a low tone together, and I could distinctly hear the first speaker urge on the physician to give me a deadly drug, should I revive. The pledge was given—the lady turned her face—it was *my wife!*

A shudder crept over my limbs, and then the blood rushed coldly back to my heart. I could see the woman come and bend over me as watching for a symptom of life; deliberately she placed her hand on my breast, I verily believe it beat not!

" He is dead! " she said and smiled, as I saw her, through my half-closed eyelids, turn away and, bidding the physician good night, leave the room.

An hour passed, and all was silent. I unclosed my eyes—the physician was asleep on a chair—no one else was in the chamber, I raised myself up, and slowly—slowly and cautiously I left the bed. Noiselessly I crept to the side of the sleeper; a preternatural strength sustained me; he had a dagger in his belt, I drew it out, I scarce knew with what intent, but the idea of harming him never entered my mind. I left the room, and mechanically went in the direction of the Queen's apartments. I entered a long passage, at the further end burnt a torch, and beneath it stood a human form. It beckoned me and pointed inward. Surely it was THE MERCHANT! or, was it but the sentry at the Queen's door, saluting as I passed? He moved on and disappeared! within SHE slept! I felt the pulse in my fingers beat convulsively against the dagger hilt! I stood still: the light of the moon fell through a window, whence might be seen the castle church; there was a marble tomb, shining like snow—it was Myrrah's; the dagger dropped from my hand with a heavy sound, it was as though a heavy weight had fallen from my heart; the tears rushed to my eyes; I looked at that black door, with its lurid torch; I knelt between that tomb and that chamber, and, for the first time a wild anguished prayer was faltered from my lips.

I arose strengthened, for my resolve was taken. Through

passages unknown to others, I left the castle; the fresh starry night was around me, and all was silence; the sentries at the unclosed gates scarce noticed the shadowy spectre gliding past them, for the bonds of discipline had been rent, and a dissolute court ruled by a drunken soldiery.

I fled on towards the mountains, till the silent city lay distant behind; the cool fresh air seemed to brace my nerves; and thus I reached the yew-tree, whence first those spires fell upon my sight. As again, and for the last time, the proud towers met my view, the course of my past life seemed mapped before me.

Some one stirred by my side. It was a father and his only son; the head of the boy rested on the old man's knee. The boy was pale with a death-wound, the man with a death-sorrow; it was I who had inflicted both!

"A curse on our tyrant, the king!" cried the anguished father.

The lips of the boy moved inaudibly as he expired; and the moon and stars glanced downward like the eyes of heavenly witnesses shining attestation. I fled on in the *shadow* of the mountains.

Conjecture was long busy about my fate. Even in my flight I triumphed; for the traitor-queen thought I had discovered her treachery, and was arming in some far province of the empire, to re-appear suddenly on their horizon with the gatherings of revenge.

The commotion will subside, the name of the champion of liberty, as of the tyrant, live but in some variable legend; the oppressor and the victim sink alike in traditionary graves; and men, when they read these annals, will doubt at last whether they are not the mere fictions of romance, instead of the realities of history. No matter! History is the strangest of romances; but the moral that it teaches is eternal.

(THE END.)

L'ENVOY.

Thus end the King's Confessions; but the end of the king is unknown. Who the MERCHANT was, remains unravelled. Whether a ruling spirit, or whether his imagined re-appearance merely shadows forth how the first impulse of our life sways every crisis of its aftercourse, is matter for speculation. The hero of the tale has lived his day. Reader, forgive his sins and take warning by his fate.

THE ROMANCE OF A PEOPLE.

A HISTORICAL TALE

OF THE NINETEENTH CENTURY. [1]

(Continued from page 18.)

CHAPTER IV.

A grand pageant closed the first day of liberty—the procession of the council to the bank, where Prince Lubecki thought it would be more out of the reach of popular clamour. The line of senators, and the thronging masses, extended over a space of two miles, proceeding slowly, on account of the great age of the venerable Niemcewicz, the bard of Poland. When the people saw their national poet thus advancing beneath the banner of liberty, they rent the air with acclamations; "All must succeed, since Niemcewicz is there!" and indeed all now appeared to prosper ; the gallant general Sierawski joined the patriots in the evening, and was appointed military governor of Warsaw ; one by one, the heroes of Poland arrived, and in the night, Chlopicki himself espoused the cause of nationality.

That night, when triumphant joy sat throned in Warsaw, a stern and gloomy man might be seen resting beneath the leafless trees and the inclement sky, before the barrier of Mockotow, and with him one, long used to luxury, one young and fair : it was the Grand Duke Constantine and his consort, the Princess Lowiczka.

After an interval of anxious suspense, Colonel Zamoyski appeared before the Prince, stating that the people and the army believed the Grand Duke was forcibly detaining the Polish Chasseurs who had accompanied him, and urged their immediate dismissal to rejoin their comrades. Constantine hesitated; he feared implicating himself with his brother, but a mighty sound came booming down the road ; it was the advancing populace.

"You have but a moment to decide in," said Zamoyski, "beyond that I cannot answer for your life."

Constantine wrote the order.

"Remember," said the Princess, "his Imperial highness permits, but does not authorise their departure."

While the Chasseurs were marching to meet their approaching countrymen, Constantine and the remnant of his Russians were flying to the frontier.

Memorable was the meeting between the returning soldiers and their comrades in arms. The former hung their heads with shame, to think they should have sided with the enemy—but one loud acclaim rent the air as they fell into the line of the procession, and tumultuous cheers welcomed their return to liberty.

That morning Warsaw was a festal place. All its youth, beauty, and valour graced the streets, balconies, and windows—old age poured its blessings on the conquering heroes.

The fifth of December beheld the revolution established, by Chlopicki seizing the reins of power, and becoming irresponsible dictator; while the provisional government had been self-instituted by Prince Czartoryski, the Castellan Kochanowski, General Pac, Niemcewicz the bard, Lelewell the teacher, and the deputies Dombrowski and Ostrowski.

A general summons to arms was addressed to the nation; all disbanded officers and men were called into active service; and proclamations issued to the Palatine Councils, directing them to meet the Diet on the eighteenth of December. Thus, the last decisive step was taken, from which there could be no return.

Constantine, with the imperial troops, was permitted to retire unmolested from Poland—a great and generous, though an impolitic act. But, in that hour, the nation was too happy to punish its enemies, and felt too great to avenge its wrongs.

The fortresses of Zamosc and Modlin capitulated, and Poland, for the time, was free.

While Poland was doing this for European liberty, what did Europe for Poland? True, it treated the Polish envoy with distinction. Many may yet remember a Polish nobleman who visited London shortly after the outbreak of the insurrection, and excited great attention on account of the tyranny of which he had been made the victim.

He was received with distinction by the aristocracy, and though he found it difficult to gain access to men in office, yet the warm manner in which he was welcomed by society in general, and the spirited tone assumed by the English press in behalf of his outraged country, seemed to hold fair promise of support from England. The cause of those exiles, implicated in the conspiracy of Lukasinski, or other equally hapless attempts, and who had fled from the fate that was denounced or dreaded, was espoused with warmth; committees were formed, subscriptions raised, and lofty names were advertised in the papers, as bestowing donatives towards the Polish fund (although, what became of the fund itself was never exactly understood); balls were given in behalf of the suffering exiles (although, most of the proceeds were spent in the arrangements of the festival); figurantes, coryphées, and premières danseuses danced the Cracovienne and the Mazurka at His Majesty's Theatre; from Sadler's Wells to Surrey, the playbills teemed with Polish names, and the audiences applauded—*rondes de jamb!*

It is true the government never gave an open ort but

then they could not commit themselves!—they could not fly in the face of great, allied, and powerful sovereigns, who had been in the habit of visiting St. James's, feasting off banquets at Windsor castle, and turtle-dinners at the Mansion-house! It is true, ministers never propounded anything distinctly; never made any pledge or promise; never said: the treatment to Poland is an outrage to humanity and an insult to enlightened governments; never said: we emancipate the *black* slave, and therefore the *white* one shall be free; we interfere in the internal polity of weak states, therefore we will interfere in that of the strong!—nothing of the kind. But they *did* say, (in secret, however,) if we bestir ourselves for Poland, then Russia may cry, "Ireland!" to our teeth; and as we *have* tyrannised, and *do* tyrannise, and intend still further to tyrannise over the *latter* country, we had best not say a word about the *former*.

Notwithstanding, they did much: even Royalty went to see the *Polish ballet;* cabinet-ministers dined at Polish dinners at the Mansion-house, and the fair lady of a high dignitary of the state was the first to introduce a Polish pelisse, from the ashes of which phœnix rose the present polka.

What more could be expected from a government, whose fleets swept the seas from the Hoangho to the Hudson, and whose armies had laid the imperial guard of France beneath their bayonets?

But they actually did even more than this! A secretary of state told an under-secretary, who told a private secretary to tell a secretary of a Polish Association, to inform the Polish envoy, that, if Poland really rose, and if it maintained a suitable policy, and formed a suitable government, the English people would, in that case, act towards Poland in a suitable manner; the meaning of which was, that if Poland rose and beat the Russian armies, and took the Russian fortresses, and established itself as a free and powerful kingdom,—then England would transfer its relations of amity from the fallen Russia to the triumphant Poland.

Justice must, however, be done to the great elements of British nationality—at that time, but subordinate—the Press, and the *People*. They spoke the language of honor and honesty, but the People have been trampled by monopoly, and the Press has turned the venal instrument of corruption.

In the mean time, the Russian ambassador made some stringent observations, and even delivered a note from his government. Accordingly, hints were dropped from certain quarters to certain editors, that it would be advisable for them to use more moderate language in their leading articles, lest they should complicate the relations of the country, and certain inducements, too, were offered. Non-interference prevailed, and the relations of the country remained " uncomplicated."

This noble effort of sound and lofty statemanship is still the glory of the party from whose ranks it emanated.

The Parisians, however, far outdid us. They ran into an enthusiasm of valour! The students of the Ecole Polytechnique talked of marching from Paris through Germany, Prussia, and Poland to Warsaw, without even asking the leave of the armies of the confederation, Vienna or Berlin! The theatres—they were like so many bits of Poland! The Boulevards—they were Cracow itself!—Kosciusko handkerchiefs and Sobieski robes, cakes, loaves, and pâtes à la polonnaise, shouts, balls, processions, dances and gensd'armes, discussions in the chambers, that never came to a result, and proud inscriptions over *cabarets* that—"France decrees the liberty of Poland," with omission of the latter half of the sentence: but does nothing to enforce it—spoke volumes for the chivalry of that tremendous nation!

And then their leading men! (French statesmen are not more punctilious about their promises than ours)—they actually *did* promise—(not those in office, but those who expected to be)—that France would *sympathise*, all France would sympathise with the "France of the North!"—let the Poles but rise! the Gallic eagle had been there before—it knew the road, could find its way again! Meanwhile addresses from the French to the Polish nation were multiplied by the press, and Russia must have trembled at these—words and paper!

Such is the courage—such is the honesty—such is the manliness of butterfly courts and counting-house governments.

The time for the second romance of our century had arrived—the romance of a *people*, as Napoleon's had been that of a *man*, and the following passages of a letter from the Palatine to his friend, Prince Adam Czartoryski, will explain the feelings of the patriot and the prospects of his country.

"We have no present aid to hope from either France or England. The feeling of either people is strongly with us, the more so, since it is their own tyrants whom they can lash under the name of ours.

" But their governments will not stir. How could they put themselves in a false position? How could they liberate abroad, and oppress at home?

" As Lafayette brought revolution from America, so our defenders would take back liberty from Poland! This the governments know; and they are hostile; they fear the people: and they are double-tongued. They hate Russia, and they would be glad to see it crippled! they hate freedom, and they would be happy to see us crushed.

" Let us be stirring, none the less. The nations are on the move, and we must be moving too. France will rise and, before long, a nobler struggle will efface the crimes of the last; the people of England will be alive, and overturn an oligarchy; the German will reject a despotism; the Hungarian, the Italian. and the Sclave, a conqueror; and Spain, an Inquisition and a Jesuit.

" Centuries may have passed in slavery, and nations may appear to be dissolved under the inscrutable dispensations of Providence; but nothing wholly perishes; the march of creation is progres-

D 2

sive, and what does not perish must *improve.* Thus *kingdoms* may fall, but *nations* never die, and thus our nationality survives our throne.

"To Poland, then my friend! Lost battles, conquered capitals, are as nothing in the struggle; after all, it is the millions against the units, and in the end, the many must remain triumphant."

The Palatine was right, but the inveterate evil was too deeply rooted to eradicate at once. England *did* stir—France rose—Italy shook itself in sleep—Spain rallied, and Germany spoke in its dreams. England gained Reform, and found it nothing; France achieved Liberty, and after three days lost it! Italy struggled, and is bleeding now; and Germany awoke with the memory of its hopes! Spain alone attained something, for it expelled the Inquisition; thus, the foulest went first, for the crime of him is light, who fetters the body, to that of him, who would enchain the mind.

In the end, man gained much, though much was lost; a pledge for the future was given; the people of the earth had for once spoken to each other in the same great language, and again the world is on the brink of change.

(To be continued.)

LABOUR AND PROFIT.

LABOUR "lives" from hand to mouth,
   Labour starveth daily;
Trade-per-cent. has rankest growth,
   Mammon's heirs live gaily.
Richard Arkwright's patent heir
   Hath a doom too splendid;
Hargreaves dwelleth with Despair,
   And Crompton dies untended.

Mammon Arkwright rolls in wealth,
   Hath too much to squander:
Mammon Arkwright, child of Stealth!
   Radcliffe starveth yonder.
Manchester homes cotton lords—
   Peels and Cobdens many:
William Radcliffe 'mid their hoards,
   Dies unhelp'd of any.

Corn-law League can cheapen bread:
 Cannot Toil be cheaper?
Are your Paupers over-fed?
 Can't you starve the Reaper?
Trade-per-cent. hath rankest growth,
 Free-Trade liveth gaily,
Saves its millions, nothing loath,
 Starveth Labour daily.

SPARTACUS.

[Sir Richard Arkwright, more than suspected of stealing his "inventions," left an immense fortune to his son, while Hargreaves and Crompton, the real inventors of the spinning-jenny and the mule-frame, died neglected and destitute. The late Richard Arkwright (son of Sir Richard), is said to have been the wealthiest commoner in England. Of his vast fortune, he had not the heart to spend more than £3000 a year; and Wm. Radcliffe, of Stockport, the inventor of dressing-machines, the veritable father of the power-loom system, died at the age of eighty years, in the most abject poverty, unaided by any of those excellent and liberal profit-mongers, whose wealth was owed to his genius. Through some indirect channel a grant of £150 was procured from government, and reached *him* in time to prevent a parish funeral.]   **S.**

THE GLORIOUS PRIVILEGE.

A TALE OF OUR DAYS.

John Wilson had inherited a little property from the nineteenth cousin once removed of a great-aunt, on the maternal side, whose second removal it was that brought him the little windfall to set him up in business. He accordingly took a shop and a wife in the grocery line. We say a wife in the grocery line, for he adapted his wife to his vocation, and, being a prudent man, sought for her amid firkins of butter, jars of pickle, and flitches of bacon. Things went on very comfortably for a time. He was very fond of his shop and his wife, his wife was very fond of the shop and him. Thus he established a fair business, was attentive to his customers, and thrived accordingly. There was one thing, however, in which he felt his dignity insulted. He had not the glorious privilege of an Englishman, the place was not a borough, he had not the vote. This annoyed him; in common with many others, he indulged in delicious dreams of how fine a thing it must be to enjoy that right; how "my Lord," and "the Banker," would "have the honour of waiting on him;" how they would pat his chubby, dirty, screaming little boys on the head, and say, "bless me! what a fine child that is! how old is it?" "Two years, my Lord!" "Dear me, how tall for its age, I thought it had been four at least!" and how my Lord would then kiss some clean spot on its face, and how he would—delicious thought!—put a ten pound note in its hand, and turning carelessly away, exclaim as he was going down the steps, "By the bye, Wilson, it *just* strikes me, hav'nt you got a vote? Ah!" turning to his canvassers, "now I recollect, to be sure you have!" and how the said Wilson, (having pocketed the ten pound note, and wishing for more,) would raise conscientious scruples, and how my Lord would take great pains to explain his views, religious and political; and, after all, how the noble-minded, free-born Englishman (that is, John Wilson,) "would take time to consider of it," and how he would hide in the cock-loft till the day of the poll, and then come down and vote for "the good of his country, his conscience and his principles," for a con-sideration!

These and other day-dreams of the kind took so strong a hold of the inhabitants of Toryden-cum-Whigsnook, that they petitioned and worried, and worried and petitioned, till they were erected into a borough accordingly, and their dearest aspirations were thus realised.

About a year and a half after this memorable event, a dissolution took place, occasioned by a remarkable circum-stance, strongly characteristic of the wisdom of the British constitution. The sovereign had been disappointed of cherry-pies one day at a Lord-Mayor's dinner, and, being very fond of cherry-pies, grew very angry. Accordingly, some of the lords and ladies of the court experienced the effects of the royal ill-humour, and not bearing it with be-coming meekness, sundry dismissals and changes took place. Now it so happened that these said lords and ladies were politically and privately connected with the Cabinet, and those appointed in their places, were hostile to the then existing government. They threatened therefore to resign, the more so as the House of Commons was at that time very enthusiastic for the sovereign. After much pro and conning, the resignation was accepted, and Parliament dissolved, to knead it up again in the new ministerial oven. Oh! those cherry-pies!

All was bustle and excitement in Toryden-cum-Whigsnook. It was only one week before the election. Such an election! Being a new borough, a shoal of candidates came down to contest it. Great attention was excited throughout the country—would the new borough be Whig or Tory? Ministerial or popular? Seven candidates came down to try. Everybody was delighted! It was likely to be a sharp contest. John Wilson, however, was perplexed which way to vote. It unfortunately happened, that his custom was divided between the Whigs and the Tories, and, exclusive dealing being the order of the day, whichever way he voted, he was sure to lose. Still there was the glorious prospect of the bribes! No, there was not, intimidation suited as well; and "if you don't vote for so and so, we won't deal with you," produced an economical contest. Well, John Wilson balanced his books, and found he had seven more Tory customers than Whigs, so he voted for the Tory. The Tory lost, and John Wilson lost half his custom.

Things began to go on very badly with our hero; "but," said he, "let there be another election, and I'll put matters straight again." Another election there soon was, sure enough. The Whig member broke his neck at a steeplechase, and a fresh writ was issued.

Another contest—but this time a new element appeared on the arena. There was a popular candidate; and, strange enough, it was the Tory. This man was a large manufacturer, and being ambitious of parliamentary influence, built cottages for his operatives. These were undrained sties, not weather-proof, but he made his workmen take them at a rental of four shillings per week, as one of the conditions of taking them into his employment. To most of them, they were useless and untenable, and numbers of these poor men let the cottages at a loss of one and ninepence and two shillings per week! But the Tory master gained his double purpose; it acted as an abatement on their wages, and it placed three hundred electors at his command. Accordingly, when the seat for Toryden was vacant, he forced, on pain of dismissal and proscription, his three hundred slaves to sign a requisition for him to contest the borough, and come forward as the working-man's friend, the *popular candidate*.

The election passed; the "popular candidate" was returned; he was considered a man of liberal and enlightened mind in the House, and the Press paraded him as one of the honest representatives of an unbought constituency. But poor John Wilson! Did he partake of the triumph? Unfortunately, the Whigs caught him the night before the poll; he went with them, for the sly rogues wore *blue favors;* they kept him drinking all night, and took him next morning to vote yellow!

The Blues thanked him. The Whigs had shunned his shop—now the Tories did the same, and the latter did not accept his excuse of drunkenness. Poor John Wilson was almost ruined with his "glorious privilege," but lingered on until another general election took place. He had determined on this time having nothing to do with the matter, and accordingly neglected to pay his rates. While he was chuckling over this clever trick, he found the liberal registrar had paid his rates for him, and that his name was on the list.

Driven thus into a corner, he thought he would now try another plan, and vote for the people, for he had been obliged to lower his prices and ticket his articles, and become a "popular shopkeeper." Accordingly, he looked out for the "popular candidate." A rich banker from the neighbouring town was the man. How could he be otherwise—did'nt he put "The Sovereign People!" on his flags, "The Rights of Labour!" "Give Labour its Own!" and "Peace and Liberty"?

The sovereign people were taken in by the sham; there were some honest men, called Chartists, in the borough, and on the nomination day, they asked him some awkward questions. But his flags answered all purposes. They asked whether he would vote for "the six points?" He answered by pointing to "The Sovereign People!" (Cheers.) They asked him whether he would vote for the Ten Hours' Bill? He answered by pointing to "The Rights of Labour!" (Loud cheers.) They asked him whether he would vote against the Game Laws? He answered by pointing to "Give Labour its Own!" (Tremendous cheers.) He told them a good deal about "Peace and Liberty;" (it is true he said little about Free-Trade), but then he inveighed very bitterly against the sugar duties; it is true he said nothing about the Church Monopoly, but then he spoke very strongly about poor men working for rich men on a Sunday; it is very true he never propounded any plan for brightening the homes of industry, but then he talked largely about a poor man's cottage being his castle, always forgetting he had no cottage at present to make a castle of; and, winding up with a touching paragraph about " civil and religious liberty," he sat down amid " delirious thunders of rapturous applause !"

Now, John Wilson had determined not to do the thing by halves this time; accordingly, he made himself very prominent in canvassing for Mr. Watermouth, the popular candidate; no man was so active as he; it was mainly owing to him that Watermouth was returned.

Watermouth, when in the House, turned out a rogue, as might be expected from a man who don't come out boldly and state his opinions at once precisely and clearly. His flags were humbug; his words were humbug; he was himself a humbug. He voted against Free Trade; against the Ten Hours' Bill, against an amendment of the Poor Law, against Church Reform, and earned the execration of every honest man in the borough.

And poor John Wilson! Of course, he came in for his share. He had taken such an active part; he must have been in the pay of the traitor; he had deceived the people; and the people turned their backs on him.

The Tory had cut him; the Whig had cut him; and now the people cut him. He was soon obliged to shut up shop; he could no longer pay his ten pounds; he was a despised outcast unworthy notice; his children became factory slaves; he was driven to the Bastile. His poor little wife was obliged to part for ever from her firkins, and her pickles, and her flitches, and her husband; and the wretched outcasts lie in a parish grave, whereon some philosophising friend has written:—" KILLED BY THE GLORIOUS. PRIVILEGE !"

———

Reader! Let those who fear giving working men the vote, ponder on this true tale. The shopkeeper elector fears the preponderance of working men's votes might injure him. Silly fear! Could they injure him more than Whig and Tory injure him? And is he not, even now, in the power of the working-classes, *if they chose to use their power,* as much as if they had the vote? Nay! he has *more* to fear from them at present, since *now* they might naturally bear ill-will for a privilege assumed; *then* they would live in the harmony of equal rights.

Again we have to sound the note of encouragement. Again, with unflinching energy, have the people stood up for their rights. But while liberty in England is rising beside the bier of paralysed faction, abroad, the old snakes of tyranny are on the watch, and the league of kings is strengthening the bonds of servitude, in anticipation of an approaching struggle. Those Powers—Christian Powers—who murdered a nation in Poland; who, at Cracow, witnessed the apotheosis of Liberty; that emperor, who sent official murderers to destroy unawares man, woman, and child in the castles of Gallicia, and then gave his imperial rewards to the assassins; who has deluged the plains of Lombardy with the blood of patriots; that king, who owes the throne of his father to the valour of working men; that monarch, cradled in revolution, who lames the hand that gave him his crown—these are forming the unholy alliance of crowned knaves against self-emancipated industry. Italy and Switzerland are the two centre points of continental liberty. Italy and Switzerland are the two especial objects of royal and imperial machination. England, alone standing separate from the royal league, has it in her power, by interposing between the hungry North and the fertile South, to atone, in part, for her perfidy to Poland, and her unwelcome interference at Oporto. That government which has disgraced itself among Christian communities, that vile old man on whose forehead "Gallicia" is written like the brand-mark of a Cain, is evidently implicated in one of the most atrocious attempts, ancient or modern history records. Italy has long been a thorn in the side of Austria and her knavish colleagues. There, the democratic principle has been progressing more rapidly than, of late, in any other continental country. Kings and pontiffs have espoused the popular cause; the sovereigns of Sardinia and Rome have been the fathers of progression. Many have been the efforts made by France and Austria, and made with partial but unstable success, to check the democratic tendency of the Sardinian king; but when popular freedom was propounded from the chair of St. Peter—when the old bonds of superstition were breaking, and thrones were being stripped of the " right divine "—when the noblest of pontiffs proclaimed the great truth, that Christianity and Liberty are one,—then, every nerve was strained to re-convert the mitred proselyte, and, on conversion failing, to destroy him. Thence, we beheld the ablest diplomatists sent to a long neglected court; thence, we witnessed the strange spectacle of a Russian emperor visiting a Roman priest, and a lusty tyrant shrinking back before an aged man. Fair means failing, foul have been resorted to, and we have this month to record one of the most diabolical attempts of modern times.

The Pope having granted an amnesty to political offenders, it was determined to celebrate it by a magnificent public festival, on the evenings of Saturday and Sunday, the 17th and 18th ult. Grand fire-works were to have been displayed on the Pincian Hill, and the marble palaces around that magnificent square were to blaze in all the splendour of an Italian illumination. A few days previously, a vague rumour of an impending disaster crept through the town : the people kept assembling in crowds. Whence the rumour originated, none could tell; it seemed like that foreboding which seized the ancient Romans at the very hour their army was defeated in a distant oriental province. On the doors of many houses the mysterious letter S had been marked by unknown hands.

The government seemed paralysed, no one knew how to act, or whither to direct his energy; when suddenly, all over the town placards appeared on the walls, some written, some printed, containing a long list of names announced as of conspirators against the people. These names principally belonged to the gensd'armerie and secret agents of the former police, to the officials of a by-gone system, including even cardinals, general officers, and noblemen.

Popular excitement had now reached a fearful height; the police feeling themselves implicated, endeavoured to tear down the placards which were immediately replaced by others. Anarchy and bloodshed seemed inevitable, when Prince Borghesi and Duke Massimo urged on the Pope the immediate organisation of the National Guard, a measure which had been already contemplated. In an instant the required organisation was effected, and the city safe in the hands of the people. Cicerovacchio, one of the leaders of the popular party, organised and guided the populace, preventing license, and arresting the accused. The plans and papers of the conspirators were now discovered. They were mostly men from the suburb of Faenza, long notorious for ignorance, bigotry, and crime; they had entered Rome in small bodies; with concealed weapons, they had mingled with the people in large numbers; and their intention was to have fallen unawares on all they met, to have fired the immense hay-stores scattered through the town, thus to increase the confusion, and to have given all the adherents and supporters of the Pope to indiscriminate slaughter. So sanguinary was their design, that one of the criminals, when arrested, said, " Blood was to have flowed that night, which the mid-day sun of the morrow could not have dried up." On Monday the 19th, Cardinal Minardi was arrested, and a clue apparently given to the whole design, pointing to the secret machinations of the Austrian government. The conspirators were found in possession of heaps of foreign coin ; and before any tidings of the above events could have crossed the frontier, Austrian troops were marching to the Roman States. Twelve hundred cavalry and a large park of artillery were moved from Verona to Ferrara, thus clearly proving on the part of Metternich, prior cognisance of what was to transpire. The design evidently was to throw Rome into anarchy and confusion, then obtain a pretext for intervention, and trample out the spark of Italian liberty beneath the cold-blooded despotism of German military rule.

The execration of Europe must rest on the hoary sinner who, with one foot in his grave, would pour out the blood of thousands, in a libation to the perverted principles of hereditary despotism.

The advance of troops on the part of Austria, called forth the threat of similar intervention on that of France, and thus Italy, between the cross-fire of two despots, calls loudly on the sympathies of the liberal and enlightened in Europe.

The only other · foreign event of paramount importance, since the ill-omened English intervention in Portugal, is the protracted and sanguinary war in Mexico. Santa Anna has again been declared dictator, on pledging himself never to treat for peace. The Mexicans have assembled an army of 30,000 men, of which 16,000 are destined for the defence of the capital. The Americans, under Scott, have 10,000 men; there are 4,000 at Vera Cruz, and reinforcements are daily expected. All is enthusiasm on the part of the Mexicans; while a terrible fever is decimating the American ranks. Skirmishes are taking place between either party, in one of which, at a place called Jago, between Calasso and Parata, 400 Mexicans with their commander have been killed.

It is with sincere pleasure we turn from lamentable scenes like these, where freedom has to pass through the ordeal of open bloodshed, or of secret murder, to our own favoured land, where progression is holding its triumphant course amid peace, order and constitutional reform.

The result of the elections has not disappointed our expectations; the triumph at Nottingham, the seats of many good men secured, the great principle established, even where Chartist candidates were not successful—all point to a not far distant, to a successful termination of the great struggle between the capitals of labour and of money. It is a great evidence of growing power, that the Charter has progressed from the hustings to the polling-booth, ay! even into the House. That seed has been sown, that feeling created, which guarantees the return of those Chartists to the House at the next election, who, at this one, have polled a minority

The government feel and know this, the opponents of the government feel this too, and therefore the Tory party, seeing the Whigs toppling, will bid more than ever for popular support; therefore they will endeavour to *popularise* the church—therefore they will, perhaps, tinker at the Poor Law and Sanitary Reform—but let them not think by local remedies, scantily applied, to cure the general disease. The Charter is the great question of the day—that obtained, Church monopolies, and food monopolies, and taxation monopolies must vanish—vanish before the voluntary system, before Free trade (not alone in manufactures and in food, but in that which produces BOTH, *Land,*)—before direct taxation, which shall distribute, in fair proportion, the burthen of maintaining government between the rich and poor.

To this question ministers must apply themselves, fearlessly and honestly, or their tenure of office is not worth the lease of a hour.

Quack remedies they have many—remedies that will but aggravate the complaint. Some talk of legislating on machinery, some talk of taxing it, some of curtailing the hours for its use. Now, we wish to see machinery transplanted from the factory to the cottage, thus making it, not the *master*, but the *assistant* of the poor. A tax like the above would only throw an additional impediment in the way of the poor man's obtaining it, and limiting the hours for its use would be a "Ten Hours Bill measure," without the good the Ten Hours Bill affords. It would only stimulate the manufacturer to carry machinery to greater perfection, so that additional power might be obtained, and fewer hands needed to watch it, and would operate as an excuse for bringing wages down. There is another plan that might be adopted, limiting the machine-power to be possessed by an individual. This would strike a blow at the competitive system, and would render the manufacturer at home unable to compete with the manufacturer abroad; it would throw numbers of hands out of employment, and derange the whole mercantile system, without affording any security for the rights of labour. If machinery is to be legislated on, we know of no way so effective, as by securing co-operative industry on the part of the people; if machinery is to be taken out of the factory and placed in the cottage, it cannot be done by a direct legislative enactment, it must be done by directing the energies of the people to the land, thus enabling them to obtain that command of capital which will lead to the purchase of machinery as an ACCESSORY to their labour; by encouraging, through legislative protection, the formation of co-operative societies on the part of working-men, thus enabling the rising power of democracy to countervail the sinking influence of the monopolist. As the CHARTER is the great means of political redemption, so is CO-OPERATION the great agent of social amelioration. It smooths the way for the attainment of those political rights embraced in the former, and, when obtained, it fits men to enjoy them with safety and security. The great question of machinery will thus find its own level, the more so as the foreign demand is irrevocably sinking before foreign competition, and the home-trade can only be created by prosperity among all classes.

We therefore caution the people against being deluded by any of the wild, visionary, but superficial schemes which the Tory party may propound, for that party will now make a desperate effort to bring the people on its side. Be it remembered, that *he who strikes not at the root of the evil only aggravates the complaint;* that we must make a stand for our principles and nothing less, and submit to NO COMPROMISE, even though we were to take an instalment.

Throughout Europe, the elements of change are at work, and, like a lull before a thunder storm, the present apparent absence of revolutionary excitement in France and Germany, points but to the rapidly approaching struggle. Frail is the link that binds the lictor's rods of France together; it is the life of one old man. Long has the conflict been preparing in Germany, between absolute monarchies and federal republics. The religious movements under Ronge fearfully tested the stability of the former; the bread riots and beer riots in Bavaria and Prussia gave it an additional blow. The constitution-tinkering of the king of Prussia has but irritated the people the more, since they beheld in it an attempt at deception and an augury of weakness. The bayonets that are bristling around the frontiers of Switzerland, are afraid to advance into that focus of freedom, lest the scarcely withheld indignation of liberal Europe should be aroused, and that crisis be hastened onward which governments are attempting to delay. Stolid, haughty, unscrupulous and blood-thirsty, Austria alone, still pours her troopers over the plains of Lombardy; still plays the midnight-assassin against Italian liberty; while Russia looks greedily on from its savage iceberg, having, however, enough to do in shattering its armies against the Caucasus, and tightening the uncertain chains of but half subjugated Poland.

Spain and Portugal are as they were, the stage where priestly rancour, stockjobbing heartlessness, military brutality, aristocratic selfishness and royal rapacity obtain the lead by turns, while enduring democracy is struggling helplessly but patiently against them.

Thus, throughout Europe, all things indicate a coming change; a general revolution, sweeping from land to land in one continuous tide, as history has often marked its course before.

England, as we have already said, will not be backward. But, while other countries are constrained by circumstances to seek their emancipation by the sword, it will be our happy privilege to obtain it on the paths of peace. Even as England has always proved itself in advance on the march to democracy, beyond most of its continental competitors, so, we trust it will prove itself again, by showing that the people have obtained a self-control, a political influence sufficient to turn its own weapons against oppression, meet legalised oppression with legalised resistance, and thus found liberty, not upon a ruin, but upon the proud foundation of once conflicting but then harmonised influences.

LITERARY REVIEW.

We have received numbers of publications for notice, the subjects of which are so utterly at variance with the progressive spirit of the age, that we have declined trespassing on the space allotted to more congenial matters by criticising them.

There is a time when combating the fallacies of opponents, and refuting old arguments, does goed : but, when the truths of a principle are once established in the minds of millions, unless a *new* argument is advanced against them, we cannot burthen our readers with the repetition of an oft told tale. Again, we have received works replete with genius, but without moral—either political, social, or religious. We would earnestly advise those talented men, who are capable of thus much, to do *something more*,—more in the matter they treat of—more in the moral they deduce. Where is the Bulwer of Chartism—where is the Knowles of Democracy ? Can no new fire be infused into what is called the " expiring drama ?"—expiring, because it has been dedicated to an expiring cause—because it has been the pander to wealth and fashion, instead of the vindicator of manhood and industry. Whenever, indeed, it has ridiculed or chastised an aristocratic vice, it has done so playfully and kindly, shewing it in a sportive light, and, at any rate, depicting how it made an *equal* suffer, not how it crushed a " subordinate." We have had the misfortunes of younger sons, the mishaps of injured daughters of noble houses, but when has the Bastile victim, when has the lost child of labour, when has the hapless operative, (the martyrs of the nineteenth century,) when have these been brought before the public eye in the drama, or when will they ? while a dramatic monopoly is kept up, in keeping with all others, that, while a censorship of the press is declared contrary to the constitution, establishes a censorship of the drama in direct violation of its recognised principle?

Critics have objected that the English dramatic author is destitute of inventive power; it is not so : but as long as he is restricted to the advocacy of monopolies, in defence of which nothing can be said, so long may he tax his ingenuity in vain, to produce that free flow of language, incident and moral, which an honest and a fertile theme alone affords the author.

Let our dramatic talent be on the look out. Chartism is marching into the fields of literature with rapid strides; the precincts of the drama it has not yet passed. Its poetry is, indeed, the freshest and most stirring of the age; as in England, thus in France, America, Ireland, and Germany, the poetic spirit has struck the chords of liberty; and the fresh vigour of its productions contrasts proudly with the emasculated verses of a fashionable school. Yet, from many we have expected more? What is Robert Browning doing? He, who could fire the soul of a Luria, and develope the characters of a Victor and a Charles,—he, who could depict nature's nobility in a Colombe,—has he nothing to say for popular rights? Let him eschew his kings, and queens,—let him quit the pageantry of courts— and *ascend* into the cottage of the poor.

Can Tennison do no more than troll a courtly lay? His oak could tell other tales besides a love story.

Can Knowles but stalk upon his stilts of Arragon, go hunting with his feudal falconers, or make a princess condescend to love a serf?

Let Mackay leave generalities behind; and while his exquisite poetry elevates the soul, point our feeling by a homely narrative to the sufferings of industry.

Let Gurney cease to sing of "King Charles," and begin to write of the sovereign people.

Let us for awhile bid good bye to "Salamandrines and Seraphim."

Let Bailey write another and a better Festus, in vindication of real (not only of ideal) humanity.

Let Horne and Powell lay conventionalism aside, and all, devoting their great talents to the great cause of the age, we shall have a literature worthy of its progressive qualities. Alas! it often happens that an author is before his age—these men are behind theirs. Those who are in advance may have the consolation that posterity will do them justice; those who are in arrear must be unnoticed to-day—will be forgotten to-morrow.

We have made the above remarks out of respect for the talents of those named : feeling anxious they should not altogether be lost to the world.

Let it not be objected to us that we are one sided—that we wish but to hear the plaintiff and not the defendant. Far

from it.   Literature is the exponent of the spirit of the age;
it is this, or it is nothing.

"Give me a nation's songs, and I will give you the character of a nation's people," is an old and valuable maxim;
the people mould a poet, but a poet directs a people.   The
noble sentiments of Southey's Wat Tyler have done more
for his fame than all his maudlin affectation in honour of
loyalty to kings.   The speech of John Ball alone would
have won him laurels; there is a magic spell in the words,
"My brethren, we are equal, equality is our birth-right."
The sentiment is the drama of nature—a bold, noble,
simple and true expression—and its author, in writing it,
gives words to the heart's aspirations, and a tone to national
character.   We say to the great minds of the day, come
among the people, write for the people, and your fame will
live for ever.   The people's instinct will give life to your
philosophy, and the genius of the favoured few will hand
down peace and plenty, knowledge and power, as an heirloom to posterity.

THE LABOURER

LORD LINDSAY.

A POEM.

BY ERNEST JONES.

Lindsay castle's jutted forth
  On the wild, old, sounding sea,
And a gallant race of the hardy North,
  As their mountains strong—as the billows free,
That monument of ancient worth
  Through long, long centuries hàve held,
Bequeathed unto the modern earth
  By the great, dim hands of Eld.

It is a mighty trust to bear
The memory of those that were;
To have a name of time to save,
And be worthy to sleep in a father's grave;
To dwell in halls of mouldering stone,
Though desert all, yet not alone '
With listeners to every word—
Each motion seen, each accent heard!
The long dim statues down the hall,
And dark old arms on the oaken wall,
Scanning everything you do,
The while you pace your chambers through;
Where, still their jealous vigil keeping,
The dead, in niche and vault unsleeping,
Forth looming from the depth of time,
Startle their children back from crime!

Thro' many a change that race had passed;
  Both sin's and honour's pathways trod:
For wealth may like an heirloom last,
  But virtue is the gift of God.

And years and wars, and storm and crime
Had worn that house of ancient time :
Its greatness shrunk,
As discord drunk
The lifeblood of its early prime :
Pageant in tournay—assault on the wall,
Valour in battle and slander in hall,
Treason at midnight and riot at noon
Soon end an old house,—'tis forgotten as soon.
A breath blows the glories of ages away—
And now the last heir unto Lindsay's decay,
With the proud blood of heroes ennobling his will,
Mistrusted a world that had used him so ill.

A fair maid came to Lindsay Hall,
  Oh ! grand was her array,
With liege and lord and free and thrall,
  And pomp of silken sway ;

And acres broad and castles high,
  And famous, old descent ;
And heart with true nobility,
  And mind with pure intent.

The mother smiled : "She brings thee gold !"
  Lord Lindsay turned away :
" 'Twas steel, that built my house of old,
  Gold saves it not to-day !"

The mother smiled : "She brings thee love !"
  Lord Lindsay turned away :
"So many said—to my fathers' dead !
  Tho' fair, yet false were they."

The maiden heard : "Since love nor gold
  "Thy brave, great heart may gain,
Thou 'rt worthy of the faith I fold
  Around it, like a chain."

Lord Lindsay's at the maiden's feet,
  A cloud beneath a star—
Uplit by her.—Oh ! love is sweet,
  But faith is sweeter far !

And as he weds that glorious bride,
  Like night to morning wed,
She breathes: "To love is to confide,
  "But doubt—and love hath fled."

Oh! There were sounds and sights of pride,
When Lindsay welcomed home his bride:
As though a charm were in the place,
Fresh fortunes flashed on Lindsay's race;
High harpers sung—and revel rung,
And laughter from hot hearts was flung,
Stirred by passion's fiery breath,
Like light foam dashed from depths beneath.
But oh! That Lady was too fair
To walk the earth without a care:
While sin's old sway must still abide,
Man brooks no angel by his side.
Though once with him they walked the sod,
Did *they* raise man up unto God?
Or was't not *he*, whose fatal spell
Dragged down the angels unto hell?

Thus, when for mortal's sinful night
Too sun-like proved her beauty's light,
A whisperer came with tale half-told,
Glance once too warm, and now too cold,
And, envying love he could not win,
To Lindsay breathed the fabled sin:
And he, with quivering lip and pale,
Listened—ay! listened to the tale,
Who, had he proved his antient worth,
Had hurled the slanderer to the earth,
And haled him to his gentle bride
  To own his slanders one by one,
And, as he spurned the miscreant, cried—
That *he* hath said—this *I* have done!
But Lindsay listened—then believed,
Nay! gave the poison he received—
And, proof and argument without,
Began the deadly spell—to doubt!

Oh! WRATH will droop with wearied wing,
  And Hate will yield to tears:
But DOUBT destroys the fairest thing,
  Creates the spot it fears.

Then o'er their world began to roll
The gradual twilight of the soul.
No wind can wave that gloom away,
And backward waft the dying day;
'Tis not a summer-glory fled,
The very sun itself is dead:
For Love, estranged by wavering fate,
Changes but once, and that—to Hate.

And Lindsay!—Did he love no more?
Oh! still more madly than before.
But Doubt, as with enchanter's art·
Placed its cold hand upon his heart;
Froze the warm glances in his eye,
And turned to ice the burning sigh;
Chilled the full ardour of his tone
To stony words from lips of stone,
And blighting thus another's fate,
Yet left himself *most* desolate.
No word was spoken to reveal,
Few signs to see, yet all to feel!
At first, so slight the altered guise,
It woke no fear—scarce raised surprise:
But hour by hour, and day by day,
Something familiar died away,—
A smile, a sigh, a look the less,
A languor in the forced caress,
Those nameless nothings, that will tell
What words could never say so well.
Though all unseen, they felt, they knew
A veil was drawn between the two;
'Twas raised by Doubt, 'twas held by Pride,
Who silent stood on either side;
It hung between, so thin of fold,
And yet so chilly, dark and cold,
The smiles of love could not shine through,
The kind glance lost its tenderest hue,
The soft endearments of the Past
Gleamed pale athwart its darkness cast:
And yet it was a thing so slight,
That mocked the touch, the ear, the sight!
Oh! It had yielded to a breath—
One little word of love and faith!
That little word was never spoken:
And souls were wrecked—and hearts were broken!

Long, long she mourned without a spot,
And where she sought love, found it not ;
And then she grieved, that such should be,
   And anger tinged her cheek with flame ;
Unconscious Infidelity
   Thus in the guise of Reason came,
And o'er her heart its shadow brought,
While still afar in lands of thought.—
When passion once asserts its sway,
Fly swiftly from the strife away '
For in the struggle, every hour
Waxes the wily foeman's power,
Who in the heart securely sits,
There hides, attacks, defends by fits ;
Defeated, to new' strife invites,
And feeds upon the foe he fights,
As skilful warriors lead'their band
To live upon a hostile land.

Then—when her heart was wearing slow,
A pendulum 'twixt wrath and woe—
A lover came, with sweeter tongue,
Each word was music, though unsung ·
She turned her from the voice so cold,
   From the dark, stern brow, she turned
To smiles, that sunlight round her rolled,
   And eyes and words that burned.
She leaned her from her lattice high,
   Her heart went down long, long before :
It was a brief, wild agony :
   She followed, when the strife was o'er.

One throb of joy, one pulse of pain,
One moment's thought between the twain :
A heart that broke—a death that healed,
So wretched that it half annealed ;
Yet, sadder fate on Lindsay's head—
A heart that beat, although 'twas dead.

Then the lot the most barren, the lot the most great,
Lindsay chose from the garner of treacherous fate :
To be hated by many, by few to be bless'd,
   To do good unto all, and receive it from none,
To wake and to watch while all others may rest,
   And to die ere one half of his task has been done.
But to die as he lived, all strange, great, and alone,
Mourned not in tears, but recorded in stone.

Soon the rumour crept and came,
Still and low as stifled flame,
That in some distant spot of earth
A vast, great spirit had gone forth
Wanderers strange from door to door,
And lands remote the tidings bore.
Uncertain, first, the echoes wild
Floated like dreams athwart a child :
A breath, a whisper, then a word,
That grew familiar as 'twas heard,
Till, quick achievement, pace on pace,
With giant march grasped time and space,
And, clearer seen in glory's height,
Forth flashed the hero on the sight !
Then shouts the mass—it knows not why—
Save, that another raised the cry ;
Those living echoes of the crowd,
From hearts most shallow, still most loud,
As answers still are shrillest thrown
From barest rock and bleakest stone.

Thus steals on time a hero-name,
Deserved, or undeserved, the same ;
From million lips in thunder hurled,
Bursts the loud anthem o'er the world ·
Then bow the nations, prostrate laid
Before the idol they have made ;
But, when temptation comes at last,
When power is strong and peril past—
Then shall we know the workman's hands :
False greatness sinks—true greatness stands.

* * * * *

Along the misty heather grey
Lord Lindsay's vast encampment lay,
Gleaming upward on the night
Emblazoned tents of silvery white,
Like snowflakes by a Northern blast
At midnight o'er the champaign cast.

The leader's in his tent alone ;
And, like a tent above it thrown,
The night lay o'er it fold on fold,
Heavy, dark, and still and cold.
The murmur from the camp around,
The muffled tread on grassy ground,
Question low and low reply,

The rustling banner's mournful play—
Like flapping wing of bird of prey,
Impatient for the carnage-day—
Sudden laugh and roundelay,
Like windgusts passing by ;
Neigh and stamp and clank of arm,
Shot at sentry-posts' alarm,
Then the single bugle-blast,
And the squadron skirring past,
Sent 'mid darkness to the fight,
Like a thundercloud through night :
In one deep hum, but dead and low,
Crept through the curtain's silken flow,
And shook them with its ominous breath,
Like the step of the coming death.
 Those small, still sounds, that fill the break
Ere long-expected thunders wake,
And start the listening watcher more
Than the loud storm's first opening roar,
 Came freezing on the humid air ;
While 'neath night's fingers, chill and damp,
The flame crouched down upon the lamp—
 Scarce light enough to show 'twas there.
Thus Lindsay sat—all spirit-cold,
While night's dark hours the sun uprolled.
The battle's eve is hard to bear,
Its fears, but not its joys are there ;
And Lindsay watched the moments fleet,
One by one, with leaden feet.
He counted them with beat of heart,
Slow to come and slow to part,
While on their silent wings they brought
Man's worst companion—anxious thought !

 On every side—anear, afar—
Slept the fiery tide of war :
Countless hearts, that, all aflame,
Should kindle when the morrow came,
Now laid in slumber, wrapt as death,
Calm as the sword within its sheath.
As from the scabbard leaps the brand,
When drawn beneath the soldier's hand,
With one proud impulse Lindsay's call
Might rouse the slumbering thousands all.
 But deem not that his eye was bright,

As kindled with its wonted light ;
His pulse their even throb retain :
There was too much to lose and gain !
The goal of all his stormy life
Is centred in the morrow's strife :
The guerdon he had toiled for long,
The hope, that made the weary strong,
The moment, that should years outweigh,
Beyond whose loss 'twere vain to stay,
When time, on-pointing to the dead,
Forbade afresh his path to tread ;
Past man's control—past thought's command—
The life—the death—'twas all at hand,
And he was sitting on the brink,
With nought to do but think—and think .

Few—few upon his musing break,
An augur from their chief to take.

There was but one—and this a friend—
Who questioned of the morrow's end.
He would not the word betray,
The word, that lost the coming day !
'Twas but one friend ! he bent his ear,
And then could scarce the answer hear ;
The gusty winds were loud without,
'Twas scarcely breathed : *" I doubt ! I doubt !"*
There was none else who could have heard
The scarce articulated word !
Yet through the curtain's silken fold,
Coldly on the midnight cold
It crept, like messenger of ill,
From heart to heart with footstep chill.
Spoken lowly and alone,
Whence did echo win the tone ?
From lip and eye, and brow and hand,
And deadness of the dull command.
O'er hearts, that every thought can hear,
Untold of tongue, unheard of ear,
In blighting circles widened out
The palsying spell—*" I doubt ! I doubt !"*

The night passed by to beat of heart,
  Like a funeral march to an open tomb ;
When sunlight mapped the heaven's wide chart,
  'Twas but a torch to show the gloom—

The gloom upon the war-helmed head
  And breast imprisoned in bright mail:
Gleamed the crest on glances dead,
  Flashed the steel on foreheads pale.

Sullen broke the battle's roar,
  Sultry dropped the cannon-flame
The conflict to the midward bore,
The banners shook unto its breath.
Music swelled the voice of death,
  And slowly rolled the long acclaim.

Reeled the battle's midward shock—
  Charges on the serried square:
As the earthquake tears the rock,
  The horse the pausing column tear.

But every arm is half unnerved—
Each rider in the onset swerved—
Rein half-tightened, lance half-thrust,
A palsy on the battle's lust,
For still each beating breast about
Is wound the web: " *I doubt! I doubt!* "

Now, gallant Lindsay! turn the war!
The moment's come to make or mar.
Now send the rally to the charge!
The serried phalanxes enlarge!
For hot volcanoes, left and right,
  Spit forth their iron hail—
Where battery flames, from crenelled height,
  Make day's red flambeau pale.

As to winds sink scattered waves,
On that deathfield without graves,
Down before the cannon-blast
Behold a living pavement cast.
And still they stood and still they fell
Before the red advancing hell:
Then turned to Lindsay every eye,
Broke from the field one smothered cry
Demanding but that single sign
To crush the foes' upgathering line.

Every horse is scarce held back—
Every heart is on the rack—
Every spirit on the rise:
It *is* the moment—and it flies!

Upon a height Lord Lindsay stood
And marked the turning of the flood;
And thrice he raised his arm on high,
Thrice turned to shout his battle-cry;
And thrice the gallant impulse dies
To fears, that throng, and doubts that rise;
It *is* the moment—and it flies!
Delay and doubt did more that hour;
Than bayonet-charge and carnage-shower.

Loud howls the battle like a gale:
But fast the fiery ardours fail,
And every brow is turning pale!
They have the heart but lack the word.
Broke from Lindsay's lip no cry,
Flashed no signal from his eye,
He neither spoke, nor signed, nor stirred,
He thought but: *"should they fail!"*

Cold on his brow was writ despair,
His army saw it lettered there;
From rank to rank, from man to man,
Like a word that dead look ran.
The impulse flags,—the die is cast—
It *was* the moment—and 'tis past!

Close! close the square! from every side,
    Hark! to horsemen's hurtling shock:
Onward pours that living tide
    Upon that living rock!

And up and down—and to and fro—
    The battle reeled across the plain,
And when its force seemed stricken low,
    Up burst the fiend afresh again;
With quivering arm and panting breath,
And battered bone and streaming vein,
But heart as fierce as it began—
A mass of horse, and steel and man!

Squadron hurtling,—shattered square,—
But still enough to do and dare ;
Beat of foot and hard hoof prancing,
Now receding, now advancing,—
The ebb and flow of the tide of death !

Then, when his bands were falling fast,
That gallant spirit dared its last.
Then Lindsay rode the foremost rank,
And drove his steed through war-pools dank,
And bravely waved his pennon high,
And loudly cried his battle-cry !
And minstrels heard the foeman say
Lord Lindsay had fought well that day.

    *   *   *   *   *

A single rider from the field,
  All worn with wounds, when day was low
With severed sword and shattered shield,
  But heart unbroken by the blow,
  That laid his life before his foe,
Rode to seek uncoffined rest
In the spot becomes a soldier best:
A warrior's grave on heather wild,
With the death of a man and the sleep of a child !

    *   *   *   *   *

The sun was trembling on the sea,
  Winds were low and clouds were high,
And one bird sung on the old oak tree
  When Lindsay laid him down to die.
It sung a song of early days,
Rich—rich with childhood's fairy lays.
Thus the robin sung on the linden-bough,
In the home of his youth as it called to him now ;
'Twas a carol of heaven it chanted him then,
And the self-same song it was chanting again.

But the world had rolled with its fiery blast,
Filling the gulf twixt the present and the past.
'Mid the mad'ning and whirlpool and roar of its wave
He knew not his cradle-song sung o'er his grave!—
  And all the spirits of his life,
His Peace, his Hope, his Love, his Strife,

Float by him wan in that solemn hour,
Bearing each a withered flower.
Colourless spectres, they cast on his sight
Forms without beauty and smiles without light!

His useless life so wildly passed!—
So many deeds and none to last!—
A sigh of regret for his parting breath;
Of all that seed but one fruit—Death!
And the Beyond?—To him unknown:
A tear—a knell—a prayer—a stone!
A sod wrapped round a soulless clay,
And a keyless gate to a trackless way!
For Death, to him all light without,
Was worse than agony—was *Doubt*.
So high a heart—so sad a fate!
Wanting but Faith to have been great.

CO-OPERATION.

"The evil day approacheth, who can save the people?"

Professor Sievers lately said, "Down with national prejudices; up with democratic institutions." We now say, too,
down with class prejudices, up with democratic institutions;
but in our enthusiasm for the glorious future, we must not
forget the means necessary to effect our object; it is not
sufficient that we will to achieve an object, it is also necessary
that we reason, prepare, and act. Let us rest assured we
want something more potent, more powerful, more effective
than argument alone, to influence the members of the
House of Commons. In honest truth, the wiseacres of
St. Stephen's are too wise in their generation to be much
affected by our logic. We have already appealed to them
by every means at our command, but they have given us
the lie direct, and sneered at that to which they could not
reply. The influence we exercise on the members of that
House must be both indirect and direct; the indirect
influence may be made powerful, it has already done
much. It is a fatal error to suppose that we exercise no
power over the government of this country; the fact is,
that in all countries, the acts, if not the form of government, are attributable to the intelligence and energy of the

people, and much of the leaning to enlightened and progressive policy of the government of late years, is attributable to the Chartist agitation. If we have not gained our object, we have taken the initiative in all good measures, and forced government to admit our intelligence, whilst they have refused to recognise the same in the representative form. The Irish Coercion Bill was damned by the English Chartists; the Masters' and Servants' Bill was sent to the right about by the same power; and before Lord John Russell, the acting manager of the Legislative drama, played the character of dustman and street sweeper, in the farce of Sanatory Reform, the working-classes of England and Scotland had collected £14,000, to buy for themselves land, build for themselves cottages, and procure for labour every necessary that aristocracy and moneyocracy will allow us to possess. It is but a few years since, in a debate on the Ten Hours' Bill, Viscount Howick, Charles Buller, and Lord John Russell were constrained to speak of a new organisation of labour—a new arrangement of things—short hours—improved modes of living, &c. It may be, that these men have forgotten to realise their promised improvements; it may be, their promises were vague and indefinite; but it is undeniable, that the progressive power of the people, that forced admission of its principles in 1843, may force concession at no distant date; and we hesitate not to inform the ministers of her majesty's Cabinet, that the time is not remote when external circumstances will compel the governors of this country to think wisely, and, if they act not well, they must resign and make way for better men. The history of these isles for the past 60 years has been a sad and eventful history; it is eventful in unbinding all the ties that united society together. In Scotland, the families of the Macdonalds and Maclauchlans have been turned out of their own highland glens, their cottages have been uprooted to make way for sheepwalks and mansions. In Ireland, unhappy Ireland, murder at noonday was lately almost the rule, and safety the exception; the pistol shot of the mad and unfortunate criminal was answered by the musket ball of the slaves hired and educated to shoot and kill the discontented. And why is this state of things? is it natural? No! it is unnatural; but money has been courted and labour has been spurned;—those ties that should bind man to home, wife and children, have been broken asunder,— and the very name of fatherland has been uprooted. This is not the result of one act of parliament, or the deeds of one ministry—it is the effect of a lawless and plundering system practised by landlords and moneymongers, supported and honoured by a government preferring the smiles of one rich and mistaken man to the comfort and good wishes of many thousands of industrious families. But the day of retribution will—it must come; yes! ere many years elapse, England, this land of seeming peace, will murmur louder and longer than she ever has done. Look around for these things, and you may now see the future coming. The black miners of the north are in a discontented state. Yorkshire and Lancashire will soon present a scene of distress, such as men living never witnessed. Already yarns are selling badly, spinning is not profitable — the products of Lowell in America are competing with those of Manchester. How much better is it for the toiler and operative, aided by machinery, that can now do the work that 150 men were required to do when spinning was performed on the old system ? "Oh !" exclaims the manufacturer, "your interest is our interest !" "Indeed," replies the operative, "if so, and the same circumstances affect both, they will rise and fall together. John Bright, in an electioneering speech at Durham, boasted that his father was at one time as poor as any man who stood before him, but he was now rich. Many families starve that the 'One Ash,' the residence of this manufacturing genius, may be enriched. The system has worked well for him, and badly for the working men of Rochdale. How have you proved that our interest is one ?"

"Every man for himself," exclaims the manufacturer; "a fair stage and no favour; what more would you require ?" "Truly," replies the slave; "but that you have not granted. Possessing capital, you regulated wages, kept down demand for labour by machinery; and controlled us by the necessities you created. 'A fair stage and no favour;' so be it, then we must begin anew; we will balance our relative stock in trade: my thrift against your prodigality, my industry against your idleness, my labour against your machinery, my savings against your robberies, and the co-operation of my class against the conspiracy of yours."

Thus arose co-operation. Unions were formed, stores established, land bought, mills built, and the great work of redemption commenced. As it is with the social, so is it with the political question: co-operation can conquer even Parliament; two £5 householders can take a £10 house in the name of one—thus, we may safely say, at least one-third of the disfranchised might obtain the vote ; that third, added to the growing liberalism of the constituencies, could carry all before it, and the Charter triumph over faction and class government.

It is by means like these we may avoid, by peaceable means, the growing storm we have above alluded to. That storm will otherwise assuredly come, and it behoves us to prepare for it. Our experienced, and well-tried general, Mr. O'Connor, is fighting the battle nobly, socially, and politically. He is building for the poor, cottages, and teaching their representatives parliamentary duties. It is not a week ago since we witnessed the greatest triumph of modern progression—some sixty men, the thinking and swarthy operatives of England and Scotland, in conference, reasoning with each other, and suggesting the best means to remedy the wrongs of labour, and secure industry against the assaults of the enemy. Oh ! it was a noble spectacle ; many a lofty and wrinkled forehead was bowed in deep and silent thought, all aiming to reach the longed-for goal, when political right will be acknowledged, and the anomaly of starvation in the midst of plenty shall cease to exist. Youth and enthusiasm were also present. A band of gallant young men who have deserted the pleasures and gaieties usual to their years, and seek for fame in the welfare of their common country — a true and noble resolve, more defined than Spartan bravery, more useful and not less honourable than the Roman patriotism of old. These men are achieving a great work, realising a nation's salvation, without the aid of the merely philanthropic ; they say, put the spade in the earth, and we will, without cannon or bayonet revolutionise England ; we will rectify her wrongs, and create for her a new industrial era. But myriads of our fellow-men will still be without our pale, to them do we address ourselves, for them do we write ; we tell them that the storm is coming—want stares them in the face—the union workhouse and county gaol are their homes—sad fact—yet how *true*.

Well ! come and join us in our struggle for right—exercise your power, and prepare for the contest ; strive onwards in the battle of life ; and if you be yet blessed with youth and health, provide for yourself a home, and you will be the better able to change the institutions of your country, and be enabled to impress the government with the justice of your claims and your power to enforce them. Senators will yet yield up their antiquated notions of classes and factions, own the Majesty of the people, and make such arrangements and enact such laws as will render every improvement in science a boon to the artisan, and every increase of national wealth a wisely distributed stream of blessings for the people. The work is ours, and we will do it—fear not—nature is no bigot in the dispensation of her gifts. Statesmen and poets are born in mud-built cabins as well as in turretted castles or lofty halls; they are to be found among labour's despised and rejected sons—rejected because feared, despised because the honest inspiration of their nature is misunderstood by the men of mere school-book and ledger philosophy. One man still lives who knows the people, and in whom the people confide; he it is that will yet live to give virtual power to that great truth which all will yet own: *vox populi, vox Dei,* (the voice of the people is the voice of God).

ROBERT TANNAHILL,

A PAISLEY WEAVER, AND SCOTTISH POET.

WE have long wished to say something of 'Robert Tannahill, the mild and unobtrusive bard of Paisley.' A child in the knowledge of the tricks of trade, but a noble hero; a true man in the greatest of all virtues, simplicity of heart and sincerity of feeling; a man who was great without pretensions; no wordy braggart, speaking much and doing little, but a worker; a valuable and worthy adjunct to Scotland's minor poets; an unobtrusive friend, almost blushing to be seen, yet never seen without a welcome, and meeting with many a hearty response from Scotland's grey-haired grandfather, to her pouting, smirking, sousie lasses.

It has been said with much truth and grace, that a great poet represents a great portion of the human family, and though Tannahill lays no claim to the title of a great poet, he was a great man, and the representative of a distinct class of Scotland's peasantry. To him was not delegated, the plenary power of the epic author, or life-displaying dramatist; his writings unfold no struggling volcano of bursting passion, no trumpet clanging denunciations of wrong. The bard never assumes the dignity of a God of justice, nor from his throne, "aloft in awful state," judges and decides with the Majesty of power, sending tyrants and oppressors to the dark and gloomy deep of terror, and settling the fate of mortals with the august supremacy of conscious right; nor does he speak to us in many voices, making us forget the lord in the servant, or the poet in the character represented. No; the poems of the author reflect the man; he hailed the simple and the sweet of nature, and loved to roam by the banks and braes that surrounded Paisley town. Born of poor, but respectable parentage, his education was of the ordinary kind, consisting of class-reading, writing, and a limited knowledge of arithmetic. Reared under the same roof with industrious and frugal parents, it was but reasonable to expect that his habits of life would be such, as would, with daily toil and hourly economy, provide for their possessor a fair supply of a poor man's comfort, affording no uncommon surplus means for mental acquirements, and offering no stubborn obstacle to a limited improvement. Under such circumstances do we find our author, who acquired a tolerable knowledge of music, such as enabled him to be a connoisseur in old and neglected airs, and also to play with considerable accuracy and execution on the violin and flute.

Such was Robert Tannahill, when twenty-one. We believe no section of the people possesses a more genuine taste for poetry than the working population of our sister, "Yont the Tweed." We have stopped often to listen to the sweet songs of her people; and travel where you may, from the old town of Cupar, to the bridge of Dee, or from Aberdeen to the banks of the Clyde, enter but one of these old ricketty weaving shops, where you listen to the strange co-mingling of the voices of men and women, and the sound of treadles, and you will see the loom-posts covered by select pieces, the lyrics of war and love, which every now and again are glanced at by the anxious learner, until committed to memory and stored away, to be used on fitting occasions. We have known many, who, in this manner, have not only acquired an extensive knowledge of their country's literature, but also a nice sense of the beautiful in poesy; and it is nothing unusual to hear some of these common weavers point to passages, and explain obscure allusions, such as would shame many professed critics; and, if such a circumstance were within the range of things probable, many of these same weavers would make the men of "cut and slash celebrity" in the region of literature, blush to the knees. Tannahill contrived to weave, at the same time, threads of cloth and lines of song; he had a rude desk affixed to his loom, and there would he, day after day, continue to hum over old airs and jot down the words that arose in his mind most appropriate to the measure, uniting the weaving and the gentle craft, and, not unlike the sweet and simple Bloomfield, "Compose at once a slipper and a song."

In his associates, Tannahill was extremely fortunate. Mr. R. A. Smith, who composed the music of "Jessie the flower o' Dumblane," and, in fact, the music for Tannahill's principal songs, was a man of taste and refined and elevated mind. A musician of note in Edinburgh, and uniting to some extent the musician and poet—most assuredly the musician and critic—his distant correspondents were brother weavers and common soldiers. The link that apparently united the friends, was a reciprocity of feeling and a oneness of affection for the neglected songs and tunes of Scotland and Ireland.

It is but natural to suppose that a friendship, based on motives so pure and honourable, would be of a lasting and agreeable character, far removed from the interested and sordid associations of the trader, and knowing no interest but a pure love of ancient melody, in many cases bordering on national patriotism; and it is with delight that we look over the few letters preserved for the reader—pure, simple, unaffected epistles, neither garnished with the ornaments of language, nor filled with the common-place expressions of laudation and compliment; never bursting with extreme gratitude, nor filled with melancholy accounts of hope deferred, but breathing in their very essence a mild and gentle spirit. Confined to a brief space, as we necessarily are, we can afford but little room for lengthy quotations, but the following letter, addressed to James King, a soldier in the Renfrewshire militia, then quartered in England, himself a rhymer, and a regular correspondent of the bard—and with whom an exchange of productions was a usage of letter writing—will give the reader some notion of the style and feeling of our author; it is dated 2nd March, 1807, and is as follows:—

" DEAR JAMES,—I received yours of the 22nd of Sep-

tember, in due time, and, according to your wish, let your
mother know that you were well. She called on me the
other night, and wished that I would write to you directly,
as she was very impatient to have a letter from you; independent of that I should have written a fortnight ago. You
are sensible of a mother's solicitude, and will not fail giving
her that gratification. Trade is remarkably low with us.
Those who have their work continued, are obliged to do it
at pitifully low prices, and those who are thrown out of employment can scarcely get the offer of any by calling
through. Lappets too have been offered at threepence nett.
However, people's minds are not yet damped so much as
you have seen on former depressions. I am obliged to you
for sending the songs in your last: ' Thou'rt fair, Morning
of May,' is a beautiful little ballad, but I would advise you
to throw out the last verse, as the subject is quite complete
without it; besides, being in five stanzas, it will not suit
any double tune. In verse 4th, line 3rd, instead of ' will
retire,' I would prefer, ' is retired.' ' The Morning trem-
bles o'er the Deep,' likewise pleases me very well.' ' Oh,
why is thy Hand so cold, Love?' possesses some merit, but
I think it inferior to the others. In my opinion, your songs
surpass your other productions, and I would advise you to
apply yourself to that department of your favourite amusement, in preference to any other. Another thing which I
beg leave to mention, and which always makes a song appear more masterly, is to make the first and the third lines
of the verse to rhyme. In the old ballad style it may be
dispensed with, but in songs written in the idiom of the
present day, it is expected, and not reckoned so well without it; but you are already sensible of all that. *   *   *
I am happy that the songs in my volume please you; but
when you mention them as equaling Burns's, I am afraid
that the partiality of friendship weighs a good deal in *that*
decision. You have never mentioned the interlude. I sus-
pect that, in general, it is reckoned not worth much. (Here
he copied the four first verses of ' The Queen's Ferry Boatie
rows light.') I don't know any air that answers the above
measure; let me hear whether you know any to it. You
will no doubt know ' Lord Moira's Reel;' I have been
trying verses to it, and will write you all that I was able to
make of it." After copying the words of the song, which
subsequently became so popular, "Loudon's Bonnie Woods
and Braes," he added, " I own I am somewhat half pleased
with the above, myself; but that is always the case when a

piece is newly finished, and it must be past sometime before we are capable of judging rightly how it may stand. Mention any defects you may see in it."

There, reader, is a fair specimen—trade and lappets—but, above all, songs and tunes. Mark the confidence and unassuming ease with which the poet-weaver expresses his opinions: such is the criticism of friendship and sincerity—thoughts well expressed—" guid gear in little bulk." There is a tone of firmness and decision which evinces a conscious knowledge of correct and well regulated taste, yet there is no trace of assumed superiority, no carping for the sake of being noticed, no attempt at either haughty arrogance or proud and despotic dictation. No! Tannahill was possessed of a mind too simple—too noble for such feelings. He owns at once the superiority of the master spirit of Scottish poetry, Burns, and with a fine but friendly discrimination, remarks that the partiality of friendship may weigh a good deal in the decision so pleasing to the poet and creditable to the writer. The poet, like most of the bardic clan, formed an attachment to the fickle fair. She was, indeed, fickle, and forsook the rhyming weaver for a wealthier hand. It is said, that before the knot was tied she relented; but the proud spirit of him who honoured integrity and singleness of purpose, could not bow even to that empress of the soul, " a first love;" he poured forth his reproach in the elegant and noble verses,—

" Accuse me not, inconstant fair,
    Of being false to thee;
For I was true, would still be so,
    Hadst thou been true to me.

" But when I knew thy plighted lips
    Once to a rival's prest,
Love smothered—independence rose,
    And spurn'd thee from my breast.

" The fairest flow'r in nature's field
    Conceals the rankling thorn,
So thou, sweet flow'r, as false as fair,
    This once kind heart hast torn.

" 'Twas mine to prove the fellest pangs
    That slighted love can feel;
'Tis thine to weep this one rash act,
    Which bids this long farewell."

Even so was it : the slighted and deceived lover remained a
bachelor for life; a circumstance we regret, remembering
that Scotland had so many lovely daughters, who, no
doubt, would have rejoiced and been proud to share the
smiles and storms of life with the author of many of her
sweetest songs. We make this remark, incurring the ha-
zard of being charged with inconstancy by those who think
that he who loves affectionately once cannot love again.
We frankly confess our scepticism to such a doctrine:
Burns adored his Highland Mary, but yet loved his bonnie
Jean ; and we seriously think a guid gudewife would have
been the poet's greatest blessing. We abhor bachelorism,
under almost any circumstances : it sours the temper of the
most amiable of mankind, and is the very mother of melancholy. In company, Tannahill was free and communi-
cative, and although on the occasion of Mr. Smith's
concerts, Burns's birth days, &c., he seems to have joined
freely in social society, yet he on all occasions manifested
the greatest aversion to the low wit and vulgar jests of the
tavern. He was the lamb of the family circle, and never
the lion of the party.

At no time did he manifest a desire to rise in the world
in point of rank: on more than one occasion he refused to
become an overseer, or foreman of a weaving establishment
—to give out yarn and take in webs was no employment for
Tannahill ; the snubbing down of wages, disputing short
lengths, having on all occasions an eye to the employer's interest, was no vocation for the muse; she could not be so
degraded, and he honourably preferred the seat board and sad-
dle-tree, plying the shuttle and eating the humble diet,
" The parritch, chief o' Scotia's food," and breathing forth in
lowly but independent strains,

" Though humble my lot, not ignoble's my state,
    Let me still be contented though poor ;
Whate'er destiny brings, be resign'd to my fate,
    Though misfortune should knock at my door.

" I care not for honour, preferment, nor wealth,
    Nor the titles that affluence yields,
While blithely I roam in the hey-day of health,
    'Midst the charms of my dear native fields."

On his name being rendered familiar to the public by
his inimitable songs—having communicated by request with
a Metropolitan Magazine, no trifling honour for a weaver

lad—he had repeated chances of being introduced into the higher and more aristocratic circles of society; but they possessed no charm for the simple-minded weaver—the bowings and scrapings of plush clad menials—the cold haughtiness of superiority based on acreage, "to feast to please, and fast for want," as poor Burns, the Ayrshire ploughman had done, was no treat for our author; he wisely spared himself the awkwardness of introductions, and the annoyance and chagrin of coming disappointment, remained at his loom, and continued to sing—

JESSIE, THE FLOW'R O' DUMBLANE.

"The sun has gone down o'er the lofty Benlomond,
 And left the red clouds to preside o'er the scene,
While lonely I stray in the calm summer gloamin'
 To muse on sweet Jessie, the flower o' Dumblane.

"How sweet is the brier, wi' its soft faulding blossom,
 And sweet is the birk, wi' its mantle o' green ;
Yet sweeter and fairer, and dear to this bosom,
 Is lovely young Jessie, the flower o' Dumblane.

"She's modest as any, as blithe as she's bonny—
 For guileless simplicity marks her its ain,
And far be the villain, divested of feeling,
 Wha'd blight in its bloom the sweet flow'r o' Dumblane.

"How lost were my days 'till I met wi' my Jessie,
 The sports o' the city seem'd foolish and vain,
I ne'er saw a nymph I could ca' my dear lassie,
 'Till charm'd with sweet Jessie, the flow'r o' Dumblane.

"Though mine were the station o' loftiest grandeur,
 Amidst its profusion I'd languish in pain ;
And reckon as naething the height o' its splendour,
 If wanting young Jessie, the flow'r o' Dumblane."

The above song, which is one of the sweetest we ever heard, has been the subject of much conjecture and criticism; first, who was Jessie the flow'r o' Dumblane, what gleg-eyed pawky quean had caist the glamour o'er him ?—town talk found two or three; but we are assured by Smith—the man of all others the most likely to know—that, in his opinion, the heroine is an imaginary one. Ramsey, author of a "Biography of Tannahill," writes, "the truth is, that Tannahill never was in Dumblane, and knew no person belonging to it; and that the words were written to supplant the old doggrel song of the 'Bob o' Dumblane'—hence the title.'' Be that as it may, the song has often been chaunted as the earnest expression of well placed love.

Some seven years ago, we remember walking on a lovely summer's evening, just as the sun had gone to rest, along the banks of Forfar Loch or Lake; the merle and mavis were humming their evening chorus, and in fancied secresy we spied a young weaver lass, dressed in her clean striped short gown, tucked above her elbows, displaying an arm brown with heajth and labour, her curls hanging carelessly over her brow, barefooted and light-hearted, with her hand placed in that of her sweetheart—a callant just merging frae his teens—who, in low rich tones, was singing to his fair one "Jessie the flow'r o' Dumblane;" and for such scenes has Tannahill found language and expression. He is not like Campbell, the Lyrist of the Ocean, making a mighty people chaunt "Ye mariners of England;" nor does he, like Burns, rouse our martial spirit, make our hearts rise to freedom, as the big drum sounds forth the warlike strains of "Scots wha hae wi Wallace bled;" he contents himself in the woods and lanes of life, giving to love a voice, and therefore he is the fond lover's favourite—and where is the poet who would not be proud of such a fame? Old Homer would not have despised it; and such an honour would be welcome to our ain sweet singing Willie Thom, another of the gifted children of the loom, a truly original man and a delightful poet. Perhaps we may give Willie a look some coming day.

Other critics, professionally of the philosophical caste, have objected to the taste of the author, and also to the taste of Burns, in his "Cotter's Saturday Night;" the objection urged in both cases being the same in principle, viz., why should the fairest and purest scenes be marred with the thoughts of evil? Human nature is not so vile as to require an expression of constantly associated villainy, and why should a shadow of doubt, a foreboding of evil, constantly combine with the loftiest aspirations of virtue, and a description of a creature so pure be followed by the lines—

" And far be the villain, divested of feeling,
    Wha'd blight in its bloom the sweet flow'r o' Dumblane."

We do not argue the point abstractedly ; it is sufficient for us that evil exists, and the fairest and loveliest of frail womankind are the very parties of all others most likely to fall a prey to the dangers alluded to by the poet. We think such thoughts extremely natural, and under such circumstances extremely , poetical : the very excess of love begets the excessive fear of danger ; that for which we care the least we are the least troubled about, and suppose the least exposed to risk ; but in the case of Jessie, in our author, and Jenny, in Burns, the love is pure, natural, and sincere—the heroines, the most lovely imagination could suggest ; the poet lifts his character to the very precipice of perfection, and of a sudden the thought starts in his heated brain—"What ! if she fall ! " It is the completeness of the bliss that suggests the thought, "Oh ! would I not curse the villain ! " Fear gives rise to anger, and Burns in the fine lofty dignity of soul, so keen in sympathy, and strong in expression, gives vent to a noble outburst of manly indignation.

"Curse on his perjur'd arts, dissembling ! smooth !
Are honour, virtue, conscience all exiled ?
Is there no pity, no relenting ruth,
Points to the parent's fondling o'er the child ?
Then points the ruin'd maid and their distraction wild ! "

How honourable are such feelings to the man, and how characteristic of genius and power is the fiery denunciation of wrong and deceit, ay, and how true to the character of the Scottish peasantry. The hardy men of olden time, who, right or wrong we judge not, did most earnestly battle for their chief or bible, have children even now who speak boldly, and in homely words, their innermost thoughts of right or wrong. We test the critics by our observation of others and knowledge of our own feelings under similar circumstances, and unhesitatingly pronounce a verdict in favour of the poets. Burns and Tannahill are true to nature—the critics true to a desirable purity of thought. The one is fact illustrated by every-day experience; the other, as yet, for all practical purposes, a doubtful hypothesis. Well, the printer says, quite enough at present. Reader, you and I will finish our gossip about the weaver poet some other day. A LEAF FROM THE ANNALS OF A SHOEMAKER'S GARRET.

THE , INSURRECTIONS

OF

THE WORKING CLASSES.

(*Continued from page* 63.)

CHAPTER VII.

The Jacquerie.

In the district of Beauvoisis the feudal lords possessed power of life and death over their serfs ; in this district the insurrection first commenced. Victims of aristocratic caprice or lordly lust, the peasants and their wives were forced to succomb to the will of their masters, while the mutilated bodies of the victims and the gibbets over the castle-fosse, told fearful tales of irresponsible power and refractory serfdom. Goaded to madness by a fresh atrocity, the peasants of Beauvoisis revolted. It was a lovely morning of May, but the bright heaven shone on a desolated earth; the fresh trace of devastating armies was trailed across the country ; the news of Parisian revolt and Parisian liberty came stirring the population like a sudden call to arms ; and that great brutalised mass of humanity that had been trodden under foot for centuries—scorned, contemned, despised—rose, like some savage beast loosened from its chains, to retaliate on its oppressors the lessons of lust and cruelty it had been taught by the practical experience of its own suffering. There was nothing definite, nothing organised in the movement. The people had long felt their wrongs—a moment came in which they felt their power ; and blind, vague, indistinct, their brute force rose against the brute force that had enslaved them.

It was but fifty or sixty men who formed the nucleus of the insurrection. A group, goaded by hunger and maddened by wrong, collected in a wood at break of day, armed with knives and clubs, but with scarce any fixed purpose or direction. They dared not attack the fortified towers ; they would not injure their own order ; they saw the smoking ruins of their cottages, their eyes glanced up at the stately towers of their lords : "To the castle! to the castle !" was the cry, and infuriate they rushed towards the gates. The warder saw no armed foe ; he marked the group of peasants; but what feudal soldier would fear the base rabble, or dream of their attack. Warder and sentinel were overthrown before they even guessed the intent of the intruders. The crowd rushed across the quadrangle, and met the hurried arming of the lord and his retainers with the fierce onslaught of their knives and clubs. The noble was torn limb from limb—his vassals killed and mangled—his wife and daughters outraged and then slaughtered—his castle fired, and in a few hours the first band of the Jacquerie planted its standard over a smoking pool of blood and ashes. Now their ranks swelled—now the cry arose of "War to the castle!" "Death to the aristocracy!" The chain once lifted in Beauvoisis, from every quarter the furious peasantry flowed to the standard of revolt. A few days beheld a band of 6000 in the field, and the smoking ruins of 60 castles in Beauvoisis, Corbie and Amiens. The insurrection spread with terrible rapidity, through Laon and Soissons, along either bank of the Marne and the Oise, over Artois, and further still progressed its march of blood and fire. There was no atrocity the peasantry left uncommitted. They murdered noblemen in the presence of their wives and daughters, whom they outraged; roasted the scattered limbs of the husband and the father, placed them, a horrible banquet, before their fair victims, and then destroyed these as well when they had quenched their lust or satisfied their revenge.

Such horrors must revolt the reader, and the superficial thinker may see in these an argument against popular freedom. A moment's thought will convince him of the reverse. These men but acted up to the schooling they had received—centuries of tyranny had brutalised their hearts—they had been deprived of all artificial education, and debarred 'the instruction they would have received from God's own lips, in the language of conscience and of nature. Degraded to abject misery, debased to menial offices, compelled to horrible prostitution of all human dignity—to their eyes earth was turned into one vast hell, whose raging waters were escaped only by those seated by wealth and birth on the high places of authority. Lust, riot and iniquity were perpetrated with impunity before their eyes; their sovereign tried to murder his father and poison his cousin; their pontiffs committed incest and rape; their nobility violated every law, human and divine; their armies robbed and slaughtered indiscriminately; their judges made an open sale of justice, and they themselves were the but of all oppression, and had to minister to this accumulated load of vice. Their flesh was torn by the lash; their honour outraged in their wives and children; their blood lavished in mere wantonness, or themselves and families as wantonly starved to death in the midst of the profusion of their masters; expressions of contempt greeted them on every side; the very name by which working men were called was synonymous with 'a term of infamy—meanwhile, they had no mild teacher to breathe the Christian love into their hearts;

no philosopher to reveal the moral truths; no instructor to inform them of their political duties! Lost—neglected—trampled on, they became what they were made; class-legislation turned the man into the murderer, the beggar into the robber, the victim into the avenger. Had equal rights existed these results, the vices of oppression and the vices of slavery, could never have taken place; those moulded in the same form, and gifted with the same soul, must have been similar, under similar circumstances; and thus the evils of despotism have created and called forth whatever evils have accompanied democracy.

Neither is it a tenable plea to admit: that things are bad; but, being bad, they must remain so, since the danger of the change would be too great. On grounds of right and moral, this argument can, of course, never be advanced; but even on the ground of expediency it is fallacious. As we have ever seen, the secret lightning keeps feeding the storm till it explodes. Tyranny breeds vice and corruption, and the unholy mass (fermenting in the dark,) is sure, sooner or later, to break the rotting barriers of one-sided law, with a violence the more terrific, the longer the crisis is delayed.

Thus it was with the Jacquerie, who are variously stated to have derived their name from the *jacques* or jackets they wore; from a leader of that name; and from the nickname of Jacques Bonhomme, given to the peasantry of France: their numbers increased with terrible rapidity, and numbers soon brought organisation; they divided their forces, now amounting to 100,000 men, into separate bands, under their several leaders, —and, amid the flames of burning castles, over the bodies of murdered noblemen, the vast wave kept rolling onward to the capital. Paris watched its progress with anxiety, till the banner of the tricolour was lifted over the divisions of the peasant-army, and the Provost saw the provinces were won. The Dauphin fled from the Louvre, and Paris declared itself a republic. Stephen Marcel completed the fortifications, organised large bodies of the National Guard, and received important succour from King Charles of Navarre. Meanwhile, the insurrection kept progressing, but losing much of its horror with its continuance. The terrific impulse was settling into an organised movement; the wild rage into a holy desire for liberty—the furious mass into a democratic army. The envoys of the Provost were busy with the peasant host, calming their fury, at the same time that they strengthened their resolution and encouraged their hopes by sending them a reinforcement of 500 horse and 1000 foot. The nobility, however, exercised a terrible revenge in the parts where the peasants had not penetrated and the population was quiescent. On the plea of preventing similar outbreaks, they put man, woman, and child of the working orders to death, in cold blood; and, as the castles burnt in one part of France, so the cottages were burning in another.

Thús the Jacquerie had progressed on its way to Paris, till it reached the fortified town of Meaux. This interval, however, the nobility, who had been flying before them in all directions, occupied in concentrating their forces and arming themselves for the decisive contest. All parties, alike, saw it was a struggle of republicanism against royalty and aristocracy; and, therefore, the royal and noble foes united against the common enemy. Even the treacherous Charlés, of Navarre, the pretented ally of the Parisians, and friend of the people, turned round to crush the peasantry. The English suspended the war, and marched their troops to the assistance of the French king and court. The Dauphin made common cause with his rival, and all this vast machinery was put in motion at once. Be it remembered, also, that the allied powers were in possession of the strong towns and fortresses; that they and their troops were clad *cap-a-pie* in the finest mail; that they were trained to arms from their infancy; skilled in the use and fortunate in the possession of the most terrible implements of destruction: while the undisciplined peasantry were scantily equipped with knives, clubs, and pikes, and exposed, in the open country, to momentary and incessant attacks from active cavalry, who could escape pursuit when they could not command success.

Despite these disadvantages, the desperate valour of the Jacquerie was carrying all before it, and the league of nobles had recourse to treachery to ensure its object. Charles of Navarre feigned to espouse the party of the peasantry, and offered to join them with his army. Accordingly, he invited them to his camp at St. Denis, near Paris. A large body of the insurgents, headed by some of their principal leaders, accepted the invitation, crossed the intrenchments, and were dispersed in different quarters. The chiefs were led to Charles, instantly arrested, and cut down; while the lines of his army were moving out of their cantonments, and gradually surrounding the devoted bands, who, ignorant alike of the death of their generals, and of the designs of their enemy, were giving themselves up to the joy of unexpected good fortune, and admiring the imposing lines of their royal ally. Suddenly those troops closed on them from every side: 3,000 defenceless men were slaughtered on the spot; the rest fled, panic-stricken, or fought their way through the surrounding masses, only to be hunted across the country, and perish in detail.

The news of this unexampled treachery, spread a deep gloom over the movement. The main body of the Jacquerie was, however, still intact. Nine thousand strong, it marched on the fortified town of Meaux, where the Dauphin had established his head quarters, and summoned the armed nobility to meet him. The court had fled to this stronghold; the Duchess of Normandy, wife of the Regent, and 300 noble ladies of France, had taken refuge in the castle; but at the time the Jacquerie approached, under Charles of Meaux and Jacques Bonhomme, its garrison consisted of only sixty knights. The evening before the arrival of the insurgents, the castle was reinforced by Gaston de Foix, one of the most famous warriors of France, who was then returning from the crusades in Prussia, and by the Captal de Buch, a celebrated commander and redoubted soldier, in the English service, who, hearing of the danger of the Court, hurried to the rescue.

The inhabitants of Meaux were secret allies of the Parisians, and at once opened their gates to the insurgent force—great banquets too, were prepared, and the night was spent in mutual rejoicing and excess. With the morning, the tri-colour was lifted, and the great living mass climbed upwards to the castle, which, frowning downward from its height, encircled the precious treasure that would place the destinies of France in the hands of the victorious. Suddenly, as their disorderly assault was pressing upwards, half drunken with excitement and nocturnal orgies, a trumpet sounded from the ramparts, the drawbridge was lowered, and the small band of knights, in their burnished armour—Gaston and the Captal at their head—rode sharply through the portal. At the same time, the Princess of France, and the ladies of her court, thronged the ramparts overhead— waving their scarfs in encouragement, and kneeling in prayer —while the glittering troop wheeled, halted, and formed ready for the charge. There was an anxious pause—a terrific roar broke from the mighty crowd—that, band rushing on band, and weltering over each other in their eagerness to be first, kept momentarily engulphing the castle height like a rising tide. Again the shrill note of the trumpet sounded the charge : " Montjoie St. Denis !" "St. George for Merry England !" And like an avalanche of burning steel, the gallant troop charged down the acclivity—while an hysterical cheer thrilled from the old battlements above, as the bold champions perilled the unequal strife.

The mass of the half-armed peasantry were cloven by the charge—their rude arms were of no avail against the finely tempered mail of their assailants; the bravest, who threw themselves into the living breach, were ridden down and speared; and then the flaming faulchions of the chivalry began clearing right and left, while panic increased their numbers, and despair prompted their prowess, till, wonderful as it may seem, 9000 men were driven like a herd before those sixty knights, with their Gaston and their Buch.

Thus far, one of the most brilliant achievements on record, might claim our admiration for its physical prowess ; but, alas ! the courage of chivalry was but too often the mere brute daring, that, unknowing how to spare, is merciless to revenge. As soon as the peasants were defeated, and returning fortune brought with the close of day the minions of misrule to the side of the victors ; these gallant knights fired the town, guarded the gates, and riding down the streets, pushed back with their lances, men, women, and children into the flaming ruins of their burning houses, till scarce a stone remained standing of the once prosperous town, and not a human heart-beat in Meaux, save those of the fair dames and damsels in the castle, and their chivalrous defenders.

The fugitive peasantry were now hunted down through France. The French army, the Navarrese, the English, slaughtered them on every side; the villages were burning all over the country, and the massacre was so complete, that hands could scarce be found to till the soil, or reap the harvest.

Following the example of Paris, and incensed at the horrid carnage of their brethren in Meaux, most of the towns now embraced the popular party; and hating, and being equally hated by the nobility, the civil war was changed, from one between the cottage and the castle, to that of the castle and the town. Fearful excesses were committed on either side,. among which, a glaring attempt on the part of the nobles to surprise and sack the town of Senlis, deserves to be recorded.

After the destruction of Meaux, the victors determined on taking and destroying, one after another, the different free towns, in the same manner as the peasants had destroyed the castles; and for this purpose they secretly assembled a numerous force of picked knights, and unexpectedly, as they thought, rushed one day through the unguarded gates into the streets of Senlis. They were obliged to chose the day time, as, during the night, they would not have been able to gain admission; but their surprise was great, when they found the city in perfect solitude, and were allowed to penetrate to the market-place without opposition. The doors of the houses were all fastened and barricaded, and the knights were appalled to see strong bodies of well-armed citizens closing in on every side upon their rear, till overpowered by numbers, and equalled in valour, they had to pay for their intent with their lives, scarcely one escaping to tell the tale of their discomfiture.

The Regent having succeeded in crushing the Jacquerie, and finding that his chief danger now arose from the municipalities, redoubled his efforts for the subjugation of Paris, justly judging, that, if the capital were reduced to submission, the provincial towns would not offer any effective resistance. To this end, he had succeeded in raising an immense force, consisting not only of French, but also of Imperial troops, of which the cavalry alone amounted to 30,000 men, 3000 of the number being knights. The head quarters of this army were at Charenton, obstructing the navigation of the Seine and Marne, cutting off all supplies from Paris, and burning the surrounding villages, the more effectually to starve the inhabitants.

The plan succeeded, a terrible famine ensued, and the impetuous populace again began to blame their leader for the faults of his enemies. They were principally incited to this by the machinations of John and Simon Maillard, two wealthy citizens and inveterate opponents of the Provost. Bought by the Regent, and jealous of the power and reputation of their rival, they had long waited the turn of events, and the imposing force of the Dauphin, backed by the fickleness of the people seemed to grant the favourable opportunity. The popular party suffered another blow—Charles of Navarre had, on his part, also been watching the course affairs were taking, and foresaw that, as famine increased in Paris, so would the adherents of the Regent grow in numbers. He feared a counter-revolution, which should place him between the Dauphin's army without, and a hostile army within the walls; and, on the plea of taking the field to repel the investing force, this treacherous ally forsook the Provost in the hour of danger. Marcel now beheld himself even more deserted than at that former crisis, when Navarre held Paris against him, the Dauphin occupied the country, and the towns remained quiescent. Indeed, his position appeared hopeless. The Jacquerie had been crushed; King Charles withdrew his support; the Dauphin was reinforced by imperial succour; the English, though allied with Navarre, attacked the citizens, and cut several of their foraging parties to pieces; and, worst of all, the people were becoming disaffected to their own cause. The municipal troops, having lost heart in the struggle, as a necessary consequence lost battles too; tidings came almost daily, of how the provincial towns, receiving no cheering news, no succour from Paris, began to flag in their zeal—how they were pressed by the still accumulating forces of the French and Germans, and how, one by one, the flame of insurrection died within their walls, till the growing darkness commenced overshadowing the capital with its gloom. In the midst of these disasters, the heart of the Provost remained unshaken. At all hours of the day and night, he was to be found either in the council chamber, or on the ramparts, confirming the waverer with his eloquence, or watching the doubtful with his own eyes. But daily the Regent's party grew in strength, and it was with difficulty that Marcel could maintain the preponderance of power on his side. He was accused of treachery, of secret correspondence with the enemy—even of collusion with the English: and the credulous people at first spurned suspicion, then listened—then doubted—then all but believed. Still John and Simon Maillard dared not openly resist his authority; the old magic of his leadership clung about him—men could not forget what he had done—could not remember one blot on his career. The conspirators, therefore, sought to effect that by violence which they could not achieve by fraud.

They fixed the first day of August, 1358, for the accomplishment of their design. The Provost was accustomed personally to inspect the different guards during the night, and for this purpose had repaired to the Porte St. Antoine some time before daybreak. It is variously stated by some that he had discovered a conspiracy, on the part of the brothers Maillard and the Royalists, to admit the troops of the Regent at this gate, and at that of

St. Honoré; by others, that despairing of holding the town against their faction, he had determined on surrendering it to Charles of Navarre, under the conviction that better terms could be obtained of this prince, who required the support of the people to make head against the Dauphin, than of the latter, who, strong in the alliance of the Emperor, waged a war of extermination against the popular cause.

Be this as it may, on arriving at the post, and finding an unusual number of soldiers belonging to the royalist party on guard, he ordered them to return to their quarters. They demurred—an altercation ensued—when John Maillard, marching up at the head of a strong detachment, countermanded the orders of the Provost, accused him of treachery and an intention of surrendering Paris to the enemy, and 'as he turned indignantly to resent the calumny, suddenly laid him dead at his feet with the stroke of a battle-axe. Maillard and his followers forthwith charged the guard of the Provost, killed six, and put the rest to flight; then seizing a royal banner, and taking horse, he and his troop dashed into the heart of the city, shouting the king's war-cry of—"*Montjoie St. Denis!*" The inhabitants were startled from sleep by the sound. The Regent's party assembled forthwith; the friends of Marcel had neither time to arm, nor leader to obey—the gates were opened — the army of the Dauphin entered — Paris was won and liberty was lost. Meanwhile, John Maillard assembled the populace—told them Marcel had been killed while endeavouring to deliver the town into the hands of the enemy; all the old calumnies were revived, all the envies and hatreds that lacquey successful daring and spurn defeated merit were in arms at once; and that people who had idolised the living now rushed to the body of the dead, tore it limb from limb, and dragged the mutilated remains with ignominy through the town the murdered hero had so often saved.

The Regent held his day of reckoning—France, Navarre, and England struggled as before—fresh generations ripened to fresh carnage, and fresh cycles of despotism ran down the range of time, till once more the same causes produced the same effects, and another revolution crumbled kingdoms into republics to rebuild them in an empire.

Thus ended Stephen Marcel. It is often the historian's fault or weakness to seize an individual character, creature of circumstances and accident, and clothing it with the hues of his own imagination, to extol the tactician into the statesman, or the soldier into the hero; but the memory of Marcel needs no adventitious aid; the bare facts speak for themselves, and history, the stern chronicler of his actions, points to the man who singly held the destinies of France at bay; the unassuming citizen, who paralysed the intrigues of kings; the obscure civilian, who kept a half-fortified town against the united armies of France, Germany, England, and Navarre; whose judgment defeated the intrigues of princes; whose honesty surmounted the temptations of power; whose constancy survived the hour of defeat; whose energy triumphed over the apathy of the towns, the slaughter of the Jacquerie, and the treachery of his ally; whose prowess broke the Royal chivalry at Corbeil, and baffled the incipient mutinies at Paris, and whose last account was rendered, like a trusty sentinel, at the post of duty! His eulogy is written in the words: *with his life Liberty lived—with his death Insurrection ended.*

THE PRICE OF BLOOD.

A TALE OF THE SOUTH.

The following tale is founded on facts, and has been made the theme of many a song and say in France and Italy. Forcibly does it bring before us the evils of proscription—setting a price upon the head of a criminal. Without such a measure, it was long contended, the purposes of justice could never be served—yet, in those countries where this barbarous law does not exist, justice is more perfect—crime less frequent. May we not reason by analogy, that, were capital punishment, against the abolition of which there is a similar outcry, at once abrogated, the results would be equally conducive to good order? What is the difference? —the one makes many executioners, the other a few;—if the system is evil, it is as evil for the few as for the many. But to our tale.

It was a summer afternoon in Italy; the scene—some miles from Naples—a spot on the great sandy highroad, where, verging from the sea, it winds past a grove—half wood, half thicket—whose coppery and dusty foliage bespoke the long drought and arid soil. The distant waters lay like a sheet of brass—the sky loomed like a brazen dome; the sunlight throbbed palpably against the earth, and one small streak of thin white smoke came oozing lazily from Vesuvius, as though the fiery mountain owned the superior majesty of the burning sun.

By the roadside, partly under shelter of the wood, that straggled up the slope of rocky heights, sat two children. The one, dark haired, with diamond eyes, curling lip, and red, swarthy cheek might number fourteen summers;—the other had the pale blue eyes, light hair, and fair face of the northern — and was the junior of his brother. They were taking their afternoon's repast of brown bread and milk, when suddenly, a tall, gaunt, wayworn man staggered before them — and, looking hurriedly around, said: " Two days have I fasted—food! children! here is food!" and with avidity he devoured the repast—then, fixing his keen glance on the brothers, exclaimed: " If any one asks you, whether you have seen a man like me, say—no! or ——" and, with a significant touch of the large knife in his girdle, he withdrew.

The younger boy, who had fled in terror, and concealed himself behind a tree, now reappeared.

" Cherubino!" said the elder—" Do you know who that man was? It was the famous robber, Lambruschini!"

The child turned still more pale.

" A price is set on his head. One thousand scudi!"

" Let us fly, Giotto!"

" He must be still in that wood—he was so faint and weak, he could not wander far. He will sleep—men grow heavy after a long fast and copious meal—we'll seek him."

Taking his trembling brother by the hand, Giotto at last found the robber asleep, as he had surmised—Cherubino tried to escape. " Hush!" said his brother, " or you will wake him."

" What would you do?"

" Kill him, and get the 1,000 scudi!"

The horror-stricken child expostulated in vain—he was almost afraid to speak, lest the robber should wake and, suspecting evil, slay them.

Giotto reminded him of their mother's poverty—that they should obtain the reward, and be rich and happy— and thus worked on his imagination, that the meek child consented to aid him in the bloody deed—and the work of two was requisite—the robber lay with his head on his rifle, and his hand on his dagger.

" I will lift the head," said Giotto, " while you draw the rifle from underneath."

Cautiously, gently, did Giotto apply himself to the task. Gradually he inserted his fingers, then his palms, under the robber's head, till it was partly cushioned on his hands, then steadily he deepened the pressure, so slowly, that he could not feel the touch, till the weary head began to rise, and Cherubino was enabled to draw the weapon from below:

Strange sight it was to see those two blooming children, murder in their eyes, stooping over the haggard face of a murderer.

"Now take my place!" whispered Giotto—and the arm of Cherubino passed under the robber's head. This was the most dangerous moment, the robber moved, and swore a horrid oath—the paralysed child was unable to move from fear —supreme caution could not have been a better guide, all was silent and still—the robber relapsed into his heavy sleep.

Meanwhile Giotto had been examing the rifle; it was loaded—no doubt with ball—but to be safer still, he tore two buttons off his vest, and dashed them down the tube.

"Now—Cherubino!" said Giotto, bringing the muzzle close to the sleeper's forehead. The boy let the head drop —and bounded back—the awakened man started to rise, but the flaming volley, spinning thro' his brain, dashed him back; he quivered and was dead.

At some distance lay Cherubino, senseless—the supernatural excitement had ceased. Giotto chafed his brother's temples with sand and leaves, water there was none; and, when restored to consciousness, laid him on a mossy bank to sleep; while he returned to his victim. There this boy deliberately severed the shattered head of the robber from the body, and enveloping it in the garment of the murdered man, proceeded with his prize, accompanied by his brother, direct to the police office in Naples.

Strange as appeared the tale of Giotto, it was nevertheless ascertained to be true, and the 1000 scudi payed over to him accordingly. The boy grasped the glorious prize, intending to proceed home at once and take it to his mother. But on his way he met the smile of beauty, he saw the flow of wine, he heard the rattle of dice; and grey morning dawned before he quitted the nocturnal orgies, in which his meek brother bore a passive part, and then they were again renewed until exhaustion bade them cease; again, and again! The ingenuous soul of Cherubino was not proof against the lure, and the child was initiated in the vices of the man. When the treasure was almost spent, the brothers lost their mother; the wild course of her children broke a heart that had been undermined by disease and want, and Giotto and Cherubino had nothing but each other on the earth. The fiery spirit of the elder drew his mild companion after him, who contrasted and yet blended with that ardent nature, like starlight shining amid conflagration. When the money had been lavished, when the mother's softening care had been withdrawn; the young men, for such this short and fearful schooling had made them in feeling, though not in years, began for the first time to think of their future. They were friendless, penniless, and their dissipation had given them a bad name, closing on them the doors of respectable employment.

"Can we not work?" said Cherubino.

Giotto smiled when he thought how hopeless would be the quest; he frowned as his proud spirit, now accustomed to license and luxury, rose scorning at the thought of servitude.

"Can we not beg?" said Cherubino.

"Ay! we will try," replied Giotto, with a proud toss of the head, as when the imperious horse dashes off the coaxing hand from his magnificent neck.

They left Naples in twilight. Cherubino was faint and hungry, but Giotto was full of hot thoughts and felt no pain, while he supported the frail form of his brother with all a mother's fondness, pillowing his white forehead against his burning cheek, and fencing with his own garments that delicate child from the dew of evening.

Presently the tramp of horses was heard, and a cavalier with his servant were seen riding sharply up the road.

"I will beg," said Giotto with a smile. "*Pro misericordia dei*——" his voice was drowned in the lash and tramp of the haughty horseman, but Giotto bounded by the side—— "we are starving, we are shelterless, we are friendless, one denaro, for the love of our lady!"

With a curse, and a lash of his whip across the boy's shoulders, the cavalier urged on.

"See! my young brother is faint, and sick, and dying," said Giotto, laying his hand on the rein, "one denaro, to save the poor child's life!" On flew the horse, "He is my all on earth—he was my poor dead mother's dearest—but one to save him for me!"

The cavalier called to his servant. "Ha! I have begged," shouted Giotto, and in a moment the horse reared back on its haunches, the cavalier lay senseless on the ground, a pistol-shot rang after the flying attendant, Giotto was in the saddle with a well-filled purse, his brother was lifted to his side, and before morning they had penetrated the dark defiles of the southern Appenine. A tear was in the eye of the young bandit, as, fearful of recognition, he reluctantly shot the gallant horse over the edge of a precipice, and then, repairing to the nearest village, lavished on his brother that treasure he had again so strangely won.

The youth, the beauty, the grace of the twain, won the admiration of the villagers, who, not over scrupulous in their notions of the rights of any property besides their own, looked on the bandit as member of an honourable profession—something better than the soldier, and something inferior to the monk.

The nocturnal robbery had closed the gates of society on Giotto, whose ardent imagination was charmed by the adventurous life of a brigand, whose vanity was flattered by the friendship of the villagers, and whose scruples were dissipated by the estimation in which brigandage was held.

"The King and the Pope are great brigands—the lawyers and officials, landlords and the tradesmen, lesser ones; they all *steal* from the poor, without the grace of courage, or excuse of danger. I will *take* from the rich—sword in hand, like a gallant knight—and in thus doing, I'm the lesser culprit of the two. What say you, Cherubino?"

Cherubino smiled a mournful smile.

"You shall be safe in some pretty cottage," continued Giotto, "Singing love ditties to some pretty maid, and I will come and see you whenever I want rest and peace."

The blood mounted to the boy's pale face.

"With you, with you,'Giotto! You shall conquer, and I will make you spare!"

The pact was sealed, and soon the brothers became the terror of the Appenine. They had formed—they had sought —no band; but, always together, the chivalrous and invincible valour of Giotto overthrew all before him; the mild courage of Cherubino won the admiration of the vanquished. Three years had thus flown—the twain had passed through Italy, in its length and breadth—their names had grown a terror—their exploits were themes of song—and the love that bound them to each other had stood many a test.

Thus Cherubino had, on one occasion, been taken prisoner and confined at Terracina. Giotto hastened alone to the place, obtained an interview on the eve of execution, took his brother's place, forced him to fly, under the terror of disclosing himself and perishing by his side, and the assurance that he had certain means of escape. Knowing his brother's nature, he complied. Giotto had no such means —calmly he surrendered himself to the gaolers, and the day afterwards was led out to execution. The death knell was expiring, the last rite about to commence—when a shout broke at the edge of the crowd, that opened, not reluctantly,

to admit a dashing troop of masked horsemen; the carabi-
neers and gensdarmes were overthrown—Cherubino cut his
brother's bands—and, laughing resistance to scorn, the fearless band dashed back to the mountains.

When released, Cherubino had sought the villagers,
and by his grief and tears, his pathetic lamentations and
prayers, wrought on some of the more turbulent to mount
for the rescue.

Incidents like these endeared the brothers still more to
each other, till this fraternal love, like one solitary flower
among a ruin, was the redeeming brightness amid the wreck
of their souls.

One evening they were sitting on an abrupt ridge of hills
that rose over a vale of the Abruzzi, with the far plains
seen through its western opening; the sun had set some time,
there was a saduess in Giotto's manner—and, to Cherubino's
questioning, he confessed to having seen a sunny girl of
Southern Italy at a farm in the valley below—whom, but
there was madness in the thought—she could never be the
bride of a bandit—and, to wrong her!—enough—he *loved !*
Cherubino smiled sadly as the words brought thoughts of
home and his mother, and scarcely noticed the fierce
watchfulness expressed on his brother's face, as he stood,
half risen, straining his sight eagerly through the increasing
gloom of night.

" What see you ?"

"That is her father's house"—pointing to a large farm-
building at the foot of the hill—and, at the same time,
directing attention to five men who were steathily prowling
about the house. A noted band of robbers were infesting
the neighbourhood, and had sought Giotto's leadership.
But he loathed that in others, which he practised himself;
and, in truth, guilt was of a lighter hue in Giotto, for he
never killed the defenceless, never struck except to preserve
his own or his brother's life, and never rifled anyone, but such
who, as magistrates, nobles, or merchants, had the brand of
tyranny, lust, or extortion affixed on their characters. We
say not this in palliation of *his* crimes; but to distinguish
them from the brutal thirst of blood and gold distinguishing
those of others.

" These are of them !" muttered Giotto, as he watched the
five stopping under a window in the garden, and preparing
to force an entrance.

With the words, noiseless and swift, he darted down the
hill ; and without a question, Cherubino ran silently by his

side. The steepness of the height towards its base forced them to make a long circuit, and by the time they arrived at the farmhouse, the murderers had entered and the work of destruction had commenced. They passed through the shattered window, and found an old man bleeding and on his knees, while two ruffians were dragging a lovely girl into an adjoining room.

"Stay! on your lives!" thundered Giotto, seizing one of the twain, and spinning him, a lifeless mass, along the stone pavement of the chamber, while the quick report of pistols told that Cherubino was seconding his brother; and the survivors, ignorant of the number or strength of their assailants, fled precipitately from the house.

Gratitude would sanction friendship—friendship would ripen into love. Giotto and Cherubino became constant visitors in the old man's house, and Giotto a constant guest in the young maid's heart.

Thus time flew on, and the lover let himself be led away by the fond lure of love, forgetting the deep gulf society had placed between them, till it was too late to withdraw; and the hour arrived in which the young spring-time of their happiness must darken beneath its first cloud.——Down the limegrove, over the meadow, past the stream, they wound in silence,—for the heavy sorrow sat upon his heart—till they climbed the rugged heights, and sat on the very spot from which he had rushed to her rescue. There he told her his past life, his present calling. She shrunk appalled. "Curse me, shun me, forget me, but forgive me!"

The large tears gathered in her eyes, but they fell not: she gazed on him fixedly, then on her home and heaven: "Yours, and for ever," she cried, and lay panting on his breast. Oh, strange were the feelings in the heart of Giotto; he felt a glowing happiness, a wild pride, but also a deep, conscience-stricken guiltiness, to think how unworthy he was of her. To part from her would have broken his heart, to join her lot with his pained his soul. Her refusal would have been his despair, her consent was his reproach.

Time passed, and a fair maid fled from the old farmhouse as a bandit's bride: a broken-hearted father sunk into an untimely grave, while the outcasts wandered for awhile over the earth in a delirium of passionate love. They were a goodly group: the noble youth, glowing with energy, beauty, fervour—the Italian maid, ripe in womanly loveliness, sunny as her clime, and fond as the fair lover of Mantua—the mild, delicate boy, contrasting with the twain as the soft moon of a summer night with the gorgeous morning and the luscious sunset.

But, after a time, the soul of Giotto grew too large for his sphere; the French commonwealth was scattering thrones and showering republics, and the young Italian longed to be a brigand on a larger scale, like the crowned or titled robbers that surrounded him. By degrees he assembled a band, and, owning allegiance to none, penetrated Savoy and Piedmont, to the confines of France. Here he fixed his head-quarters, on the top of an almost inaccessible rock, that rose abruptly from the plain on three sides, but on the fourth was separated from rocks of similar altitude by an abyss of about thirty yards in width, and 1000 feet in depth, down which dashed and boiled a black and roaring cataract. Here he established his home, here he left his Marie, when, like a feudal chief of old, he went on his predatory excursions, from which he was ever wont to return successful, with increased daring and accumulated wealth. Many sought to join his band, but he steadily refused to admit them : his followers were all picked men, and, Napoleon of robbers, he chained them to his fortunes by that wonderful mastery of will, that enthusiastic loyalty, which enables him who commands it to achieve what to those less favoured would prove impossibility.

The same fondness still existed between Giotto and his brother, though now shared, not only with Marie, but with the offspring of their love—a lovely infant, born, like a young eaglet, on this sterile rock.

The affairs of France becoming more settled, the government began to look after the internal administration, and the fame of the daring bandit soon attracted a strong body of gensd'armes to the neighbourhood. These were dispersed by the outlaws, and after having in vain endeavoured to surprise the rock, or resist its defenders, a regiment of riflemen was ordered to their assistance.

We are now approaching the extraordinary scenes attending the close of our hero's life.

The troops sent to invest the robbers' stronghold soon cut off his communication with the surrounding country, and, in endeavouring to break through their lines he was repulsed, and lost two thirds of his men. Seventy-five alone succeeded, with their leader, in regaining the rock, where they prepared themselves for an obstinate and protracted defence.

Not expecting the advent of any regular force, they had

neglected to supply themselves with provisions, though well provided with ammunition and warlike stores. A few days after their defeat, they were summoned to surrender, and the offer being spurned, an attack was made on the rock. It was escaladed wherever practicable, but the bold outlaws, hanging from the precipice, picked off the assailants with a deadly aim, hurled the loosened crags upon their heads, and scattered death around, while not one of their own band received a single wound, or ever came within reach of the enemy.

The colonel commanding the regiment soon saw that it was hopeless to attempt taking the place by storm, and, therefore, resolved on starving the besieged into submission. A strong chain of posts was stretched round the foot of the rock (the fourth side was, as we have seen, guarded by an abyss and torrent,) but even on the heights opposite, sentries were placed within hail of each other, and a disposable body of troops held ready for any emergency. Thus six weeks elapsed, and no sign of surrender. Nor was there a sign of life visible on the rock. Flags of truce were sent from time to time; and pale, haggard faces, as of famished men, peered over the precipice and conversed with the envoy. On one occasion, the latter saw dead bodies cast into a grave, but no one spoke of submission. "They are weak now with hunger," cried the impatient colonel; "we will attack the rock." The Directory blames me for detaining a whole regiment so long to take a handful of robbers!"

But as they climbed the rocks, savage eyes glared on them from sunken sockets: again they met the deliberate aim; again the lossened crags spun crashing down; again the discomfited troops were forced to seek their cantonments without any result, but that of having suffered a heavy loss.

"It is evident they have no provisions," said the colonel, "how do they contrive to live?"

A soldier volunteered to go and see.

"Give me a purse of gold and 50 lashes," he said, "and I will bring you word in a fortnight."

His strange request was granted; and at night, with a mangled back and a daring heart, he climbed to the robbers' stronghold.

"See how they have served me!" he cried, when brought bound before Giotto, and he showed his bleeding back.

"What seek you?"

"Revenge! and death with the free, sooner than life with the slave!"

His manner pleased, his tale was believed; he was placed in probation, and acquitted himself so well in moments of danger that he won entire confidence. To obtain this, his plans were well laid; he had arranged with the Colonel, that, some days after his departure, another attack should be made. Accordingly, on this occasion he distinguished himself much, slew, unscrupulous as he was, many of his comrades in arms, and was admitted a member of the outlaws' band.

During his stay, he noticed that three of the band absented themselves daily for some hours in a mysterious manner; and then returned with part of a lamb, or hare, or poultry—never with empty hands. They evidently went by rotation. At last the turn came to him. He went with two companions to the edge of the crag—two were lowered by a rope down the precipice, then to a ledge of rock, whence, scrambling for some distance, they reached the brink of another abyss, where he was lowered by his companion in a similar manner, till he arrived parallel with an EAGLE's NEST. Here he found young eaglets, already fledged (but, with their wings tied, so that they could not escape,) and the food the parent birds had brought them. According to his instructions, he took part of the food, leaving enough barely to sustain the fledglings—and was drawn up by his companions.

The secret was discovered! That night the spy fled back to his employer, and on the following morning the Colonel was up by times, and called the best marksman of the regiment to his side.

It was a bright morning and a clear sky.

"Do you see yon eagle?" said the Colonel. "Well, then, name your reward, if you can bring it down."

"Were it as small as a pigeon, it is dead!" Magnificently the glorious eagle swept in mazy circles, like an aerial bather in the golden waves of sunrise; the marksman aimed warily and long; never more that eagle rose to its mountain nest. Dismay seized the heart of Giotto, when he saw his eagle fall, and with an agonized glance he looked at Marie and his brother. The pale girl sat clasping her hungry child to her foodless breast, lulling it, but in vain, to sleep. Cherubino—not the lovely boy, but a living wreck—sat by his side, ministering with fond forgetfulness to her wants, till Giotto loved him more and more for being kind to her; while the uncomplaining boy concealed the pangs of hunger, and cast a smile before the advancing march of death.

Most delicate, he sunk the first, and died in the arms of
Giotto and Marie; she wept—his sorrow was past weeping.

The sun was flashing his last over the far chain of cones
and peaks beneath their eyes when Cherubino died; no
word escaped Giotto's lips, but he read the solemn prayers
for the dead with a sepulchral voice; the famished band
dug the grave of their mild brother, and moistened it with
their tears—holy tears of sorrow from reckless hearts offered
to the good, now lost from their midst.

They buried him proudly, those outcasts, with the honours
of war; and three salvoes of musketry rung over his grave,
while the old mountains gave as full an answer from their
stony hearts, as if he had possessed a soldier's patent to rob
and slay upon a larger scale.

The vollies surprised the encampment below—that sign
of death had been the only sign of life on the rock for
days; but time passed, and still the outlaws refused to surrender. Astonishment filled the minds of the besiegers.

"The eagle's mate!" suddenly exclaimed the Colonel,
and again the marksman was called forth—again sped the
shot, and the stricken mother perished in her mountain-nest.

"How long can a man live without food?" asked the
Colonel. The regimental surgeon specified the extremest
limit. "We will double the time," said the officer, "and
then storm their stronghold."

The last hope of the outlaws had fled. Days past and
death was waiting for his prey. "We will surrender!"
cried one. "What! to be chained to the gallies for life?
What! to break the oath that binds us?" And the desperate, but unbending men, spurned the very thought.

"We will fly!" calmly said Giotto. The incredulous
bandits smiled. "Every man be ready at midnight!"
continued the leader, and calmly stood watching the retiring day.

At twelve the band were ready. Their weapons were
tied around them; their hands were free, by their chief's
directions. Giotto went first—the bandits next—Marie
last. He proceeded to the edge of the abyss separating
them from the rocky chain. Wood crested the other side—
one thousand fathom deep, thundered the torrent—exactly
opposite rose two trees close together. Giotto pulled forth
a cord, to the one end of which was tied a staff; he threw
it across the chasm between the trees, then pulling it back
towards him, by the end he held, the staff rested trans-
versely against the trunks, and tying the rope around a

stone beside him, a strange, precarious bridge was thus formed. The outlaws passed first, then Giotto, bearing Marie and her child. Strict silence was enjoined, for the sentinels were ranged within hearing of each other along the rocks. They gained the opposite side in safety, and were threading their way through the enemy's posts, when the infant woke, and cried !

"Hush the child !" hoarsely whispered Giotto, and the frantic mother tried, but vainly, to still its crying.

The lives of all depended on that moment ; the brave men who had sacrificed all for him—his own—*Marie's !*

"*Qui vive ?*" cried a sentry.

"Silence the child or we are lost !" In vain ——! With quivering lip stood Giotto ; his giant frame rocked with agony—it was but a moment—he tore the child from its mother's arms, and it lay lifeless on the ground !

They had escaped ; the lines of sentries were passed ; the open plains were crossed ; and a mountain-wood sheltered the fugitives.

"What have you there, Marie !" said Giotto, as the bereaved mother pressed some object in her shawl close to her heart.

"*My child !*" she answered, as she rocked and sung a lullaby to her dead baby.

As soon as the flight of the outlaws had been discovered, a price of ONE THOUSAND SCUDI was set on the head of Giotto. Some days passed ; the brigand's camp was fixed in a gorge of the western Alp ; still the mother nursed her cold babe—when Giotto took from her her repulsive charge, though force was needed—and buried it.

Night closed above the infant's grave—the watch was set, and slumber sunk on the little camp.

"You are weary, sentry !" said Marie to the watcher at midnight.

"To the death, mistress !"

"Go sleep, and I will watch for you."

The outlaw hesitated—"*He shall never know*," she added.

The outwearied sentinel consented, and resigned his carbine. That night a sudden shot startled the outlaws.

"It is mere accident," said Marie, "Hush ! the captain sleeps !"

In the morning, the headless body of Giotto was found where he had laid him down to rest, and shortly afterwards a woman claimed the blood-price for the bandit's head.

To a convent in Piedmont, a young penitent was admitted.

She paid 1000 scudi to be spent in masses for the soul of a murdered child; and sister Marie died some months after her arrival, with a broken heart and a wrecked mind, but amid the tears of all who knew the mild sorrow that succeeded her grief-wrought madness.

MONTHLY REVIEW.

As meeting after temporary absence enables the observer to trace more effectually the growth of youth or the decay of age, so does our Monthly News-note bring more vividly before us the changes in our political life.

In ENGLAND, the triumph attending the great progress made at the recent electoral contest, has not yet died away, and before the exultation for the past tames down, preparations for the future are being made. If the deity were before angered with the people, and sent a famine, it now follows, as a matter of course, he must be pleased, since he has sent a plenteous and abundant harvest. At the time of the famine the people were sunk in political apathy; at the time of the plenty, they are roused to political life—thence the Archbishop's arguments may be turned against himself—God favours the people and frowns upon oppression; and, indeed, the more liberty prospers, the greater will be the plenty and the peace.

Co-operation, the great lever by which the POLITICAL ARCHIMEDES of our age is lifting the dead weight of slavery into the light of freedom—not in Herts, Worcestershire, and Oxfordshire alone, but in the heart of every thinking man, of every hoping slave—has exemplified its giant power at the late Land Conference at Lowbands, where schemes, once called Utopian, are realised, and further plans have been propounded, at which none now dare sneer. At Nottingham, the social reformer has proved that political regeneration is within the grasp of honesty; that an election can be pure; that a vote can be disinterested; and—honour to the land that bears such men! the poor toilers who sentinelled their chieftain's camp, whose crust is steeped in misery, whose heads find but precarious and uneasy shelter—these heroes, the non-electors of Nottingham, refuse the gold they have so justly merited, and pay themselves with triumphs of their victory! Who would despair of a cause—despair? who would, for a moment, doubt of success, with such leadership and such following?

Against these are arrayed a retrogressing army, that marches backwards from the field it would maintain. Its outposts are driven in from the factories and the mills: the manufacturing counties are half conquered, and now we are marching to their green and leafy gardens of delight, in their Lincoln and their Dorset, in their Wiltshire and their Kent, waving the Charter-flag in their eyes, and crying: "Justice! justice!" to the landlords and their serfs. The brutal murder of a man by a superintendent of police at Sleaford, in Lincolnshire, and the refusal of the magistrates to take cognizance of the same, at once proves their incompetency, their partiality and their intent, and draws up articles of impeachment against a system open to such atrocities. By such means they are hastening the triumph of the people, since they might linger on among their rotten institutions if they kept quietly and cautiously among them; but by firing the cannon from their ruined ramparts, they shake down with their own artillery the wall they would defend. The saying, "*Quem Deus vult perdere prius dementat,*" is as true as it is old.

In SCOTLAND, the Holytown ejectments remind us of middle age barbarism. Two thousand workmen have their wages abated, without a reasonable pretext, by one shilling per diem each—making an amount of £200 per diem saved the masters—and when the poor men refuse to submit to such an arbitrary proceeding, 800 families are forthwith ejected from their tenements, that the sight of their starving and shelterless wives and babes, exposed on the bleak heights to the inclement weather, may reduce the refractory slaves into obedience. To offer a comment would be to insult the hearts of our readers. In the face of this, men dare come before the public as philanthropists, without one blast of indignation on their tongues, without propounding one remedy for their social and political evils. But these mockbirds of policy—these drones of society—are fast vanishing before popular denunciation. The perfumed dandy, who, scarce fledged, was launched from the drawing room to represent a county, has been made to bow to the stern, calculating money-getter; but he, in turn, is being taught that the jingle of silver is not the music of a nation—and Labour claims the jury right of Englishmen, to be judged or legislated for BY ITS PEERS.

And IRELAND—Ireland, where Whiggery has been weaving a modern Penelope's web—asserting, truly, the land was not half-tilled, yet breaking stones, instead of digging fields; buying food abroad, yet sending that which was in the country out of it; making roads, yet at the same time creating railroads to supersede them—Ireland is that which it was: the Niobe of the nations, and the rock on which Finality will split. One only medicine can cure it—giving the Irish their own, restoring the soil to its children—but the physician must be a Home government, established under the banner of Repeal.

In FRANCE, also, decay is smoothing the way for progress: the decay of old shackles, as the growing limbs of young democracy expand beneath them, till they burst and fall. The depravity of the French aristocracy becomes daily more apparent, yet six leading Paris journals have been confiscated for daring to say so. The defalcation of ministers, the sale of appointments and insignia, the fearful immorality in the upper classes—constantly apparent, and now fearfully illustrated by the Duke of Choiseul Praslin's murder of his wife, that he might live in uncontrolled infamy with hired wantons—the gross villainy of the traitor-king, who, without one spark of manhood in his breast, lays a plot against the virtue of his own niece, Isabella of Spain, trying to blast her reputation after he has ruined her health and blighted her happiness, — these are bringing aristocracy and monarchy into merited disgrace; the tricolour again begins to feel the breeze of Freedom, and the power of its awakening shout will sing above the grave of its crowned oppressors.

SPAIN prepares her annual revolution; the Carlists are gathering up, Narvaez is recalled from London, and, amid the chaos sits a feeble, sceptred girl, with a broken heart, but an earnest will— taught by the treachery of princes to trust the honesty of her people: may she not swerve! She has but one alternative—to become the popular leader or the royal victim.

In PORTUGAL the queen is showing her old faith by levying (if she can) 10,000 more troops, while the people are struggling at the elections, and, if beaten there, preparing to fight again.

In ITALY, Pope Pius has thrown down the gauntlet

against Austrian tyranny. The full designs of the assassins of Faenza have become apparent; the Pope was to have been carried off a prisoner; Rome fired; and the Austrians to have deluged the country. The firmness of the Pontiff, and the courage of the people has disappointed them; but, baffled, they would show their vengeance, and thus seize upon Ferrara. If a poor man steals a turnip, he is sent to prison; if an Emporer steals a town and the rights of a people, shall none dare murmur? Shall such open robbery be perpetrated in the broad day-light of the nineteenth century, and in the face of England?

In Albania, an insurrection has broken out, likely to affect the position of Turkey, but whether only to supplant a foreign despot by a home one, or for a nobler cause, remains unknown.

A fresh wreath has been strewn on the path of Poland's resurrection, by the heroic deaths of Wiszniewski and Kapuscinski, two Polish patriots, hanged at Lemberg, by order of the Emperor of Austria. They died nobly, shouting to the last: "Long life to Poland!" Poland can never die, as long as she has such children

Germany, like the beam between the balance, is agitated to and fro, according as the democratic or despotic scale obtains the ascendancy. Let liberty shine forth in France or England and she will not be behindhand. Already her Teutona is waking from sleep amid the mountain fastnesses of Switzerland; the motion has at length been carried in the Diet for remodelling all the cantons into one great republic; and while France is threatening the Swiss with troops along their frontier, bidding them respect the treaty of Vienna,—they throw a challenge in her teeth, bidding her do the same, and, in compliance with that treaty, restore to the canton of Vaud the Valley of Dappes, which they have taken from it, and incorporated with the Departement de l' Ain.

America presents but little news. In Mexico, Santa Anna is gaining 'time by negociation, and the Americans are being thinned by disease, and harrassed by guerillas.

Thus, whichever way we turn, we behold, indeed, the powers of evil at work; but, at the same time, we see the people making a bold front. At home as well as abroad, the brave task is going onward, and with true soldiers, an honest cause, and the blessing of God,

"THE PEOPLE BY AND BY WILL BE THE STRONGER."

THE LABOURER.

A TREATISE ON THE LAND.

During the most active and enquiring years of my life, I made practical agriculture my choicest and most cheering study. I presume I acquired the taste from nature, as it is the natural pursuit from which youth derives most pleasure, and to which old age looks for solace and comfort. The practical knowledge I acquired of agriculture naturally led to a closer and more interested intimacy with the peasant class, and to the affection that grew upon me for their order I attribute the formation of my character. I could not see a peasant labouring for my benefit throughout the day without feeling some interest in his condition, and the necessary mode of arriving at a knowledge of that condition led me to a perfect knowledge of the difficulties and vicissitudes against which the peasant class had to contend. This course of education led to further thought; thought developed further dependence and oppression; and the desire to remedy the several grievances, brought me into that contact with law, privilege, and authority, which has led to the bitter enmity of those who obtain a livelihood by, and consequently have an interest in, upholding that degrading inequality by which the few lord it over the many.

All this process of practice and thought, I have undergone under the most rigid discipline of body and mind before I ventured to propound my cherished remedy for social abuses, whilst, strange to say, the ignorant and self-sufficient scribblers of the press affect a kind of magical knowledge and intuitive wisdom upon a subject which has cost me so many years of thought. The world has been convulsed by the several versions of political economy propounded by the several brainless quacks, who ventured to discuss the principle upon no other grounds than those of self-interest, and while labouring under a thorough ignorance of the great question upon which alone the super-structure of political economy can be built.

In arguing this extensive and unprovable dogma with the free-trade professors, I have shewn that the indispensable ingredient, RECIPROCITY, has been altogether omitted by their orators and writers; and I am sure it is unnecessary to remind my readers of the fulfilment of every one of my predictions, dangerously hazarded against the pompous and accepted prophecies of the league; and had I not the power of recalling the past to your recollection, the propounders of some new Utopia would still possess sufficient influence to convince you of the certain realisation of their most extravagant professions in return for your witless and extravagant confidence.

It so happens, however, that, although proscribed by the advocates of freedom, I have wormed myself into the affections of freemen. The silence of the press, the contumely of fools, and the ignorance of the uninformed, have not, unitedly, been able to stifle my voice, or secure your indifference. And I am now about to open a treatise with the predictions of one who fifty years ago was banished from his country for advocating the very principles which I now defy monarchs to retard. I give you a chapter from Arthur O'Connor's " State of England," from the only copy of that work in existence, and from it you will learn the difference between the political economy of the philanthropist and the political economy of the speculating blood-sucker!

. You will mark, that the writer of this treatise is now in the fiftieth year of his banishment, and that the advocacy of the principles propounded in that treatise, and not his revolutionary propensities, was the cause of his banishment. I invite you to a minute and critical perusal of this, the ninth chapter of his work, and to a sorrowful reflection upon your own present sad and melancholy condition, and then to ask yourselves, whether or no the poor man's political economy, in this day, possesses more ardent advocates than the same principle could boast of half a century ago.

, Here is the chapter.

"CHAPTER IX.

" That this system, by creating a derangement in the natural direction of the capital and industry of Great Britain is injurious to the people of England, as well as to the nations of Europe.

. " The moral, which prescribes to the individual to make justice the rule of his conduct, and to seek his happiness by a strict observance of those laws which nature has made the condition of health and tranquillity; the moral which teaches him to seek happiness in making the miserable passion of sordid self-interest yield to an ardent and lively sympathy for his fellow-creatures; in a word, the moral which teaches man, that to be happy he must cherish an ardent love for his species, and look on this life as a game of alliance, where, to gain the assistance and friendship of others, he must generously give the example, is as necessary for nations as it is for individuals, upon the broad principle of an enlightened self-interest.

"It is in this light, I propose to demonstrate, that, however brilliant the career of Great Britain may appear to a superficial observer, the happiness of the great mass of her people, her internal security, and even the amount of her wealth, would have been infinitely greater, if, instead of her mercantile system of monopoly and conquest, she had adopted one where every species of trade and of industry was perfectly free, and where the most sacred regard had been paid to the independence of the rest of the world.

"Leaving the advocates for the present system of monopoly and mercantile conquest to value the profits Great Britain has drawn for this century past, from her foreign dominions, at the most extravagant rate, the whole would not amount to the tenth of what it has cost her to keep and defend them.

"The West Indies are cultivated by British capital in the most extravagant manner at present. A proprietor in France or in England cannot cultivate a farm in his absence at 50 miles distance by agency, without sustaining such losses as have long rendered such a mode of cultivation, with men of good sense, in a view of profit, too losing a game to be adopted. The eye of the master is necessary at every instant, without which the temptation, the neglect, waste, and dishonesty, have been found too strong to be resisted.

"If this be true of an absence of a few miles, what must we think of the loss, waste and dishonesty, which a proprietor must experience, who, residing in London, cultivates his estate in the West Indies, at 3,000 miles distance, by means of agents and by slaves, whose price, wear, tear and subsistence, are at his expense. It is clear, such a manner of culture could never repay the proprietor without he was assured a monopoly price; which monopoly operates against the people of Great Britain, as well as against the rest of the world; all this waste, extravagance, and dishonesty, instead of falling upon the West India proprietors falls on the consumers.

"If these islands were free, their freedom guaranteed by America and Europe, and cultivated by resident proprietors, the greatest possible spur would be given to increase the quantity of West India produce; whereby the people of

Great Britain might purchase the quantity they consume at a fourth of the price they pay at present. A few wealthy West India proprietors are the sole gainers, while the people of Great Britain are made to part with four times the quantity of the produce of their industry, to be four times worse supplied than they would be, if the Antilles were free.

" In the same manner, the whole of the East Indies has been given in monopoly to a Joint Stock Company, whereby all the waste, extravagance, mismanagement, plunder and robbery of its servants, at 10,000 miles distance, fall upon the people of Great Britain, as consumers of East India produce, as well as on the rest of the nations of Europe.

" If the commerce of India were free, its produce would come infinitely cheaper to the consumers; not only from the vast superiority the thrift and good management of private adventurers has over the waste and extravagance of a Joint Stock Company, but as the quantity of capital which would be embarked in the trade, not only from Great Britain, but from all Europe, would, form a vast augmentation, the East India produce would come no comparison cheaper to the consumer; the best management would be exchanged for the worst; the freest competition for a monopoly; and the capital of all Europe for the capital of a single company.

" The whole order of political economy has been reversed and destroyed by this monopoly of the East and West Indies. It has been a preposterous attempt to encourage national industry by creating an extravagant price; whereas, by the most obvious principles in political economy, industry is to be encouraged by creating the greatest possible number of effectual demanders; the one rests upon monopoly, the other upon the freest competition.

" The interest of these monopolists, into whose hands the East and West Indies have been committed, is to keep the market understocked; the interest of the consumers, which comprehends the whole of the people of Britain, is to have the markets the most abundantly furnished; the interest of these monopolists is to get the greatest possible part of the produce of the industry of the people of Great Britain for the least possible part of the produce of India; and the interest of the people of Great Britain is, to get the greatest possible quantity of India produce for the least possible quantity of the produce of their industry. No two interests can be more directly in opposition with each other, than that of the monopolists of the East and West Indies, and that of the people of Britain.

" It is not only that the whole people of Great Britain
suffer as consumers by this monopoly, but such are the
inveterate, incurable vices which grow out of the institution
of a Joint Stock Company, that even with all these advantages against the people of Great Britain and Ireland, and
against all Europe, the affairs of this Company are every
now and then at the brink of ruin; they are at this moment
overwhelmed in debt; and it is but lately they were obliged
to throw themselves at the feet of the Parliament, to save
them from bankruptcy and ruin.

" But assuredly, of all the evils which have befallen Great
Britain from this part of her mercantile conquest, the
habits of extravagance, the habits of plunder, and the vast
increase of corruption, in more ways than one, with which
they have contaminated the morals and poisoned the freedom of Britain, are the most deadly, which strike at the
root of those virtues and of that liberty upon which every
thing dear to them rested.

" In forming a system to make Great Britain the manufacturer for the rest of the nations of Europe, the whole
has been rendered insecure and artificial; it has caused
a violation of the order which would have been established,
if her industry had been left to follow the natural order of
things; and, as might have been expected, it has generated
an infinite number of evils, and exposed her to an infinite
number of dangers.

" By means of this forced augmentation of her manufactures, the agriculture of Great Britain no longer suffices to
subsist her population

" As a considerable part of her population is wholly employed in manufacturing for the other nations of Europe,
according to the natural order of things, this part should
reside in those countries which give it employment; for it
is on those countries that this part of the population of
Great Britain is dependent for its provisions; by which
means she is exposed, not only frequently to suffer the evils
of dearth, but to be menaced with the horrors of famine.
Such are the effects of the vicious direction her capital has
received from the laws which impede the free circulation
of her landed property, and create a monopoly in commerce, and an excess in manufactures—that at this day,
Great Britain contains twenty-two millions of waste acres
in common. Would it be believed, if it was not affirmed
by the report of a committee of the legislature, that one-
third of the lands of this nation, of whose exports and
imports there has been such vaunting, is without culture

or produce ? To which must be added several millions of acres, of which the monopoly of land, by the laws of primogeniture, &c. prevents the improvement.

" A few years ago, before this system of mercantile conquest, and this excess in the manufacturing part of her population had made the progress they now have—Great Britain had corn to spare, and was a considerable exporter ; now she is reduced to pay several millions annually to supply her consumption. A few years ago, her most accurate writers gave the average ordinary price of wheat at 28s. the quarter, of late its ordinary price has more than doubled; and in 1795 it was at 108s., in 1796 at 100s ; in 1799 at 94s., and in 1800 at 134s. Prices for the first necessary of life so enormous, and attended with such famine and misery, as are alone sufficient to prove that this system is vicious.

" It is to this derangement of the natural order of industry, that, in a great measure, we must attribute such a rapid increase in the number of the poor in Great Britain, that six millions annually are insufficient to provide for them as miserable paupers at present.*

" If the proportion between the agricultural and manufacturing parts of the population had not been deranged by this pernicious system, these deadly evils could never have happened. Those who live by agriculture raise a stock of provisions for the year for them and their families ; and if they chance to fall sick, they are not instantly reduced to misery and want; whereas, if a manufacturer meet with any misfortune which prevents him from working, or that his particular manufacture is not in demand, from this very moment he and his family are instantly a charge on the nation, or reduced to beggary and famine.

" By this forced system, which aims at manufacturing for Europe, millions of the people of Great Britain depend on the caprices and changes which take place in the surrounding nations ; whereby, all at once, whole classes are deprived of employment, and, in full health, reduced to the

* That all this indigence does result from this forced system of manufactures, is confirmed by Sir Morton Eden's inquiry into the state of the poor of Great Britain ; where it is fully proved that the number of the poor of those who are employed in agriculture, are as nothing compared with the number of those employed in manufactures ; and that for the last 200 years the poor rates have kept such exact pace with the increase of the manufactures, as to leave no doubt that the attempt to force this branch of the national industry has been punished with all that misery and dearth to which we see this class exposed in Great Britain.

condition of beggars; by which the poor and the poor rates of Britain are greater than those of all the nations of Europe together.

"When we see millions of British capital employed at 3,000 miles distance to cultivate the Antilles, by the expensive means of agents and slaves; at 10,000 miles distance in the East Indies; and that no man finds it his interest to employ one shilling to cultivate any part of this waste half of Great Britain; who will maintain that this system of mercantile conquest is not as injurious to the people of Britain as it is to the other people of Europe? When we see the people of Great Britain dependent on America, and on the nations of Europe for bread; when we see them, year after year, suffering a dearth, whence thousands die of disease, and even of absolute famine, and the poor rates at more than six millions; who will deny that this system of mercantile conquest, and forced manufactures, is not as injurious to the people of Great Britain as it is to rest of the world?

"The labour and capital employed in agriculture are more productive for the nation than in any other way whatsoever; but is it not always so for the individual whose labour and capital have been suspended. By the unjust and impolitic laws of primogeniture, entail and settlement, and the equally ruinous law of commonage of lands, at least one half of Great Britain is without culture or produce. By the law of primogeniture, vast tracts of lands are made the estate of an individual who cannot sell them, or even lease them, except for a few years. But it can never be the interest of any man to expend his labour or capital on uncultivated lands, where a considerable part of the produce is to be paid to another as rent, and on a term too short to enable him to get back his capital. No man will work that another shall reap the fruits of his labour; yet it is on this principle that the advocates for the laws of primogeniture and commonage of land, expect that men will expend their labour and capital. The only man that can have an interest to improve these waste uncultivated lands is a small proprietor, for he alone has the whole produce to enable him, and a perpetuity to induce him; yet there are men who assert that a tenant on a short lease, paying a considerable part of the produce to a landlord, is a better cultivator than the proprietor who has the whole and for ever.

"On the same reasoning, it has been asserted that the produce of the lands of Great Britain would be diminished, if the labour of an additional million of her population were employed in her agriculture. By which arithmetic, a million of sickly manufacturers, whose precarious existence is hourly threatened with beggary and famine, and when the nation pays annually seven millions for corn, is preferable to a million of healthy, vigorous peasants and farmers, who produce their own food and a surplus for others.

" Thus, immense estates in the possession of an individal, immense farms in the hands of one farmer, are accompanied with the depopulation of the country, towns crowded with half-starved manufacturers, six millions for paupers, one half of the soil without culture or produce, with more crimes, more executions, more prisoners, more punishments, and more misery than is to be found in the rest of all Europe altogether.

" ' Ill fares that land, to hastening ills a prey,
Where wealth accumulates and men decay
Princes or lords may flourish or may fade,
A breath can make them as a breath has made ;
But a bold peasantry, its country's pride,
When once destroyed can never be supplied ! ! ! '

" When we consider the hundreds of millions of her revenue Great Britain has expended ; the hundreds of millions of debts she has contracted ; the blood she has lavished ; the taxes with which she is loaded, in order to support this system of mercantile conquest and forced manufactures since 1688, it will appear as clear as the sun in its meridian, that the whole has been expended, not only for nothing, but to cause ruinous derangement in the direction of her capital and industry ; by which one-half of her soil lies uncultivated, the most extensive system of poverty is created, and the nation reduced to a precarious subsistence. While, so far from establishing the most lucrative trade with the Indies by the mode she has adopted, the people of Great Britain are made to pay four times the quantity of the produce of their industry, to be four times worse supplied with the Indian produce they consume than if the Indies were free ; and so far from the other part of this war system (this excess from forced manufactures) being beneficial to the people of Great Britain, it has deranged the natural proportion between the part of the population employed in agriculture and the part employed in manufactures ; whereby Great Britain, no longer able to maintain its inhabitants, is dependent upon other nations for subsistence, overwhelmed with poverty, afflicted with dearth, and menaced with famine."

Can the reader of the foregoing chapter fail to ask himself, wherein the political economy of the present day agrees with the political economy of half a century back, propounded by the expatriated rebel? I now turn to the question of the Land, and shall be able to demonstrate that its subdivision into the exact parcels capable of employing the labour of the peasant and his family, is the only possible political economy by which England can be saved from a bloody revolution, and the estates and capital of the wealthy from confiscation. Having already instructed you in the alphabet of the Land Plan, and having made the question of that importance which now forces itself upon the press and the country, I shall proceed to shew you how I propose to realise my prophecy, that

ERE LONG THE PLAN WOULD BECOME NATIONAL.

Who, two short years since, when the bird was hatched in St. Martin's Lane, would have ventured to calculate upon its growth and strength? Who, when he gave his assent to the then novelty, could have imagined that it would have been carried into practical operation, before many schemes antecedently propounded had been sufficiently digested to warrant even experiment? Who could have thought of even eighty peasants being rescued from the garret and the cellar, from the gin-palace and the brothel, from the sickly town and artificial slave market? And who could have contemplated the fond hope and joyous anticipations of the thousands, and tens of thousands, who are now cheerful participants of a niggardly fare, with the view, with the satisfied view, of a better hereafter, strengthened by the consolation that the penny now saved will add to their future store? And who could have anticipated that any reptile, any hired mercenary, could be found base enough to aim his poor pointless arrows at a plan so calculated to disseminate peace and happiness amongst the industrious? But so it has ever been, and so it ever will be; so long as society is divided into a master-class and a slave-class, so long will mercenaries and scribblers be the hired agents of the wealthy, to crush and denounce all who would venture to assist the poor.

From the moment the Land Plan was established to the present, my desire, my aim and object, has been:

FIRSTLY.—To make it national.

SECONDLY.—To place it beyond the possibility of becoming a prey to lawyers and the law : and,

THIRDLY.—To secure for all who entered the Company, more, if possible, than the realisation of the promised benefits.

Firstly, then, I shall treat of the mode by which I propose to make the Land Plan national ; and I have no doubt—no more than I have of my existence—of the accomplishment of this, my first and primary object.

CHAP. I.
Mode of making the Land Plan national.

Being not only an advocate of, but a religious believer in, the principle of Universal Suffrage, and feeling convinced of the damage that the popular cause must sustain by the slightest violation of trust or confidence reposed in the most humble of its leaders, I have resolved upon testing the opinions of all, before I venture upon the realisation of this, my primary object, and to that end it is my intention, prior to the meeting of Parliament, to call meetings in the several large towns of England, Scotland and Wales, to which the members shall be invited, with the view to taking into their serious consideration the propriety of making the Land Plan a National Plan, by the following means ; but, without the concurrence of an overwhelming majority, I shall not have recourse to those means. The means then that I propose, are—

To transfer the whole affairs of the Company to the management of the Government, under a special Act of Parliament, by which the government shall be bound :—

Firstly.—To dispense with all patronage that would tend unnecessarily, to diminish the funds of the Company by a farthing.

Secondly.—To guarantee the continuance in office, as long as they conducted themselves properly, of the present directors as the managers of the Company.

Thirdly.—To pass a special Act, whereby the members of the Company shall be exempt from all Stamp Acts and Stamp Duties ; and

Fourthly.—To raise a sufficient amount of money upon the faith of the Government to locate the several members who shall constitute the Company, within the shortest possible period ; and to erect school-houses, in the proportion of one to every one hundred occupants, upon the free and voluntary principle.

Now, if the government accept those conditions, I pledge myself to hand over to the Chancellor of a very needy Exchequer, at the least a quarter of a million of money, by the first week in March next, and a further lodgment of half a million of money by the following first of September. Independently of government interference, we shall be in possession of more than a quarter of a million of money by next March, and by the end of the year, at which time our sections close, I estimate the number enlisted in the Land Company, lowly, at ONE HUNDRED AND FIFTY THOUSAND. This number will be constituted of the poorest and most confiding, and may be truly designated "The Chartist Co-operative Land Company;" but I do not propose that those enlisting under the banners of national faith shall be placed upon the same footing as those who enlisted under the banners of national confidence. The majority of those constituting the Chartist Co-operative Land Company will be of the order of 'fustian jackets, blistered hands, and unshorn chins;' while the majority of those constituting the Government Land Company will consist of the perfumed Athenæum gentlemen, and those I propose should pay a larger amount of qualification money for the greater advantages to be derived from government protection. In the event of government assuming the management of the Land Company, I propose raising the two acre shares to £5, the three acre shares to £7. 10s., and the four acre shares to £10, and I will pledge my existence, that, under Government patronage, one hundred thousand of the aristocracy of the trades would enrol between the 1st of March and the 1st of September, and taking them at the medium standard of three acre shareholders, their paid up shares would amount to £750,000. This is giving them six months to pay £7. 10s., as the Government might insist upon a section of that amount paying up within that period,* and the amount would not be more than £1. 5s. a month, while the removal of that number from the highest classes of the trades would leave a vacuum to be filled up by the lower order of the same trades. Let us then see,

FIRSTLY.—The advantage that the system would confer upon the shareholders.

SECONDLY.—The advantage that it would confer upon the government.

THIRDLY.—The advantage that it would confer upon the trading-classes; and,

FOURTHLY.—The advantage that it would confer upon the labour-class.

The advantages it would confer upon the shareholders, would be to secure them against the possibility of loss; against legal exactions; against the pressure of stamp duties, and to give to them those facilities of rapid location which the greatest co-operation of individuals could not possibly secure.

I trust that the most ardent well-wisher and advocate of this plan will not allow his false notions of democracy to urge a single objection to its adoption. I trust that no man will falsely argue, that such a course would place the working-classes of this country at the disposal of the government, or at the mercy of the government, while upon the contrary, reason should convince all that the adoption of the plan would place government at the disposal, and under the absolute controul, of the working-classes themselves Not of the working-classes only who became members of the Land Plan, but of the working-classes generally who have an influence over those of their own order, who had an influence upon the government. The government of this country has cunningly professed a desire to see that distinguishing mark of popular improvement which would justify its leaning to popular principles, and in my soul, and in my conscience, I believe, that out of the chaos of contending parties there is no ground upon which a strong government of all can unite, except upon some principle which manifests so palpable an improvement in the working-classes, as to justify the government in setting the opposition of their enemies at defiance. This is the political economy to which my uncle looked for your redemption fifty years ago; this is the political economy to which I look for your political redemption now; for, believe me, as the old general said when he saw the enemy advancing, "There's the enemy, if you don't kill them, they'll kill you;" and so I say of the political economy of the Capitalist, "If you do not kill it, it will kill you." This is not just the place to remind you of the fallacy of their predictions, nor is it my wish to direct your attention to an abstruse and unproveable dogma, from a simple and proveable proposition. I wish you to get the possession of the government, and I defy mortal man to devise more speedy or certain means, than by proving to the government, that, in its distress, the most neglected were the most stable, most trustworthy and most wealthy. No man is to suppose that I would allow this holy institution to be handed over to the government upon other than the most honourable and defined conditions, and no man is to suppose that I would relinquish my own controul of its economy, or my own honourable situation of unpaid bailiff.

Government patronage I shall "protest" against; the unnecessary expenditure of a fraction of the funds I shall contend against; nor would I vote for any measure of transfer which, after being deliberately drawn up, and after deliberate consideration, was not acquiesced in by a majority of the members; nor would I acquiesce in any measure which would deprive me, under the most rigid government controul, from carrying out the plan in faithful obedience to those principles on which it was established, and in compliance with those rules, under whose faith the several members joined. In short, I would, as now, receive the monies each week, and within the same week pay them over to the credit of the Chancellor of the Exchequer.

Such are the great legal guarantees that the government could . accord to the company, and now I shall state the pecuniary advantages to be derived from government patronage. For all public purposes undertaken by the government, building materials are admitted free of duty. Hence, the government, from this principle, as well from its power of contracting upon more beneficial terms than any individual, or corporate body, could build a house for £70., which would cost an individual £100. Here, then, would be a saving of 30s. a year to a two-acre occupant in his house alone; thus government would be enabled to lease two acres of land that cost £45. an acre, and a house, as cheaply as an individual or a company paying duty, could lease the same house and land if the land cost £30 an acre. It may be argued, that this would be a loss to the government, in the shape of tax, raised by duty upon those materials; but my answer is, that such would not be the case, because, if the government had not so stipulated, the quantity of required materials would not have been used, and, consequently, the government would not have received the duty upon those articles. It cannot be advanced, that the persons located would be under the influence of government, because, upon location, each member should receive his conveyance for ever, conditioned to pay a rent charge at the rate of £5. per cent. upon the capital expended and advanced; and hence the occupant, upon receiving possession, would be as wholly independent of the government as he is now.

Under such an arrangement, all stamps or conveyances

made by vendors to the company would be saved, as well as all stamps upon the conveyance from the government to the occupant. In point of fact, the arrangement would have this advantage over the enrolment of the company; namely, protection against the assaults of lawyers and the litigious. Moreover, the government would have a facility of purchasing land that individuals never can possess, and the power of protecting titles without the slightest risk of litigation.' Such are the advantages that the members would derive from government patronage, and I shall now state the advantages which the government would derive, and especially during this unsettled period of the labour market.

Firstly.—The government would receive a weekly amount of subscriptions, which, under such an arrangement, I would estimate lowly at £50,000 per week.

Secondly.—Presuming that government undertook the erection of 10,000 houses at a time, and allowing that ten persons of all trades, classes and denominations would be employed in the erection of each house, 'and the necessary agricultural pursuits, this of itself would give employment to one hundred thousand persons directly, independently of the incalculable amount of trade, that such employment would lead to.

Thirdly.—Government could raise money in abundance upon the security of that landed property, at the rate of $3\frac{1}{2}$ per cent., and would consequently derive a benefit of $1\frac{1}{2}$ per cent. from surplus of rental above the interest, and which sum, now constituting our sinking fund, I would cheerfully abandon for government protection and aid, and a full equivalent for which each occupant would receive from the positively lower rent, measured by the cheaper erection of his house being released from the payment of duty upon building materials; and the further greater advantage derived from the principle of wholesale purchase, and the government being able to give to the company a more extensive advantage of this principle than individuals or corporations. For instance, where a company should confine its operation to the purchase, say of £20,000 worth of land, upon which amount it would secure a saving to the members of at least 4 or 5 per cent. over and above the investment of £4,000, £5,000 or £6000 in the purchase of land, and, government being able to purchase to any amount, would, upon the larger operation, secure a saving to the company of an additional 5 or 10 per cent., ranging above £20,000., so that, in point of fact, the abandonment of one per cent., the amount saved between four per cent. paid by the bank and five per cent. received as rent, would be but a very trifling sacrifice for the several advantages otherwise gained.

. *Fourthly.*—The Expense Fund, to release the govern ment from casualties, being established at the same rate as at present, would be amply sufficient for that purpose, because expense does not increase in the same ratio as increased means to meet it, derived from an increased number of members.

Fifthly.—Presuming that our Company will number 150,000 at the end of the year, and taking £4 in round numbers, as the average to be paid by each shareholder, this would give the government a capital of £600,000, and presuming, which I do presume, and which would be verified within one-half the period, that 200,000 of the labour and trade class would become members in the year 1848, and presuming that this number would be four-acre members, it would give the government an additional paid up capital of two millions sterling, making a paid up capital of £2,600,000, for which the government would never be called upon to pay one farthing in the shape of interest; and here is a feature in the Land Plan which the poor miserable creatures, who write about, and presume to doubt its stability, have never taken into calculation. It is this, that, even as at present established, the Company pays no interest upon the paid-up shares, and this is its stability above any other Company in the world, while as a compensation, it guarantees advantages which no trading Company assuming to pay the largest money interest upon paid-up capital can by possibility guarantee. For instance, supposing that capital to the amount of £400,000 was paid-up by 100,000 members, for that capital the trustees of the Company pay no interest; but, on the contrary, receive an annual rental of £20,000 a year, or £5 per cent. upon the paid-up capital—it is the trading capital of the Company, and which, at the winding-up of the affairs, of each section, is restored in its proper proportion to the members of that section, together with their shares of all profits made by the sale of estates, by the Land Purchase Department, and by the Insurance Company.

.Now I beg to call your particular attention to this one striking and irrefutable fact; namely, that the stability and solvency of the Company is guaranteed by this simple fact, that the Company pays no interest upon its paid-up capital, while, by a very moderate levy, by the profit upon rules, and the strictest economy, more than a sufficient amount is brought in to cover all the expenses consequent upon our multifarious operations.

Sixthly.—The advantages derived by the government in the shape of increased trade, increased consumption, diminished poor rates, and increased tranquillity, would be incalculable.

Seventhly.—The government might then set at nought the political handle now made of Drainage and Health of Towns' Bills, of Schools, and sectarian Education schemes, as the working-classes would wait patiently until they could educate their children in their own school-houses, and breathe the fresh air in their own well-ventilated cottages.

Eighthly and lastly.—Government may then say to the foreign despot and domestic factionist: "Behold I was the the slave of one, and the tool of the other, measuring national honour by the nation's ability and willingness to pay the expense of a war, and domestic policy by the expediency of truckling and succumbing to those whose will or caprice was capable of hurling me from office. But now you see my volunteer legion capable of defending me against the tyranny of the one and the vengeance of the other. You now see my exhausted treasury replenished by domestic industry. You now see me independent of your caprice, independent of your will, because I have realised the purest of all political principles—that Labour is the source of all wealth, and ought to be the source of all power. I was YOUR TOOL——I am now the PEOPLE'S MINISTER."

THIRDLY.—I shall consider the advantages that such an arrangement would confer upon the trading-classes of both orders—the aristocracy and the democracy.

The wide spread notoriety and the incalculable advantages that the Press would then give to, and explain in favour of the Land Plan, would very speedily thin the overstocked labour ranks of thousands and tens of thousands of competitors, which, bear in mind, has ever been the primary importance that I attached to the undertaking. While I defy you to show me a trade, whether it be the mason, the bricklayer, or the slater; the carpenter, the joiner, or the plasterer; the wheelright, the blacksmith, or the nail-maker; the painter, the glazier, or the plumber; the tailor, the shoemaker, or the hatter; the glover, the haberdasher, or the linendraper; the ironmonger, the stone-quarryman, or the slate-quarryman; the sawyer, the limeburner, or the coal-miner; the papermaker, the printer, or the publisher; the type-founder, the cotton manufacturer, or the blanket-maker; the cabinetmaker, the upholsterer, or the paper-hanger; the schoolmaster, the music master, or the dancing master; the silk mercer, the hosier, or the grocer; the tobacconist, the cornchandler, or the miller; the spinner, the weaver, and the blockprinter; the butcher, the baker, and the seedsman: in short, I defy you to show me a trade, except the church, the army, and the law, that would not be benefitted by this increased impetus given to the cultivation of the national resources. We traverse the seas in search of customers for our produce. We attach importance to the emigration of Britain's hardy and industrious sons, upon the false and unchristian principle that they become consumers of our produce at the distance of thousands and tens of thousands of miles, burdened with a tax of speculation, freight, risk, and insurance, ever blind to the grand principle of reciprocity, by which, if encouraged at home, they would create a market at their own door for English produce, discharged of those manifold impositions. This, my friends, is Free Trade; this is God's free trade; this is religious free trade; this is reciprocal free trade; this is unalloyed political and domestic economy, which allows every man, without molestation, let, or hindrance, to coin his own sweat into an exchangeable medium to barter with the rest of the world for commodities of which he may stand in need, and may more advantageously purchase than produce.

FOURTHLY.—I shall call your attention to the advantages that the more extensive realisation of this plan would confer upon the labouring class generally.

I sometimes smile in pity when I think of the miserable hack who writes placidly about the prudence and discretion of disinheriting the operatives of the North, by throwing them for some weeks upon the clemency of the autumnal season, and an abundant vegetable crop, which, of course, under the circumstances, is meant to be common property during this SACRED HOLIDAY; while the same drivelling reptile dares to make calculations as to the probable, the comparative, or the possible condition of the freeman housed in his own castle, free to cultivate his own labour field, and whom no domestic tyranny can consign to some weeks of idleness, while he is willing to labour for his livelihood. I have frequently drawn the picture of 3000 acres, cultivated in a parish by a thousand peasant farmers, as compared with the condition of the same parish, cultivated by three slaves of an autocrat landlord; or can I draw a picture from a better subject than that which I now daily witness? I have come to a poor parish—poor, because the farms average nearly a thousand acres in extent, and because the whole labour that should be performed by man is performed by oxen and horses that devour the fruits of the earth, and what should legitimately belong to man, that is, if man is of paramount importance in the eyes of his Maker. Well, I found this parish poor, eaten up with poor rates, and now I have set the bee-hive, and the busy bees—called drones, vagabonds, and idlers, by the pompous and the idle—swarm to make honey from the blossom of co-operation. Here then is the best answer that can be given to Kohl, the German defamer of the English working classes, and to all other such hirelings, who justify the tyranny of their oppressors upon the plea of popular idleness, popular ignorance, dissipation, and unthriftiness. From the centre, and indeed from all points of this estate, can be seen the strongest, the most irrefutable condemnation of the rulers of Britain, the gorgeous poor-house where unwilling idlers are pent up as vagabonds, servile dependents, and willing idlers, for no other earthly purpose than that they should augment the competitive reserve, upon which capitalists may fall back to reduce the wages of the comparatively satisfied.

Will any man deny—can any man doubt—that the wages standard of Britain is now tyrannically and ungenerously measured by the standard of insult and degradation that the family-loving, liberty-loving, and kind-hearted peasant will endure, rather than be subjected to the slave-brand, the pauper's fare, or pauper's dress, and a pompous overseer's haughty contumely and dominion? and can the greatest sticklers for the new-fangled principle of political economy, taught by a new race of speculators in low wages, contend for a system, which simultaneously renders barren and sterile nineteen twentieths of our land, while a tenth of those hardy peasants, who would cheerfully cultivate it, are consigned to beggary and degradation, to pauperism and starvation, lest their generous, natural, rightful, and legitimate employment should tend to the more equitable distribution of the national income, secured by the better cultivation of the national resources?

I have burned the fact upon your memory, that the monopolising class would prefer a national annual income of £300,000,000, to be unequally divided by class legislation, to an annual income of one thousand millions to be equitably distributed amongst capitalists, honourable speculators, and producers. The Land Plan, then, secures to the labour class a competitive market, far preferable to that in which they are now obliged to compete upon the destructive principle of underbidding each other to insure the privilege to labour; and I venture to predict, that, however inviting the hay and harvest standard of wages may be to the several located occupants, that every man of them will discover the fact, that what his labour is worth to the employer it must be worth to himself.

It is impossible, my friends, to separate this great social system from our political system. It is impossible to divest the mind of the fact, that the Emancipation of the Catholics gave great additional weight, influence, patronage, and protection to the Roman Catholic people. That the Reform Bill, which meant the representation of the owners of capital and machinery, and the speculators in trade, conferred incalculable advantages upon that body; That the growing obscenities, the tyranny, the injustice and neglect of duties, by State Church Ministers, is hourly strengthening the hands of the several dissenting sects; and it is impossible to lose sight of the self-evident fact, that no minister of England, with the single exception of Sir Robert Peel, has ever been the minister of a principle, or the continous though not comprehended advocate of a steady unswerving policy, which means the preparation, the "trying up," the dovetailing, and putting together of those several disjointed fragments, upon which the success of the principle must depend; but, upon the contrary, the undeviating principle of all other ministers has been reduced to the pitiful circle of place, and their policy the best means of securing the influence and support of that party most capable of preserving them within this narrow circle. Many of you are old enough to recollect how the reforming ministers bid for popular support, boasted of popular intelligence, and contended for a sufficient amount of popular confidence, only to secure the principle, " THAT TAXATION WITHOUT REPRESENTATION WAS TYRANNY AND OUGHT TO BE RESISTED." Well, why was popular sacrifice, popular intelligence, popular courage and confidence, sacrificed by the minister the moment the shout of triumph ceased ? Simply because he had conferred power, not upon that class for whose interests he professed to struggle, but upon that class whose profits and whose presumed station in society depended upon the slavery of the working people, and upon the subserviency of the minister. Let us, then, deal with ministers as mere machines, as they have dealt with the people, machines to be oiled by the national sweat, and propelled by the national will.

Let me now draw a figure for you, só clear and comprehensive that the most ignorant can understand it. A figure haunting every man's mind in the kingdom, but never before familiarly painted to the common understanding, so that all may judge of its proportions. Now, mark this figure; I will not daub it, nor so paint it that its exhibition shall require any particular shade of light, but all shall comprehend it at a view. Education has been paraded as the legitimate source from whence representation should spring. Property is now the standard, or rather has been the standard, and that property of that description upon the possession of which the faded and exploded constitution was said to be based; namely, Land. But I will show you that education lost its influence in the exact proportion in which trafficking, cunning, and commercial subtlety increased.

The landlords of yore educated their families better, according to the prescribed course marked out by the constitution, than the trading classes educated their families. But, not requiring any other description of education than that which would secure a qualification for clerical advancement, military promotion, or governmental fitness, they of themselves remained like a stagnant pool, wallowing in their own unstirred mire, resting satisfied with that protection with which their institutions fenced and preserved their exclusive rights and privileges, and the distinctions and eccentricities of their order. They had the wealth, but in proportion as the trading class progressed in cunning and subtlety, it was discovered that the arms of the Church and the Land, which are the SWORD and the BIBLE, were inoperative weapons against that subtlety and cunning which has now become the literature of England. Hence you find the wealthy, welleducated landlords firing their fanciful pellets from behind their smouldering ramparts in the Lords and the Commons, merely " standing up to receive " the shots of this very cunning and subtlety amid the derision of the new professors, and to be scoffed at by the world. Hence, neither property nor education longer constitutes the title of the landlord class—it has faded before the new literature of commercial policy and Free Trade. This transition arose from the fact, that the oppressed and those who have to contend against monopoly see the necessity of being prepared with an attacking power, while the confiding dupes of the secure system rest their chance of defence upon the legitimacy usurped by their order.

Let us now apply this figure to the Church. The supporters of the right divine of Kings to rule and reign, the recipients of the third of every man's capital, labour, skill and industry, suppose themselves to be the right arm of the State, and

"The pulpit—drum ecclesiastic—"

was always the sentry-box of the State. The same anathemas and denunciations that were successfully thundered against jacobins, levellers, and papists, were relied upon as the pulpit artillery; as the reserve to uphold the ascendancy of the patrons of the Church, and to destroy that growing spirit of inquiry which asked for solution of the words in holy writ, "He that will not work, neither shall he eat." Passive obedience and non-resistance was preached, but the Catholic priesthood, whose flocks were oppressed by this all-absorbing State Church, precisely as merchants and traders felt themselves oppressed by the monopoly of the landlord class; these Catholic priests, by a like impulse, instructed themselves in that description of theology which was calculated to exhibit the ignorance of the State Church preachers; and the consequence is, that, as education and property have ceased to constitute the qualification of the landlord class to govern, so the presumption of State Church religion will, ere long, cease to constitute the qualification of the Church of the few to laud it over the conscience, the industry, and the zeal of the many.

Now reverse the picture, and suppose that the trading community had been the best informed, and the wealthiest, and the most powerful, and had rested its title to its ascendancy upon the prescriptive rights secured by custom to its order: in that case, the intellect of the oppressed landlords, whetted by persecution, would have become a powerful competitor against the legitimacy of trade, built upon the fragile foundation of presumed wealth and knowledge.

Again, as regards the Church: had the Catholic religion been the State religion, and had its preachers relied upon State protection instead of theological knowledge, and the deep inquiry into the solution of those presumptions by which one class of religionists usurps to itself the right to live as freebooters upon the industry of another class, and to denounce all who will not subscribe to their doctrines, in such case the oppressed Protestants would have been the new lights of the age, and their discoveries, as regards freedom of religion and liberty of man, would have been used by them in a religious sense, precisely as political economy and Free Trade have been used by the cunning traders and subtle merchants against the monopoly of the confiding, and therefore ignorant, landlord class.

Now, I draw this picture for you to prove that no government, that no power, can prescribe the course of education, or the amount of property that will constitute the qualification of an elector or a representative ; and the conclusion which I would draw from the inference is this, that as the increasing knowledge of the middle classes broke down the ramparts of the landed aristocracy, and as the burning denunciation of Catholics and Dissenters has all but consumed the decaying body of the State Church, so a perfect knowledge of the injustice of the trading class, and the enlightenment of the people as to the equitable mode of transferring legitimate power to the many, teaching their opponents how they would use that power, not for the destruction of others' property, but for the most extensive cultivation of the national resources, in whose increase all would have an interest, because all would be equitable participants according to their skill and industry. These are the poor man's qualifications —his labour is his money qualification, and his knowledge how its proceeds should be applied for his own sustenance and the State's honour, his educational qualification. And, my friends, I defy mortal man to devise the means of securing those two qualifications other than by throwing industry upon its own resources, and allowing every man to be the undivided recipient of the fruits of his own industry, resting satisfied that he will not be niggardly of what the State may honourably stand in need of—that state which returns protection for allegiance, and that the honoured pastor, who administers spiritual consolation, will be supported like an honoured shepherd, by a bountiful, a generous, a confiding, and loving flock.

This, then, is my aim and object, to teach the minister that in these days of sudden transition, and of doubtful ministerial ascendancy, the working classes, the industrious classes, the honourably speculating classes, and the justly regulated trading classes, are the rock upon which he must henceforth build his title to govern ; and, as sure as water will find its level, so surely will power find its level ; and that power, which alone can constitute ministerial security, is to be found in the just and equitable government of the working classes. Question has succeeded question, and the rapid rolling of antagonistic interests have revolved in such quick succession, as wave succeeds wave in a storm, that the minister, sitting upon the billow of the day, if asked what principle or policy he represented, should point to the most

recent swell of discontent rising in the distance. His station
must be uncertain; his principles must be equivocal; his
policy must be capricious; until he can sit firmly upon the
levelled breakers, waves, and billows, which will constitute
the safe harbour for ministerial integrity. Landlocked by the
affection, the strength, the confidence, and the interest of that
wall of British hearts which may defy the indignities of the
foreign despot, or the assault of domestic factions.

My friends, as I purpose this to be a treatise to keep, and
to which you may refer when the policy at which it aims
to establish shall be the accepted policy of the rulers of
Britain, I shall make no apology for the introduction of
elementary matter, which to the studious and thoughtful
will appear as an indispensable ingredient in the discussion
and consideration of the Land Plan.

Indeed it is so comprehensive a question, and so minutely
connected with every apparently irrelevant part of our constitution and system, and its magnificence becomes so developed as I proceed, that I shall not limit myself to one
number of the ' *Labourer* ' for its illustration if I find that
more space is required for its complete and perfect developement, and in such case I shall continue the treatise
in this work until all shall be masters of the subject.

CHAP. II.

Treatise on the Land Plan.

The previous chapter has been written upon the presumption that the members of the National Land Company
will be happy to possess themselves of government protection, and to release me from individual responsibility. In
that chapter I have endeavoured to point out the advantages
to be gained by the members in case government should become the patron, and I have very imperfectly delineated the
advantages to be gained by the government. I shall, therefore, devote this chapter, firstly to a more perfect illustration
of those advantages, and secondly to simplify the mode by
which government may be induced to accept the proffered boon. I have shewn you that the paid-up capital of
£600,000, subscribed by the 150,000 members, the number
that I confidently assert will be enrolled before the close of
the year, together with the two millions paid up by two
hundred thousand persons within the year 1848, would
place at the disposal of government a sum of two millions
six hundred thousand pounds, upon which no interest
would be payable, or no deductions to be calculated upon

to meet consequent expenses, as the Expense Fund would be more than ample to meet exigencies and contingencies, and I shall now show you what the further advantage to government would be upon the completion of the affairs of the Company, say, numbering altogether three hundred thousand.

I will estimate the amount required for the location of each member at £200, making a total of sixty millions; which would bring in a rental of three millions at £5 per cent. upon the expended capital; and which capital of sixty millions the government could raise at three-and-a-half per cent., or less, upon the security of the land, and would be liable to an interest of two millions one hundred housand pounds, thus leaving to government a net profit upon the rent of nine hundred thousand pounds, or nearly double the amount expected to be realised by the Corn Laws. Hence I clearly show, that by an expenditure of sixty millions raised by the government, the Chancellor of the Exchequer would receive two million six hundred thousand pounds, for which he would pay no interest, and also an annual income of nine hundred thousand pounds. If, however, the large amount of sixty millions for peace, prosperity, and domestic happiness purposes is considered too large a sum, let us reduce it to the amount paid to the West Indian planters for the manumission of their slaves, £20,000,000; that sum, expended on the location of one hundred thousand independent husbandmen, would leave the Chancellor of the Exchequer a bonus of nearly one million, upon which he would pay no interest, and a profit upon the rental, paid by those husbandmen, of three hundred thousand pounds per annum. How far the large amount of sixty millions would go in the direction of foreign conquest, to force trade and manufactures upon the other nations of the earth, the reader will learn when he has perused the review of British policy, written by Arthur O'Connor, nearly half a century ago. Surely, then, if we tax England to liberate those who could not bear the oppression leased by England to the slave owners of the West Indies, we may, with great honour, propriety, and justice, raise the same amount of money, the interest of which would be cheerfully paid by the contented husbandman for the liberty of Britons.

I will now carry this figure farther, and I defy the M'Gregors, the M'Cullochs, the Taylors, the Lloyds, the Humes, to refute one single part of my argument, or to disturb a single one of my positions; unless their controversy is based upon their own false data of their own false principle of political economy, adopted to square and level the accounts of profit and loss of British speculators. I have only shown you the amount of capital that the Chancellor of the Exchequer would receive in the shape of entrance money, and the amount of annual profit he would receive in the shape of one and a half per cent. in rent, over and above the amount of interest guaranteed by the government for the purchase money of the land. But I have yet a further and a larger item to add, which is guaranteed by our rules, and compliance with which is a boon and not a hardship to the occupant. It is this—the government, we assume, would locate a member for £200; we will, then, take fifty of those members to constitute a location; those fifty would have cost the government ten thousand pounds—and upon which the occupants, at the rate of five pounds per cent. upon the capital, would pay a rent of £500 per annum, or £10 a man. Now, no man is better acquainted with the fact than I am, that a cottager, holding a cottage and a few rods of land, will purchase it at any price that the landlord chooses to ask, rather than abandon it. It is a fact, clear as the sun at noonday, that a shopkeeper in business, and holding his premises upon a lease, sets his heart upon the purchase of those premises at an exorbitant price, and that he will give more for those premises than any other purchaser. But, how much more forcibly does this argument apply to the husbandman, whose castle is placed in the centre of his labour field, and whose whole thought and affection is set upon the prospect of being one day able to say, "This is my own, this is my manor, and I am the lord of this manor." But, to keep the figure plainly and simply before you, the government has paid £10,000 for this location, and receives £500 a year rent upon that outlay. Now, that rental, if sold to the several occupants at twenty-five years' purchase, which is five years' purchase under the market price of land, would fetch £12,500, or 25 per cent. in money, over and above the original cost—that is, the man who paid £10 a year for a house and allotment, which cost the government £200, would cheerfully pay £250, or twenty-five years' purchase, to make himself proprietor in fee.

Now, this is a fact that I can speak to better than all the political economists in the world, and for this reason, that I could now sell every estate that I have purchased for the Company, without laying stone or brick, at a profit of 50 per cent., in small allotments. The reader must understand, that I do not impose this further condition of purchasing at twenty-five years' purchase property which is leased to him for ever, because it is already a stipulation in our rules, the difference being, that upon the winding up of a section, the profits arising from this department would be divided amongst the members in the one case, but would go to the government, and necessarily to the country, in the other case. I say, necessarily to the country, for this most simple of all reasons, because, under my auspices, the government of this country is as sure to fall into the hands of the industrious classes, as night is sure to follow day, while the management of the plan being accepted by the government, would have the simple effect of hastening this desirable object.

Thus I show you that government, upon the sixty millions expended, would receive a further profit of 25 per cent. upon the purchase of allotments by occupants, or a further sum of fifteen millions upon the purchase of the several allotments by the several occupants. I have asserted over and over again, and I now repeat it and defy contradiction, that every man of common industry, located upon as much land, at a fair rent, as he can cultivate beneficially by his own labour, will support his family well, and buy the fee simple of his allotment in less than five years; but I will presume that the process of purchase under the more favourable prospects presented by government management would take even ten years to wind up, and then I will show you how the government would stand. The government would have paid sixty millions for purchase, and would have received two millions six hundred thousand bonus from members, fifteen millions profit upon the sale of allotments, and about twenty-five millions seven hundred thousand by the consolidation of the nine hundred thousand a year, made upon the one-and-a-half per cent., the amount charged in rent over and above the three-and-a-half per cent. for which the government was liable. Hence, if not an allotment was sold, the government, by funding the nine hundred thousand a year profit, would realise a capital of twenty-five millions seven hundred thousand pounds, and a further capital of two millions six hundred thousand pounds, making a profit of twenty-eight millions three hundred thousand pounds, and by the sale of the allotments would make a further profit of fifteen millions, making a total profit of forty-three millions three hundred thousand pounds, the original sixty millions borrowed from capitalists being paid off by the sale of the several estates to the several occupants, at the low rate of twenty-five years' purchase. Hence, upon the winding up of the larger transaction, that is, the location and purchase of three-hundred

back their sixty millions,. the government would have re-
'ceived a profit of forty-three millions three hundred thousand pounds, and England would have a national militia of
'one million five hundred thousand soldiers, as the men
would fire, the women would scratch, and the children
would bite the invader that attempted to attack the home-
'stead; I estimate each family at five.

Now, to realise less than I propose to realise myself,
'namely, the location of a hundred thousand, the only
difference in the figure would be this, that the Chancellor of
'the Exchequer would receive a trifle less than the third of
the two millions six hundred thousand, paid by members as
entrance money, because, under government patronage, I
would propose to double the amount of shares as a tax upon
the want of popular confidence; but, even upon the hundred thousand members enrolled upon the present terms,
the government would receive nearly , a third of . the
£43,300,000, or something over fourteen millions, upon the
winding up of the affairs even of the fustian jackets, the
blistered hands, and unshorn chins.

My readers will understand, that all my life I have been
teaching the people what they are capable of doing for
themselves without government aid, and, seeing the
imperfections of our system, I have been labouring incessantly to bring that system and its supporters into
disrepute, and therefore, complicated and elaborate as this
treatise may at first appear, when taken as a whole it will
be viewed as the superstructure of that national system
which some government or other will be bound to adopt
and carry out as the only means of satisfying the appetite
of the age.

If I had confined myself to the mere exulting shout of
"the Charter and Liberty for ever," the public mind would
not by this time have reached the exalted position. it now
occupies, and therefore, while the idle gentlemen, who are
too proud to work and too poor to live without labour,
were boasting of their heroic devotion to the glorious cause
of liberty, I was silently and unnoticed sapping the walls of
corruption. Although the people were unconscious of it, I
was leading them from madness to sanity; whereas, if I had,
coward-like, refused to take my full share of that medicine,
administered by the government to the insane of that day,
I might have been justly looked upon as a quack, creating
delirium that I might traffic in the malady; but I thank God I
have received copious draughts of the government elixir, which
has given the people an amount of confidence in me that no

Of course, I have not made a table of the increased consumption under increased conveniencies of every description of article which gives profit to government, profit to commerce, profit to manufactures, profit to trade, and profit to industry; but, if I were to estimate the increased consumption of those three hundred thousand husbandmen and their families in every department of traffic, by ten pounds a family, or two pounds a head, it would give the ocean skimmers and the new world seekers for customers, an amount of certain trade at home, larger than the whole continent of America has furnished, does furnish, or is likely again to furnish, and without risk of hostile or ruinous exchanges, of being cut off by war, or sacrificed to over production; while, upon the other hand, those industrious husbandmen would create, as a fair medium of exchange, the most valuable of all commodities, for the importation of which, consequent upon an imperfect state of agriculture, England is now compelled to bend her head to every petty state of Europe, lest a just and honourable intervention should insure the jealousy of some rival corn growing country.

I think I hear the artificial visionary, some Baptist Noel, or John Bright, inspired with a magnanimous affection for the yet unborn, exclaiming, "What! thus allocate one million acres of British land to three hundred thousand of the present generation, regardless of the fate, of the condition, or comfort, of generations yet unborn!" To such philosophers I answer, firstly, in the words of Holy writ, "Sufficient unto the day is the evil thereof," and "Let men be wise in their own generation." The curse of England has been the expectant policy of her ministers, who have ever juggled the living by pretending to mitigate their sufferings by sharing them with posterity; while one of the greatest oppressions of the church is, the hypocritical pretext of acting rigidly as trustees for successors. But if I am compelled, by the ignorance of the short-sighted, to furnish a more direct and natural argument, my answer is, that no child born within the next century will ever live to a sufficiently old age to see the subdivision of the lands of England, Ireland, and Scotland carried to an extent that would be injurious to the living generation; but on the contrary, the more the principle is extended, the more will the whole of the national resources be cultivated, the more will the kind and generous feelings of man be developed, and the more will his grosser passions and evil propensities be controlled, as in my conquence I believe, virtue, unalloyed virtue, is the natural characteristic of man; while cunning, hypocrisy and vice, are the evils engendered, fostered, propagated and encouraged by a corrupt, a selfish, unjust and monopolising system.

Can I possibly use a better illustration of the effect of injustice upon man's character, than the insertion of the following lines, this moment received from an Ashton correspondent?

> " If I'm designed you rich man's slave—
> By nature's law designed—
> Why was an independent wish
> E'er planted in my mind?
> If not, why am I subject to
> His cruelty or scorn?
> Or why has man the will or power
> To make his fellow mourn?"

I shall conclude this chapter with a few brief observations upon the collateral, but not unimportant advantages that government would derive from the project.

FIRSTLY.—It would save all the items which may be classed under the head of Education Grants.

SECONDLY.—It would relieve the government from the dangers of an overstocked pauper market.

THIRDLY.—It would enable the government to relieve itself of the major portion of the police tax, and,

LASTLY, but not least, it would make it independent of a Russian loan, of foreign aid, of Bank toleration, or of the caprice of the capitalists, ever measured by government necessity; while, upon the other hand, before I would consent to invest the Company's prospects and money in the hands of the government, I would contend for the addition of a minister of Agriculture and Public Instruction to the Cabinet, and that every single benefit guaranteed to the members by our rules should be guaranteed by the government—that is by Act of Parliament; and still further, as my object ever has been to make the plan national, and to secure as little delay as possible between full payment of the share money and location of the member, I would stipulate that the mode of selection by ballot should be altogether done away with; that the Company should consist of but one section, and that whenever a certain number, three or five thousand, or five hundred, had paid up, that then that number should be at once located, and, upon location, that each member should receive a conveyance of his allotment for ever, upon condition to pay the stipulated amount of rent, and with the power reserved to him, at any time, to redeem his land in fee by the payment of the stipulated purchase money, or, by instalments of not less that £10, to reduce his rent by the standard of twenty-five years' purchase. Thus, every industrious man would have an opportunity of purchasing his allotment, in fee, because the government would not have the power to sell to any purchaser but the occupant, and would not be compelled to mortgage, and upon the redemption of each allotment, the government should be compelled to relieve it of that portion of the nine hundred thousand pounds profit rent, to which I referred as being funded, but which the government might more conveniently reserve for an annual income; and, in case the nationality and extension of the plan led to the inclosure of race courses and common land, I would stipulate that all such property should go, not to the members only, but that it should constitute a labour fund for the unwilling idlers, who should have the option of becoming agricultural labourers for their own benefit, or, if operatives, mechanics, or tradesmen, should be furnished with the raw material out of the proceeds of the national property, to carry on their several trades upon the principle of the poor laws of the 43rd of Elizabeth.

Now, throughout, the reader must bear the one prominent fact and object in view; namely, that my desire is to give to every willing labourer, of whatsoever calling, the opportunity of enjoying the full and undivided fruits of his own industry, and to make willing idleness a crime; and I should much like to see the minister who acquiesced in this project, defeated by the House in carrying the arrangements necessary for its operation, go back again to the country upon the simple question of

ENGLAND FOR THE ENGLISH
AND
IRELAND FOR THE IRISH.

I think the result of such a contest would be at least one hundred Irish members, with so large an English majority, as, backed by English intelligence, would shake the citadel of corruption to its very centre, and paralyse the nerves of all factious opposition. But as it is my intention to make a tour of England, Scotland, and Wales, upon my return, for the express purpose of instructing myself as to the state and new growth of Chartism, and personally to inform myself upon the state of public opinion upon this subject, until then, I shall abstain from further comment upon the advantages likely to accrue from the proposed course; merely announcing, that as the founder of this plan I will be in every way guided by a large and unmistakable majority of the members, and will not commit my child, now becoming a giant, to any foster-father, nurse, or protector, in whom a majority of those who have an interest in its growth and health cannot have entire, implicit, and undivided confidence; guarding them against the supposition, that, if protection was guaranteed by Act of Parliament, and the fulfilment of the conditions set forth in our rules also guaranteed, that any government, no matter what its principles might be, could violate those conditions, or any one of them, any more than that government could now refuse to pay fundholders their dividends, soldiers their pay, or judges their salaries. In fact, that even after the consent of the government to accept the management of the Company, that a Conference, chosen by all the members of the Company, should sit in London for a month, if necessary, to deliberate upon the Act of Parliament by which government would be bound, and my suggestion would be, that the vote of three-fourths of that Conference should be required to acquiesce in the proposed plan. Surely, then, if the advantages to be derived from the further extension of the plan, from the fact that all timber, bricks, and building materials used for the benefit of the Company would be free of duty; that the protection derived from Act of Parliament against the possibility of litigation; the exemption from all stamp duties; the cheaper terms upon which government can buy land, and perform all the required work, and the rapidity with which operations would progress; if all these advantages are taken into consideration, it must be admitted, that the Land Plan would be then national, instead of sectional, the great object which I have always had in view; and above and before all other considerations it must be admitted, that I have discharged my trust faithfully and honestly, especially when it is understood, that, setting my face against patronage, I hereby renounce any payment from the Company, or from government, from neither of whom will I ever accept of place, pension, or emolument, of fee, favour, or reward, for labour or service performed for the people, for their social or political redemption; while, discharged of all pecuniary responsibility, and acting as unpaid bailiff under the government, that is, such a government as the people would then have, I would have fifty-fold the inducement and none of the annoyances, that I now have, while I could make myself a thousand times more useful. But you will always bear in mind the GREAT FACT tha is the astounding effect that our Land Plan must have upon the government of the country; and the certainty, the inevitable certainty, that a representation of the principles that it enunciates will lead—must lead—to the social and political redemption of the ·working-classes of this country.

I have ever thought, and still think, that the selfishness of leaders is the one great barrier that stands between the people and their rights; and I trust that I shall be acquitted of this crying sin when I thus offer to surrender an amount of power which no man in the world ever before possessed, for, to me, the largest amount of payment that the world can afford—the payment of happiness, pride, consolation, and comfort of having, by my own ingenuity, energy, courage and honesty, redeemed a faithful, confiding, and industrious people from penury, degradation, and want, and placed them upon their own resources—having given them a sufficient amount of intelligence and power to throw the idle, who have lived upon their ignorance and disunion, upon THEIR OWN RESOURCES. And now, to wind up this chapter, I will sum up in a word the principal motive which induces me to seek this protection for the Company and myself. It will be found, then, in the fact, that the amount of patronage which this extensive concern is calculated to bestow upon me, and my resolution that not a fraction of the people's money shall go in that direction, will inevitably bring me into unenviable contact with many zealous and ardent agitators, in whose spleen and envy would be found their justification for abuse of the whole system, and whose sharpness, though not worth a pin practically, would then be enlisted on behalf of a popular measure, which it would be useless and unprofitable to assail; in short, my every thought, my whole thought, is centred in the exulting pride I shall feel when the Land Plan is secured against the credulity of the weak, the cunning of the artful, the venom of the jealous, and the folly of the theorist.

CHAP. III.

Perhaps one of the most remarkable circumstances connected with the Land Plan, is the unsparing abuse it has received from the brainless hirelings who conduct the press of this country; creatures, who are ready to prostitute themselves to any faction or party able and willing to pay them the price of their prostitution; creatures, who will advocate railways, navigation bills, building societies, benefit societies anti-slaver societies education societies draina e and health of towns' societies, early shop-closing societies, poor men's guardian societies, and old women's societies, or any societies, however absurd, if they can but secure the advertisements of those societies ; and from my soul I believe, that the spleen of the press to our great national society—our Britain redemption society—will be found in the fact, that the funds have been devoted to a better and a holier purpose than to the seduction of the press. And yet, strange to say, this painted old bawd, this enervated and exhausted old harridan, has been obliged to confess the advantages to be derived from the Land Plan as a foundation for its argument, that the promised benefits must be protracted to an almost indefinite period.

In the first instance, these miserable, brainless opponents talked about the impossibility of a man supporting himself and his family upon the fruits of his every day industry throughout the year, until I drove them from this position by the announcement of the plain and simple fact, that, if others lived and fared sumptuously upon their slave labour, while they pined and starved, and wasted and withered under the lash of capitalists, and the harsh dominion of capital, it was natural to presume that they could have sustained themselves upon their free labour.

Driven from this position, the slave writers, the fettered hacks, began to talk of the danger of the squatting system, and this objection was a mouthful of comfort until I showed to them, and proved to you, that such was the monopoly of the aristocracy of all classes, that society would stand in no danger from the squatting system for yet a thousand years to come.

THE HONEST ADVOCATES, thus driven from their second position, then began to mouth about the possibility, but dared not urge the probability, of my deceiving, cheating, and plundering the people. Driven from this position by your confidence, they were obliged to assume the doctrine of chances, and to talk about my demise. As to the prospect of my deceiving the people, or wronging the people, it is as unlikely, and the people know it, as that the sun should change its course, or that the tide should cease to flow. And as to the prospect of my death, though professing legal knowledge, the scribblers were not aware, or if aware, would not put you in possession of the fact, that if a hundred millions worth of property was vested in me, and not raised or contributed for a special purpose, but was my own property, I could, by simple deed or will, convey that property to trustees for the intent and purpose for which it was raised, with as much security, and greater facility, than it can be done by enrolment, registration, or Act of Parliament. The simple arguments with which I have driven the assailants of the project from their several positions has led them to a calculation as to the time it will require to locate a section; and supposing, and naturally, that the working-classes are anxious to avail themselves of this mighty project for their redemption, they place the promised fruit at a distance from their reach, in the hope of dissuading them from becoming participants themselves, or aiders of others in the great design.

With this view, several arithmeticians have puzzled their pates with figures, until it was impossible for the cleverest man living to understand their premises or their conclusions; but I will now place this branch of the subject so simply before you, that each member will be furnished with a ready answer for each arithmetician. I will take a section, numbering 6,000, and I will presume the paid-up capital of that section to average £4 a member, or £24,000 in the aggregate. Those £24,000, presuming that it would take £200 to locate a member, would locate no more than 120 occupants. Those 120 occupants, upon that amount expended at £5 per cent. would pay £1,200 per annum, and the arithmeticians, forgetful of the principle of reproduction, presume that with this location the Company's operations cease, while I invite you to take this view of the subject:—the Company receives £1,200 a year as interest, in the shape of rent, upon the £24,000 expended, and the Company, at 4 per cent., (an amount of interest not guaranteed by any Bank in the world, and with the security not guaranteed by the Bank of England, or by the government itself,) can raise £24,000, its original capital, paying £960 of the rental of £1200 a year, thus leaving the company a profit of £240 a year, or one per cent. upon the whole capital, arising out of rent not guaranteed or secured upon the mere purchase money of the land, but upon the labour of the occupant and his family as well. I may be answered, that our rent is capricious; but my reply is, that there is nothing on earth so solid. I may be told, that our rent is capricious; but I answer, that if it was double the amount, three times the amount, or four times the amount, that not a man who has tasted the sweets of free labour, free home, and a free life, would become a defaulter during the whole of life.

Again, it must be understood, that this Land Plan is not a partial labour question, but a whole labour question, and it must be understood, that those who are anxious to assist their brother labourers must be enlisted in the plan as well, by confidence as by interest, and that to the Bank we look for the reproductive principle; that is, that when we expend £24,000 in the purchase of land, and the erection of buildings, and the licence of labourers to receive the full profits upon their own industry; that in such case, the labouring classes having monies invested in the savings' banks, at a paltry interest of £2. 18s. per cent., will, from interest, and from devotion to their own principles and class, prefer vesting that money at an interest of four per cent. upon the security of land, house and labour, to investing it in any other description of security. Thus, the moment we expend £24,000 in these operations we have a right to calculate upon the return of that £24,000 in the shape of bank deposits, and so on, according to the extent of the subscribed capital, there can be no impediment or hindrance to the further purchase, the further location, the further raising of capital upon the further rental: thus, upon each £24,000 expended, leaving the Company a sinking fund of £240 per annum, or one per cent. in rent over and above the four per cent., payable as interest.

But, I would go further, and take it out of the caprice of the banking system altogether, and I would assert without fear of contradiction, that when the plan is sufficiently developed, the Company could raise upon mortgage of land, house and improvements, the whole amount expended. For instance, the estate of Lowbands has already been increased in value by nearly £1,000 in labour and capital expended by the occupants; and while the occupants would not be liable to a purchaser, mortgagee, or depositor, for more than the stipulated rent, yet every man understands, that a property worth £600 a year rent, and increased to £800 a year by the expenditure of labour and capital, will be a better security than the property in its original state, worth £600 a year.

There is another question, and a very important question too, which is, the amount of money now placed, and according as profits come is likely to be increased, in the Redemption Department. Upon this department the company makes a profit of one-half per cent., and it immediately becomes reproductive, and at once applicable to the location of other members; so that, in point of fact, as I have often stated, as far as the success of the company, and the rapid location of occupants depends, I would prefer the loan of a million of money, at four per cent. to a paid-up capital of £400,000, for which I paid no interest whatever.

If this reproductive principle were to be argued in favour of a fool our correspondent, A. B., must be, to doubt the security of Mr. Mortar, the most respectable builder, and a man of the highest character and integrity; true, Mr. Mortar may not start in business with a large capital, but he has that which is preferable to capital to sustain him, integrity and a good conscience; but, independently of that most valuable of all securities, cannot our correspondent understand, that when Mr. Mortar has expended £1,000 in building operations, that his own labour, ingenuity and skill leads to the legitimate presumption, that capitalists, of which there are no lack, will advance the amount expended by Mr. Mortar, receiving his ingenuity, labour and skill as the best of all collateral securities, and thus our correspondent might have understood, that, upon this £1,000 capital, Mr. Mortar may erect a city, and leave ample security to all who assisted him in his praiseworthy undertaking, besides a handsome remuneration for his own ingenuity, labour and skill."

Now such would be a newspaper puff for Mr. Mortar the builder, who ventured a thousand pounds capital in speculation upon other men's labour, but for this puff Mr. Mortar would also pay out of the proceeds derived from his ingenuity, labour and skill, or, what is more likely, out of some poor slaves' labour. Now, my friends, I will lay down this simple fact for you. In the first instance of our experiment, it took me nearly a year to build 35 houses. In the second instance, I built 45 houses in little more than three months, and now I am engaged in building 100 houses, and which I hope to perfect within a shorter period than three months; and when our plan is sufficiently understood to enable me to proceed with a thousand houses, instead of a hundred, I will find less difficulty and much, greater economy in building that number than in building a hundred. I mention this fact to disarm the brawlers of the argument, that it will take such a time, and such a time, to admit of the principle of reproduction, that is, to complete one location and, apply myself to another. Those persons who argue about the time it will take to locate a section are hired to write, or they write because I nipped them of their anticipated patronage and anticipated plunder. But yet, see how this plan does go on in spite of all their machinations, and now, mark the facility with which I can raise a large amount of money, independently of the Bank. I will illustrate this by the nature of the five estates I have purchased. Upon Herringsgate, 1 might have allowed a large portion of the money to remain on mortgage. On to the amount of over £7,000. Upon Snig's End there is a mortgage of £7,000, payment of which the mortgagee will not accept of, and at £4·per cent, so there is a loan of £7,000. Upon Minster Lovel there is a mortgage of £5,000, which is to stand for seven years—there's a loan of £5,000. On Mathon, there is an annuity payable to an old lady, and by that annuity we become our own insurers and get a loan of nearly £3,000, so that upon those three last purchased estates, there is a loan without a farthing expense in raising it of £15,000, precisely the same as if it came through the bank, with this exception indeed, that it costs not a farthing expense, requires no trouble, and cannot be called in without due notice of six months.

Now, if I had not intended to make this plan a stepping stone to the achievement of political as well as social rights, I could have located a hundred thousand people with as great facility as I could now locate one thousand, thus—I could take a long lease of farms that were to be let to any extent, improve those farms by the addition of a cottage to every two, three and four acres, and then raise money by way of mortgage on the improvements; but then such holdings, for however long a term, would not confer the franchise, and although they might extend over a period of ninety-nine years, yet the father, and the mother too, would calculate upon the sad day of reckoning, when the idle capitalist would absorb the fruits of their industry, of their children's industry, and of their grand-children's industry, and the holding would lose that charm which ever belongs to MY OWN FOR EVER.

But if ever the labouring classes of this country shall be satisfied with such a tenure as a lease for years, I would very speedily put them in possession of a large part of the kingdom, as every landlord who wanted to sell would lease his land to us, for the mere purpose of enhancing its value, by the erection of houses and the expenditure of labour, which would one day become the property of the descendants of the purchaser. I think I have now shown you that the aid of the Bank alone would be sufficient to locate, in rapid succession, as many thousands as chose to become members of our Company; while I have also shown you, that, without the Bank, the additional value given to the land by the expenditure of labour and capital, would by mortgage (if we were driven to that alternative) enable us so to reproduce as to locate all our members; while I have further shown the disinclination of parties now having mortgages upon land to allow them to be paid off.

the press in the case of railway speculations, building speculations, insurance speculations, mining speculations, steam
navigation speculations, liquid manure conveying speculations, benefit societies speculations, and the thousand and one
bubble speculations, not one single one of which has the slightest
foundation or permanency beyond the amount of confidence
that the press can enlist in their behalf? and if this Land
speculation had been adopted by money-mongers in the City,
and the certainty of four per cent. secured upon land, instead
of five per cent. upon land and labour, the waters of the
Stock Exchange would have been convulsed by the diving
of the sharks, each contending for the first plunge; and, long
ere this, the shares would have been at a premium of 200 '
per cent.; but the solution of the riddle will be found in this
fact—THIS IS THE SPECULATION OF THE
PEOPLE.

CHAPTER IV.

The produce of the land is the thing, the only thing in
nature, which gives value to gold itself, and value to every
other commodity that is purchased with gold.

The land is the only raw material upon which permanent
and unchangeable security can be given. No man will lend
his money upon mortgage secured upon cotton, upon wool,
upon cows, upon horses, or cloth.

The land is the only commodity that sells in the market
with something like regularity of price.

The land is the only raw material out of which the
husbandman can coin that exchangeable medium which he
can barter for every necessary of life and every luxury.

The land is the only raw material, by the working of
which the real value of labour can be ascertained.

The land is the only source from whence man can draw
every article of consumption and every article in use.

When a man sits down to his breakfast, every thing in the
room, every thing on the table, the table itself, and the room
itself, is produced from the land.

When a man rises from his bed, he should understand
that the bed, the bedstead, the furniture, sheets, blankets,
counterpane, and everything in the room is produced from
the land.

When a man dresses himself, he should understand that
every stitch upon his back, and every particle in which he
is clothed, is produced by the land. If he reads, he should
understand that the paper, ink, and covers, are all produced
by the land. If he drinks, he should understand that the

smokes, the pipe and tobacco are the produce of the land. So that, in short, every thing useful, every thing usable, and every thing exchangeable, comes from the land; and, therefore, the land is the MINT OF LABOUR, from which the moneyer coins his livelihood.

The land has ever given distinction to class, because its possession was considered to carry with it a superiority over the possession of any other commodity, varying in price and fluctuating in value, in consequence of the capriciousness of its use. But not so with land. In China, princes hold their titles not by the amount of blood their ancestors have shed, or the amount of plunder they have committed, but upon the condition that upon a certain day in the year they shall hold the plough and cultivate the land.

In France, a population of thirty-five millions is more satisfied with the representation springing from two hundred thousand electors, than England's population of thirteen million is with a representation springing from a million of electors; and simply because the land of France is sub-divided and cultivated by small farmers.

When walking in the domain of my exiled uncle, which once belonged to the Mirabeaus, I have seen the peasant walking through my uncle's meadows and fields, with his basket and his spade, and his children after him; I have seen him turn into his acre or half acre, in the middle of that domain, and which belonged to himself, and my uncle has told me that men of that class would not take ten times the market price for their spot of land, because they knew the value of it.

Saxony is a country of whose revolutions and emeutes we never hear, because the King is a wise man, and has compelled the aristocracy to sell their land at the market price, for the use of those who were willing to cultivate it. The King of Saxony, knowing that the possession of the land alone could confer security upon the throne and comfort upon the subject, issued a commission to value the estates in his dominions—the aristocracy imagined that the object was to subject them to a graduated scale of taxation, and the King allowed them to furnish their own estimate of the value, and at that price he compelled them to sell the amount required for the employment of the people.

In Belgium, a labouring man will stint himself half his life to make wherewithal to build his nest, from whence no bird of prey can drive him, and to purchase a labour field where he can secure a market for his industry; and for that land, although in some instances at a distance of two miles

instances, £500 per acre.　He first rents it at a rent of
£6, £7, £8, or £9, an acre; and then, by the fruits of his
own industry, he becomes the proprietor, and is happy.
But I venture to prophecy, that the new rage for manufactures will, ere long, place the agricultural population of
Belgium at the mercy of speculators, and hand her industrious
sons over to the tender mercy of a poor law Bastile.　The
manufacturers of Belgium will kidnap, buy, or steal, the
agricultural population of Belgium, as the English manufacturers kidnapped, bought, or stole, the agricultural
population of England.

And in all those countries, whatever amount of rent
the husbandman pays, he is the most happy, most
cheerful, most healthy, most innocent, most moral, and most
independent, of all classes.　Can any man tell me, then,
what there is in the nature of an Englishman, in the character of an Englishman, in the love of independence of an
Englishman, or in the quality of the English soil, which
would render England and the English less valuable for
agricultural pursuits than the land or the people of any
other country? or in point of political economy, in which
they have been abundantly instructed by the professors of
that science of late, have the English people discovered the
greater advantage to be derived from capricious labour and
from slave labour, than from continuous labour and free
labour? Or, have I again to remind them, that the landlord's
rents, the parson's tithes, the tax-gatherer's demands, the
farmer's profits, the blacksmith's profits, the wheelwright's
profits, the tradesman's profits, and the shopkeeper's profits,
are one and all derived from the profit made upon labour?
Need I remind the slave labourer, that the employer may
measure his wages by the standard of his own cupidity, his
own avarice and daring, and that with the proceeds of this
slave labour he is obliged to go without what he himself produces, while he is obliged to purchase the produce of the
land at that capricious retail price which the producer or
monopolist and forestaller may please to demand for it; that
he is obliged to purchase all of the worst quality, at the
highest price, and to the greatest disadvantage, being compelled to deal at the truck shop of the master, or to pay a
tax of 25 per cent. for credit to the shopkeeper; while if he
was even paid in the produce of his own labour, he could
not exchange it beneficially, because it is upon the wholesale principle, and on the aggregate of the labour of
thousands, that the capitalist makes his profit.　And even
beyond that he is obliged so to demean himself as to insure
f h　　　at la　driver: he has no house

that he can call his own, he has no resting place whereon to lay his addled head and aching limbs; he has a partner whom he calls his wife, but whose interests are too often at variance; he has children, ay, daughters, who become lodgers in his own house; he cannot calculate upon any certainty; he lives from hand to mouth, he gains credit upon the presumption that his labour will continue; he may rent his house by the year, and make his domestic arrangements upon the calculation of permanent employment, and upon Saturday night the will of his employer may constitute him unwillingly a defaulting tenant and a debtor, unable to meet the demands of the shopkeeper.

Still, though unemployed, the rent goes on, and if he is to live food must be provided; and if, in his unwilling idleness, he is ready to confederate with his fellows to resist or overthrow this unnatural state, he is tried as a conspirator, bludgeoned as a rioter, or shot as a rebel. Such is the real picture of the condition of an artificial slave? But, mark how different the condition of the free labourer, and above all of the free labourer who is tenant of the Land Company. That man is rescued from the caprice of the capitalists and the slave drivers; from the uncertainty of employment, from the casualties of trade, from the unearthly cellar or tottering garret, from the monopoly of the retailer and the mercy of the shopkeeper, from the gin palace and the beer shop, from disease to health, from the man-made town to the God-made country. And, although the economist who professes to write the *Morning Chronicle* laughs at the idea of man being his own producer, the free labourer can, nevertheless, produce what will exchange for every commodity in the world, and need not surfeit foreigners, or overstock foreign countries, with the surplus of his produce, while he himself is starving; because, if he has a surplus pig, a surplus quarter of wheat, or a surplus cow, he'll be sure to have a surplus pair of breeches, while probably the man who made them may be without a pair to his back, while his surplus of necessaries may give the artificial slave a better chance of procuring them, free from the caprice of foreign speculators and monopolists.

Again, let this simple fact be borne in mind. Let us take even a less average of wages than that stated by John Bright to be earned by operatives, and let us presume that those operatives would now be but too happy to be insured four full days' work in the week. If we estimate the slaves' earnings, then, at 2s. 6d. a day, out of which is stopped a large portion for " batings," " usages" and " fines;" and if he is idle two days in the week, he is defrauded of five shillings a week, and has to pay rent for the week, and to live for the week, and to clothe his family and buy fuel for the week, out of the four days' earnings; and then let the landman reflect upon this startling fact, upon this irrefutable fact—that 5s. a week is £13 a year, and that the rent of four acres, of a house, with convenient rooms and splendid outbuildings, and interest upon £30 capital, will not altogether amount to as much as the loss of the two days' labour to the artificial slave. And would not those of Lancashire and Yorkshire, of Nottinghamshire and Derbyshire, be now rejoiced, ay, to madness, at the announcement that they should be insured four full days' work in the week? Would not tailors, would not shoemakers and hatters, leap for very joy at such an announcement?

The four-acre allotments here, at Minster Lovel, will average less than £12 a year with interest of capital and all; and now let this arithmetical fact, this indisputable fact, be engraved upon every operative's memory, that the occupants of the Land Company pay less rent for four acres of good land, a beautiful cottage, and outbuildings, and £30 capital, than the operative pays for the loss of two days' labour in the week. Now will not every man impress that fact upon the mind of his simple neighbour, and will it not force itself upon the consideration of the farmer and the shopkeeper, who, as a consequence, will be compelled to pay an additional amount of poor rates.

After this irrefutable fact, I shall not further compare the condition of a free-labourer with that of an artificial labourer, but I will compare the condition of a free-labourer, located according to the rules of the Land Company, with the same class of small proprietors in other countries. Here, then, is the difference.

A Belgian occupant, a Swiss occupant, a Prussian occupant, and a French occupant, in general lives at a distance of a mile, and sometimes three miles, from his allotment, and in every one of these countries, I have seen two children yoked to a wheelbarrow, drawing dung a mile; while, upon the contrary, a Land Company's occupant lives in the centre of his allotment, and saves from two to six miles a day of a walk. In France, the small farmers, for the most part, live in villages, as was the custom in Ireland in the time of the Danes, and to a more recent period, when the people there also lived in towns, and hence the denomination of land called town's-land; but the allotments most generally lay at a considerable distance from the town.

Again, the rent or purchase paid by an English occupant, will not average one-fourth of that paid by the generality of foreigners. Again, the English occupant is in the very market, that others send their produce three thousand miles to; but, above and before all, the English occupant's spare labour, at the periods of the year when its sale is most profitable, commands a higher price in England than in any other country. For instance, as I have frequently asserted, a man and his family may receive for hired labour as much, during hay-time and harvest, as will pay the whole rent of a four-acre allotment, leaving him about forty-two weeks in the year, allowing ten weeks for hay-time and harvest, to cultivate his own land, and the whole of the produce for his own consumption. And the tradesman should understand, that there is a shorter apprenticeship required for agricultural labour than any other craft, and that, according to an old Irish saying, "Every woman is a good man in harvest," when farmers want men, and men, women, and children can make hay. Such, then, are the social and pecuniary advantages which the English occupant would have over the foreign occupant, while, in a political point of view, his holding confers the franchise, as well as parochial and local rights, which it would not in any other country. And though last, not least, it places him within view of that school-house where his children are to receive an education that will teach them how to defend the rights that their father purchased for them.

Then there are advantages which cannot be at all estimated, and which, if taken in the aggregate, would secure another saving of five shillings a week, of which the artificial labourer cannot avail himself; for instance, last week, the occupants at Lowbands co-operated and bought forty tons of coals, and had them delivered at six shillings a ton under the price that I was in the habit of paying for a single ton. They bought a large quantity of flour at eight shillings and sixpence a bushel, for which retail, and of a worse quality and poorer weight, they should have paid twelve shillings a bushel, and so they will co-operate for everything else; for, taking them for all in all, there never was a better or more industrious set of fellows.

Now, I will mention a fact, a fact that will startle you by its very repetition, although I have often mentioned it before. It is this, that an occupant living in the centre of this estate, which is a fair criterion, will put out more manure with a wheelbarrow and a boy, than the farmer who lived here before me could put out with six horses and six men; and those living at the extremity of the land would perform more of the same work in the same way, than a farmer would do with ten horses and ten men. Now then, take the average and put down the six horses at five shillings a horse, thirty shillings; and six men at two shillings a man, twelve shillings; total, forty-two shillings. And not to say a word about wear and tear, and loss on horseflesh, I show you, that what costs an occupant three shillings, costs a farmer forty-two shillings, besides the cutting of his land, and the injury to the roads which he has to pay a tax to repair; and this is but a small farm for the district, being but three hundred acres, and, therefore, what must be the comparative disadvantage to a farmer cultivating a thousand acres. It is these farms, these unprofitable farms, that have led to the slavery of the English people, and there is nothing now to secure their redemption, but the subdivision of those farms into such allotments as will secure to the nation the largest amount of produce, and to all classes the smallest possible amount of pauper rate; and it is because I wish to see the thing done by magic, instead of by slow degrees, that I am ready and willing to surrender an amount of power, which in the hands of one man is too much, in order that it may be placed in the hands of those who would be compelled, in obedience to the laws of political economy, to cultivate the national resources to the greatest possible advantage for the greatest possible number.

A word of comment upon the blessings of this plan and I have done. It was established in April, 1845, by the few confiding spirits of Chartism, amid the jeers and scoffs of the ignorant, and now behold its giant strength, and wholly consequent upon the confidence vested in a foreigner, who has, by his own unremitting energy and industry, instructed a nation in a new science, from a knowledge of which their askmasters industriously excluded them. No man in England who is a member of this Company ever dared to aspire to the thought of one day being located upon his own land in his own castle, and yet the mock sentimentalists no sooner heard of this transition from absolute slavery to positive freedom, than they began for the first time to sympathise with those whose ignorance, dissipation, and unthriftiness they urged as a disqualification to the possession of political rights. These hypocrites had not the honesty to canvas and expose the plan, when exposure would have been justifiable, if their presumptions had been well founded; but, like Chartism, it took them by surprise, and jumped, with a sudden bound, over their heads and beyond their power of resistance. And what is a remarkable feature in the history of the Press is the fact, that, previous to the establishment of the Land Plan, the hirelings were loud in praise of the allotment system, which meant the gilded link of slavery, by which the serf was bound to the loved spot for which he dearly paid, and affection for which induced him to starve in quiescence rather than risk its loss by an appeal to charity. Then half a rood, the eighth of an acre, was a principality—now four acres is perfect starvation.

Did these quacks not know that a poor stockinger, or frame work knitter, would cheerfully grub and clear a piece of woodland of roots and stumps for the poor privilege of growing two crops upon it, and then restore it to the owner worth ten times the original value, improved by the poor man's labour?

Did England, or the world, ever before hear of, read of, or dare to think of, the assignment of comfortable cottages and outbuildings, with two, three, and four acres of land, to those who had'nt a foot of ground to call their own? And was ever the reward of mortal man so great as my reward, when I now see the sickly, puny, drooping slave, and his ill-treated wife and stunted children, with the smile of freedom in their countenances, the blush of health upon their cheeks, and the ste of soundness in their gait? and then talk to me about the delusion practised upon the thoughtless and the ignorant, when the whole of this gigantic, this national, and about to be universal project, has not, in puffing or printing, cost the members the fraction of a farthing.

Had I made merchandise of their necessities and their enthusiasm, as the Irish liberal press trafficked in the ignorance and enthusiasm of its votaries, my bill for advertising would be something like twenty guineas a week. But in spite of all, and though compelled to plod on, worming my way into still greater confidence, I will make this Land Plan socially, what I have made the Charter politically—a shield to the virtuous and a terror to the evil-doer. I have shown the ripe fruit over the garden wall, and it is now optional with the oligarchy and aristocracy of England, whether they open the gates to the willing purchaser, or see the wall tumbling before unwilling idlers. The world, and all the armed forces of the world, cannot now resist the Land Plan, as the English people are now too well versed in the science of political economy to believe in the advantage of depending upon foreigners for their food, while they work like slaves to produce what the foreigner may or may not purchase. The English people are now political economists to a man, and their political economy teaches them that self-preservation is the first law of nature, and that, in obedience to that law, they must be their own producers, in order that they may be assured and cheap consumers, and all the rubbish of the *Times* and the *Chronicle*, the *Daily News* and the *Globe*, the sun, moon, and stars, will never convince them of their error, and therefore it is as useless as it is hopeless to attempt to arrest the progress of the Land Plan; and the duty of all is, and the aim of all should be, so to direct it, as to make it the harbinger of peace, instead of the demon of revolution.

For myself, although I have never made professions of the sacrifices that I was prepared to make, I nevertheless solemnly, sincerely, and unhesitatingly declare, that I would rather live in a garret upon bread and water for the remainder of my days, than see the progress of the Land Plan impeded, or attempted to be forced onward by revolution; or, if necessary to secure its success, I would cheerfully risk my life against incalculable odds; but I never have boasted of what I was prepared to do for a people who were not prepared to help themselves, and who, if prepared, would not require any individual sacrifice. I now conclude my treatise upon the land in these words :—

I WILL DIE OR CONQUER.

CHAP. V.

THE BANK.

I fear the shortness of the space allowed me for the consideration of this subject, will compel me to take another opportunity of analysing the question more critically. Never-from the delay, inasmuch as I have already explained the whole system so minutely, in the *Northern Star* and *Labourer*, that the most ignorant could not fail to comprehend it; but thus it ever is, and ever will be, with people requiring repetition upon repetition of matter already fully explained. I the less regret my want of space just now, because in the *Star* of the 18th, in my reply to Messrs. Hibbs and Selsby, I have entered rather minutely into the advantages to be derived from, and the stability of, the National Land and Labour Bank.

As to its stability, it is the only bank in the world that offers landed security unincumbered to its customers; and as to its value in connection with the Land Plan, it is inestimable; indeed, its value may be estimated by the following fact. If a bank possessed sufficient confidence to insure the investment of any amount of money at an interest of four per cent. upon the best landed security, the proprietor of that bank might, without the slightest trouble, make two per cent. profit upon all the monies lodged—simply by the purchase of unincumbered estates, leased to occupants at a rent of £6 per cent. upon the outlay, and not a tenant would be a defaulter in twenty years; and if he was, the bank would not lose a fraction as others would be but too happy to clear the out-going tenant's arrears, and step into his shoes upon his conditions. Upon the other hand, a Land Bank, established for the purpose of buying and leasing estates as security to the depositors, would be a very unstable bank, inasmuch as the rents of large farms may fluctuate considerably, according to the price of grain, while the rent of the small occupant would be regulated by his ability to live upon it, and the security of the bank would be enhanced by the constant expenditure of his labour and the consequent improvement of the soil.

Messrs. Hibbs and Selsby have asked me, what security the Land and Labour Bank gives to depositors? I ask what security Sir Benjamin Heywood and Co., or any other private banker, gives to its depositors, beyond the security of confidence, while the National Land and Labour Bank gives the security of £5 a year for every £4 for which it is liable, and receives itself £4.11s.3s. as the interest upon Exchequer Bills, for its unappropriated capital. The security of the Land and Labour Bank is, that it does not issue notes which may be called in when its capital has been applied to the legitimate purpose for which it was intended—the purchase of Land. The security of the National Land and Labour Bank is, that its proprietor would not, and could not, speculate hazardously with the funds. Would not, because the wealth of the world would not compensate him for the loss of that confidence which is indispensable to the success of his project. Could not, because the open mouthed press, and the eaves-droppers upon 'Change, would very soon proclaim it to the world—that the demagogue was speculating in railway shares, in stocks, or in fascinating bubbles.

The National Land and Labour Bank is secure beyond all other banks, because a fictitious high rate of interest would not tempt the proprietor to discount the bills of s eculators in corn speculators in cotton, or speculators in railways, and thus jeopardise the property of its confiding dupes.

The National Land and Labour Bank is secure beyond all other banks, against the failure of Glasgow firms, Liverpool firms, Belfast firms, Mark-lane firms, London firms, and Dublin firms.

The National Land and Labour Bank is secure beyond all other firms, because the property which it guarantees to pay interest upon must be increased, and cannot be diminished in value.

' The National Land and Labour Bank is more advantageous to the small depositor than any other bank, because it gives a larger permanent amount of interest than any other bank.

The National Land and Labour Bank is more secure than any other bank, because its depositors are not only secured in £4 interest upon £5 of landed property, but they are further secured by the additional value given to land by labour, by the additional value given to the land by additional buildings and improvements made by the occupants themselves, and still more by the amount of money in the Redemption Fund, which the occupants cannot withdraw.

' The National Land and Labour Bank is more secure than any other bank, because its proprieter's name is not affixed to bill, bond, or note, to the amount of a guinea.

The National Land and Labour Bank is more secure than any other bank, or rather its insecurity can be more easily detected, inasmuch as its proprietor gratuitously and cheerfully undertakes to submit a statement of its condition, and to publish it, annually.

The National Land and Labour Bank is more secure than any other bank, because its expenses are less, and its profits more certain.

' The National Land and Labour Bank is more secure than any other bank, because the depositors cannot capriciously make a run upon it, and make it bankrupt with a surplus, but not immediately available, capital.

' The National Land and Labour Bank is more secure than any other bank, because its proprietor repudiates the bare notion of making the banker's profit upon the concern, because universal confidence reposed in him is dearer than the world's wealth.

And yet I did not, and would not, undertake to establish the Bank on my own responsibility, until I had received the clearest and most explicit opinion of the ablest counsel, that the Bank could only be safely established in the name of one individual, whereby the trustees could assign the landed property of the Company as security for the funds lent by the Bank to them, for the purpose of purchasing land. If a Company start a bank, they are entitled to divide the profits between them, and they are obliged to pay up a certain amount of money, in shares, before they can commence banking operations, and then they become licensed gamblers; whereas, an individual banker is not hampered by partners, does not, as

Messrs. Hibbs and Selsby suppose, require to have his bank registered, nor even to take out a license. He may rent a sentry-box, or a stall in the market place, and proclaim himself a banker.

I think I have now said enough to convince the most sceptical of the security of the Bank, and the advantages it offers to small capitalists, and I shall wind-up this treatise with the most simple and complete description of the banking operation. The Land Company, we'll say, is in receipt of 1,000*l.* a year in rents paid by occupants. The Company requires to raise a loan of 20,000*l.* upon that rental of 1,000*l.* a year, to enable it to make a further purchase, and, in order to raise that sum, the trustees of the Company hand over the 1,000*l.* a year as security for 800*l.* a year—four per cent. upon the 20,000*l.* invested by depositors. Now, what can be more simple, or what can be more understandable;—or what can be more bothering and ridiculous, foolish and nonsensical than to suppose, that what's done by all other classes every day in the year, and makes fortunes for them, cannot be done by the co-operation of the class upon whose industry and wealth all live in idleness and luxury? We have now, in land and property, what represents 4,000*l.* a year at 5*l.* per cent.—that is 80,000*l.* I am the banker, that property is now vested in me for the benefit of the Company, and as soon as the Company is completely registered, the property to that amount will be conveyed to the trustees, liable, as security, to the depositors in the National Land and Labour Bank ; as the poor who have confided in me may rest assured that I will deal equal justice to the occupant who has land, and the depositor who enabled him to get the land. And in conclusion, I will only add that all my own spare funds go into the bank, without interest, and if I had a million to invest, and a banker that I could confide in, I would cheerfully entrust it to the safe keeping of an establishment, which could not lose it by traffic, diminish it by speculation, risk it in speculation, or risk it on what is whimsically called commercial traffic. I have now done. I have finished my treatise, with an assurance, that all who entrust their monies to the National Land and Labour Bank shall punctually receive four per cent. for the capital, and the principal undiminished whenever they require it, according to the conditions on which it is lodged ; and that the world shall have an annual opportunity of seeing how an unpaid banker, and an unpaid bailiff, can perform cheerful service for an oppressed and confiding people.

Your faithful friend and representative,

FEARGUS O'CONNOR.

Minster Lovel, Oxfordshire.

Sept. 23, 1847.

DEATH PUNISHMENT.

BY HENRY GRACCHUS.

What art thou, Death, that men provoke thy rage,
And sanction murder in this iron age ?
Did not the Ruler of this world decree,
That all his creatures should submit to thee ?
Who dare resist thee ? who thy will control ?
Thy boundless empire goes from pole to pole.
Oh ! ruthless tyrant, who can understand,
As none escape thee, why some dare command
Thy scythe, that gathers in one common urn
The dust of life that never shall return ?
This is the crime that I so much deplore,
When men dare take what they cannot restore.

Awake, my muse, our task to-day shall be
To spurn the crime that shames humanity :
To ask despotic man, why he pretends
To murder others for peculiar ends :
Crime heals not crime, injustice cures no wrong ;
Man's life and death to God alone belong.
No prince on earth, whatever legists say,
Confers the right to take man's life away :
God—only God,—who, in his mercy, gave
A life to man, may life destroy or save ;
Might is not right, this all men must allow ;
Who first shed blood, then murder'd, just as now.

Come, righteous muse, let us with care proceed,
To view the horrors of this awful deed ;
Let us all tyrants, all the world defy,
Condemn the crime that none can justify :
Truth shall direct, while reason we employ,
To shield the wretch his fellow-men destroy.

'Tis time to wrest from tyranny's red hand
The bloody axe, the halter, and the brand :

K

No more these symbols shall the earth disgrace,
Or stain the annals of the human race.
This be our theme.   When vice, in every clime,
Unbares its brow—to spare it were a crime.

Hear courts pronounce between the poor and great,
Both act alike, but share a different fate :
The poor is guilty—who his cause defends ?
Bereft of fortune, influence and friends.
The great is innocent—though bad the cause,
His guilt provokes the magistrate's applause !
And this is justice ! No, I shrink with awe,
From what our rulers dare miscall the law—
There is a law, eternal and divine,
That simplifies what men cannot define,
Resumes all justice, in a word or two—
"As you'd be done by, learn, in turn, to do."
By this great truth this other I maintain—
"Whate'er the guilt, death should not be the pain."

And first, I say, that nature is the school
Where all may study this unerring rule,
That should direct us in our short career,
And make us pity what to God is dear.
For is not man, although by crime defil'd,
His maker's image, and his noblest child ? .
Why take his life then ? Why his dust profane ?
Why break a link in the immortal chain ?
He has shed blood !—I grant it, but his crime
Is not-effac'd by blood—it may by time.
If you allow, the guilty may repent,
Tears cancel crime; but not your punishment:
One tear, but one—the wretch may be forgiv'n,
Repentance weeps, and mercy comes from heav'n :
But man his fellow-man cannot forgive,
Though Pity spare, and Mercy bid him live.

Well, let the guilty fall, if fall he must,
Confound his paltry ashes with the dust—
Think you his blood one spirit can restore,
Or make his victims what they were before ?
Have not the efforts of mankind been vain,
To banish guilt by cruelty or pain ?
Blood cannot mend the manners you detest,
While villains perish, others cannot rest:
Some brave all perils for revenge or gold,
Although the axe, the scaffold they behold.

Yes, 'such is man, and this none can deny,
The slave of wrath all perils will defy ;
And gold, the root of evil, is far worse ;
Man's best and latest friend, or greatest curse.
What crimes, what horrors does it not create,
Throughout all empires, both in Church and State !
Condemn and punish, threaten as you may,
The hand of guilt by blood you cannot stay ;
Man will alike your threats, your terrors brave,
And fly through danger to a certain grave.
The child of passion, he pursues his course,
Forgetting danger and without remorse.
Spare, spare his life, he may one day become
What he is not, within a living tomb :
The world the guilty wretch may well endure,
If from temptation and from crime secure—
I little care what chains the culprit load,
How he may labour, or where his abode,
Let him his life, his agony prolong,
Do all you please—but never wrong for wrong.

Thus reason speaks, and can we hesitate
To spare the wretch, whose fate may be our fate ?
Who to misfortune can refuse a tear,
But little dreams what end he has to fear
To-day erect, to-morrow on the ground,
We rise or fall, just as the wheel goes round.
What one man does, all men, in turn, may do ;
This Terence said, and what he said is true :
No man is happy 'till his latest breath,
And Crœsus calls for Solon at his death.
Experience teaches what I inculcate,
We spare the guilty, lest we share their fate.
'Tis nature's law, the wisest and the best,
Observe but this, and you fulfil the rest.

And next, the civil law can't constitute
The fearful right that I to man dispute ;
Who gave to all, what no one man can claim,
The right to kill ? that right is but a name.
From this one principle I can infer,
When all pronounce, they may in judgment err.
Numbers increase, but still the right must be
Just as before, the right of unity.
And do not say, the body may control

The right of members, to preserve the whole :
'Tis but a sophism, as if you said,
Throw gold away, we want no gold when dead
Men never had what they did not receive,'
They may usurp, as mountebanks deceive :
'Tis all presumption, but you may rely,
None have this right; no more than you or I.
Man's sacred right was with creation laid,
The rest is but convention, and was made.
All men possess, to them must be supplied
By God or man, this cannot be denied :
I grant to millions power, but not a right ;
Sure one poor man cannot with millions fight ;
Yet though the stronger may the weak oppress,
The right of all is neither more nor less ;
'Tis that which strength or power constitutes,
And the exclusive privilege of brutes.
Thus, when you men in the same cause unite,
You make a body, but create no right ;
You may increase your numbers, add still more,
The right of one, of all, is as before :
Hence I conclude, whatever others say;
Men have no right to take man's life away.

And, thirdly, one more proof, ere I conclude—
I will be brief, lest some might think me rude—
To me it seems decisive, and combines
All that's requir'd by all the best divines.
The word of God, that, no man can deny,
May baffle reason, though without reply ;
Can teach philosophers how they may find
The light of truth, the rule of all mankind.
I take the volume, read each sacred page,
And find man's history from age to age ;
One time a rebel, then a slave to sense,
He is subdued by God's omnipotence ;
Until, at last, Jehovah's son is given,
Who teaches all that *love's* the way to heaven.

One time we see an erring child reprov'd,
Revil'd by all—the master stands unmov'd;
But not his heart, that cannot turn away
From her whom folly had thus led astray.
All now accuse her, as they stand around,
She hides her face, falls prostrate on the ground ;

While her sole friend, her meek, unerring lord,
Confounds the guilty, but unsheaths no sword;
" If you be innocent, cast the first stone,"
The guilty fled, and mercy stood alone.
He turns and sees this wayward child deplore
Her faults, her frailties, and he asks no more.
" Hath none condemn'd thee?" " None, my Lord,"
    she cried;
" Nor do I, woman," her good Lord replied;
" Go, sin no more." Is this not clemency—
A lasting lesson to posterity?

    Again, another whose weak, loving heart
Had been ensnar'd by man's seducing art,
Comes forth in tears, not knowing how to meet
An injur'd God; she sinks upon his feet;
Her streaming eyes her anguish now betray,
While with her locks she wipes her guilt away;
Her master sees—he speaks but to forgive,
Then takes her by the hand, and bids her live.
" Arise," said he, for tears can pity move,
" Thy faults are cancell'd by thy ardent love."

    Such are the rules our master left behind,
To teach the world and to instruct mankind;
All shar'd his mercy, all retir'd with joy,
He came to save, but never to destroy.
Through life he taught and practis'd charity,
Man's noblest virtue and best policy;
To spare the guilty, and their faults reprove,
Is all the law—a law of mutual love
There's eye for eye, and life for life, 'tis said:
None can deny that blood for blood was shed.
All this and more, perhaps, I may be told:
But the new law's more perfect than the old;
The weak may doubt, the tyrant argue still,
Although the precept stands, " Thou shalt not kill."
And if in olden times some blood we see,
The right was then that of theocracy;
But since a God, to cancel all our woe,
Has shed his blood, man's blood should never flow:
Upon the cross, the altar where he stood,
He wash'd away the right of shedding blood:
He cried aloud, and his expiring breath
Absolv'd the guilty and abolish'd death.

The earth shall perish and all men decay,
But God's eternal word not pass away ;
Enough, to prove what none but 'fools deny —
If I be wrong, they will, no doubt, reply :
'Till then, they must allow me to be right,
My task is done—I bid them all good night

THE INSURRECTIONS

OF

THE WORKING CLASSES.

(Continued from page 129.)

CHAPTER VIII.

The Revolt of Rienzi, 1341—1357.

It may be a matter of surprise to some, that while insurrections shook the northern and more recent kingdoms of Europe
to their foundation, Italy, the old mother of empires, should
remain a dull and quiet spectator of the scene. In the
states of new formation, the vital action was still fresh, the
forms of society were not yet consolidated, and more susceptible
of sudden derangement. Italy, on the contrary, was like an
exhausted volcano. Her people had been worn out by cycles
of slavery, and corrupted by ages of misrule. Italy exhibited,
in the fourteenth century, the spectacle of a moral desert, in
which the destructive elements were not urgent, the regenera-
tive powers scarcely perceptible. True, there had been changes
and commotions—true, the sword of the conqueror had mowed
down her cities and obliterated her institutions ; true, when
the old band of the lictorial fasces had been sundered, and the
scattered rods turned into so many independent sceptres, sem-
blances of republics arose—but they were the republics of gold
and aristocracy, of hierarchy and arms. The mantle of old
Roman dominion had descended, in a certain sense, on the
apostolic monarch—to some extent, the mediæval purple was
tinged with its shadow, but even this band of union had become
more weak ; scattered and incongruous, the fragments of old
empire stood each by itself; this—in a pseudo-republican attitude ;

that—in a guise of palsied royalty; while each tottered as the blasts of war and innovation swept howling and furious across their crumbled Babel.

Here were the seeds of change, here were elements ready to the hand of the reformer, while the immediate scene of action chosen by Rienzi, and the special circumstances under which he acted, though apparently unfavourable, alike justified his undertaking and insured its success.

The contentions of personal ambition had weakened the papal power. Pope and anti-pope had struggled with each other, exposing their mutual vices, and urging their individual claims, until at last the people of Italy began to believe in the former and doubt the latter—and the apostolic succession became the plaything of faction and offspring of intrigue. Unhonoured in Rome, the pontiffs crossed the Alps, bade Italy adieu, and removed their court to Avignon in France. That authority which their misconduct had undermined, their absence obliterated, and the seven hills were left to the dictates of the turbulent aristocracy, who, hitherto growing under the shadow of imperial or pontifical power, were now content no longer with a delegated authority, but, fortifying their castles in town and country, assumed the character of independent chieftains, desolating the humbler orders of society, deranging trade, and crippling industry by their implacable and ceaseless feuds. Though, in some instances, a republican *form* of government existed, its existence was apparent only in its relation to other states. A senate would meet, a parliament deliberate on peace and war ; but the voice of the magistrate was unheard in the internal administration—the rights of nobles were decided by the sword—their vassals were the objects of irresponsible caprice, and the injury inflicted on the vassal of one lord by another lord was retaliated, not by punishing the noble, but by inflicting a like injury on his followers. Thus, whenever the feudal tyrant took cognisance of a wrong, it but aggravated the evil, while the great mass of the toiling population, crushed beneath the shock of these contending powers, looked vainly for redress, and could only hope to escape the general ruin, by breaking through the shadowy restraint of the laws, and setting up on their own account, as freebooters and banditi.

As a necessary consequence, here, too, great calamities afflicted the working-classes; and, while the vast contributions of the Jubilee or Holy year, (a centenary festival, that at last the rapacity of the pontiffs renewed after an interval of thirty, and then of twenty-five years !)—while these enriched the hierarchy to such an extent, that, night and day, two priests were stationed at the altar of St. Peter, raking the untold gold with precious rakes into their coffers ; while the aristocracy were gathering the richness of the fields and obtaining the tribute of the merchant; while their followers levied arbitrary contributions, laid tolls across the very streets of cities, and swept the seas with their piratical gallies : the people were starving, the people were stricken by pestilence, the people were lost in wretchedness, and yet historians have been found to laud 'the republican institutions of mediæval Italy.

Among the numerous tyrants of Rome, the most powerful were the rival houses of *Colonna* and *Orsini*, whose hereditary feud was prolonged through a space of two hundred and fifty years. Pre-eminent above the surrounding aristocracy—few of whom refused to merge their independence under one or other of these mighty factionists, they disputed the chief magistracy and the papal chair, and after the retreat of the popes to Avignon, a compromise was effected, by electing annually a senator from each of the rival parties, to act as joint-governors of the Roman state. While their feuds exhibited such features of atrocity, that defenceless children were massacred in the streets, in retaliation for past injuries—(thus a young Colonna was slain by an Orsini before the door of a church,)—and renowned warriors of the rival house surprised and murdered (thus the bravest of the Orsini was killed by the younger Stephen Colonna,) these men 'were called to mount the seat of justice, and enforce obedience to the laws." Still, they were clothed with a panoply of awe and veneration by the mass : they derived, or affected to derive, their descent from the heroes of ancient Rome—their magnificent castles, whose hoary towers had witnessed remote centuries, seemed to frown defiance on plebeian innovation ; the circumstances that surrounded their lives appealed to the imagination, and, in the person of Stephen Colonna the elder, the virtues of ancient Rome seemed for once united with the chivalry of mediæval Italy. Added to this, all the institutions of the country were calculated to uphold an awe of feudal power ; its 'possessors were cased in the double armour of spiritual and temporal ascendancy—and daring, indeed, must be the heart that should conceive resistance to the aristocracy and hierarchy of Rome in the fourteenth century. Much of this power was, however, superficial. Secret vice and open profligacy had done their work on the public mind, while personal feuds 'and national quarrels of nobles or kings showed, that while disunion impaired the strength of the oppressor, it was granting opportunity to the oppressed.

The son of a washerwoman and an inkeeper, born in the humblest quarter of Rome, Nicholas Gabrini Rienzi, undertook the mighty task of regenerating his country. He had, strangely enough, received a liberal education from his parents, an unusual circumstance for one in his position of society, and availed himself of the advantage, by haranguing his fellow-countrymen on every fitting opportunity, and obtaining thus some notoriety among his compeers in the ranks of labour.

His fame reaching the ears of the great, they took him by

the hand as a democratic plaything—a dangerous one for aristocracy—admitted him to their houses, laughed at his sallies, and smiled at his enthusiasm.

An embassy of the three orders being about to depart for Avignon, to negociate matters of importance with the pope, Rienzi was chosen as one of the thirteen deputies of the third estate, whose spokesman he was made, and accordingly addressed Clement the Sixth in a speech, the democratic truisms of which must been great indeed, if they were sufficiently understood by the obtuse aristocracy of Rome to cast him from their favour and plunge him into beggary.

For a time he supported himself on charity ; but once more the gates of fortune were opened to receive him. He had undergone the lesson of adversity; he had learned how bitter it was to bear. It was feasible to suppose that, eschewing a second error like the first, he would now subside into a selfish but useful tool of those who relieved his wants and flattered his ambition. The appointment of apostolic notary, however, while it placed him in a position of comparative affluence, enabled him to see more plainly the corruption of those in office, and the vices of the still higher powers that delegated their authority.

He had now beheld both the effect, in the misery of the order from which he had risen, and the cause, in the vileness of the classes to which he had been raised; and, lest his spirit should sleep over the moral, providence decided his course by a significant incident.

His brother, to whom he was deeply attached, fell by the hands of an assassin, against whom, as he belonged to the privileged orders, justice and affection cried in vain. From this moment the vast plans of the Reformer appear to trace their developement, and we must admire the strange admixture of boldness and caution with which they were brought forward. At first allegorical pictures were pasted against the walls, or carried through the streets of Rome, emblematic of the vices of the aristocracy. The names of the leading families and their crests were derived, significantly enough, from beasts of prey—thus the

" *Orsi, lupi, leoni, aquile, e serpi,*"

"bears, wolves, lions, eagles, and serpents," of whom *Petrarca* sings, were the names, or badges, of different noble families. These Rienzi grouped together in large paintings, exhibiting the deformity of character proper to the beast, and equally apparent in his aristocratic prototype. The populace gathered, gazed, wondered, and inquired—at last they began to trace the hidden meaning. His pictures were received with favour and applause—they were straws thrown up to see which way the wind blew—and then Rienzi himself stepped forward, explained their meaning, and expatiated, with an earnest and fiery eloquence, on the wrongs of the people, and the crimes of their rulers. His words came home to the feelings of his auditory : there stood the injured husband, the plundered artisan, the scourged serf ; there rose the palace and the church—the fortress and the prison ! He spoke of these—he pointed to the glorious harvests and the starving poor : language could not exaggerate the people's misery, and a voice alone was wanting to direct their despair. Thence he went back to the past, and spoke of their lost rights, their former power : his audiences increased, his influence spread, and he now determined on mounting a loftier stage, and agitating on a larger scale.

In the church of St. John Lateran was inscribed an antient decree of the senate, in which the Emperor Vespasian had extorted despotic authority from a coerced, or venal senate. Here Rienzi convened an assembly of nobles and working men, to hear an historical lecture on the subject of this inscription, and the delegation of power from its true source—the people. Subtly and cautiously the orator brought before his readers the gradual change—the antient rights, the present slavery of the masses—how the delegated authority had degenerated into irresponsible despotism—and shadowed forth a faint prophecy of the GOOD ESTATE, or the period in which the people should be restored to their legitimate power.

Attracted by the novelty of the idea, a vast crowd congregated to hear his lecture : the multitude wondered, applauded, and appreciated—the nobles, who attended in great numbers, sunk in haughty apathy, failed to understand his meaning, or scorned its application, and might smile or frown at the gaudy appearance of the plebeian lecturer. But, in the parade and mystery with which Rienzi affected to enshroud himself, lay a part of his influence and impunity. The dazzling robe, inscribed with mystic characters, with which he appeared before his audience, was not the trapping of the mountebank, but the disguise of the statesman. The people had been accustomed to the pomp and pageantry of the Roman church, to the munificence of the barons—they were not yet sufficiently enlightened to admire simple grandeur—but, to win attention and applause, Rienzi found it expedient to throw mediæval tinsel around the severe forms of antient Rome. He gained, also, another object : he lulled the suspicions of the nobility, who thus beheld in him but the clever charlatan, striving to amuse, instead of the patriot, endeavouring to instruct. Thus time passed. Rienzi was the admitted guest in the palaces of the great—he was the welcome teacher in the hovels of the lowly, until the " Good Estate" grew into familiar words, and men began to strive for that which they had learned to admire.

Rienzi had now patiently reared the foundation for his undertaking. He had gathered the scattered elements ; he had imbued them with new life ; he had directed the spirit ;—it now remained for him to organise the physical force. The measures he adopted for this purpose were astounding by their suddenness and vigour.

A proclamation appeared on the church doors of St. George, summoning the people to hold themselves in instant readiness for the re-establishment of the Good Estate ; and the same night Rienzi convened a meeting of one hundred citizens, on Mount Aventine, to carry the proclamation into effect. He there explained to them his plan, and the facility of its execution, and induced them solemnly to pledge their co-operation. On the next day the fearless band marched down Mount Aventine, and summoned, by sound of trumpet, the people to meet on the following evening, unarmed, before the church of St. Angelo. The procession, strangely enough, appears to have passed uninterruptedly through the streets; and the conspirators beguiled the suspense of the night by the performance of religious ceremonies in the church—a master-stroke on the part of their leader, inasmuch as he thus pointedly showed that he was not hostile to the established faith—and invited the co-operation of its ministers. Indeed, he endeavoured to enlist the hierarchy on his side, by reminding them of the oppressions they suffered from the temporal power, and dwelling on the gratitude the pope would feel to be relieved from its imperious vassalage. He succeeded in his object : the priests, for once, espoused the cause of liberty, and the papal vicar, Bishop of Orvieto, sanctioned the undertaking by his presence and co-operation.

With the first dawn Rienzi, the bishop on his right-hand, issued from the church of St. Angelo, at the head of his hundred conspirators. He was bare-headed, but in complete armour : three banners, emblematic of freedom, peace, and justice, waved over the procession, and, as it descended the steps of the portico, the wild cheers of the gathered multitude rolled up their loud encouragement. Slowly it wound through the dense masses, on its way to the Capitol—from every street tributary streams swelled the human tide, while the nobles came forth from their palaces to gaze in stupid wonder on the scene—awed by the congregated, although unarmed thousands, and undecided how to act, in the absence of Stephen Colonna, the most redoubted of their order. Meanwhile Rienzi had reached the Capitol—entered without opposition, and, issuing on a balcony, made proclamation of the GOOD ESTATE, expounded its laws, and received their ratification in the plaudits of an enthusiastic audience.

Thus the new government was established, by an unarmed people, in the centre of feudal strongholds—by a plebeian patriot, in the centre of a warlike and terrible aristocracy.

The meeting had dispersed—the casual stranger would have seen nothing to attract attention, and Rome seemed to have resumed its customary quietude, when Stephen Colonna, who had been summoned by the nobles on the first alarm, returned to his palace. Rienzi forthwith despatched a messenger to inform him of what had transpired, and demand his allegiance. "Tell your master," said the haughty noble, "that I will cast him at my leisure from the windows of the Capitol." As soon, however, as the messenger had borne this answer, the great bell of the Capitol began to sound the alarm—the people poured into the streets at the well-known signal. "To the Colonna palace!" rose the general cry;—the proud Colonna had scarcely time to save his life by flight, with difficulty escaped the rapid torrent of the populace, and scarce rested till he had reached his stronghold of Palestrina, in the country. Rienzi forthwith issued an order, commanding all nobles to quit the city and retire to their estates. They obeyed with alacrity, glad to escape so easily, and their departure, and a strict watch at the gates, by insuring the present tranquillity of Rome, gave Rienzi time to digest his plans and consolidate his power.

The Roman people, in the enthusiasm of re-conquered liberty, were now desirous of testifying their devotion to Rienzi by conferring a royal or imperial crown, or reposing irresponsible power in his hands. The patriotic citizen might inwardly pardon, but wisely reproved, this attempted violation of the democratic rights he had just been founding; while the purposes of government, and the ambition of governing, were better assured by the less sounding but more popular dignity of TRIBUNE, which, in its modern acceptation, combined the legislative function with its old duty of protecting the commons.

The Tribune now proceeded to complete his code of laws, by which he purified the judgment seat of venality, the justice hall of perjury, and freed the revenue from peculation. The remission of taxation, though accompanied with great public undertakings—and the startling fact that, notwithstanding this, in five months he trebled some of the principal branches of the national income—must have revealed to the plundered dupes of aristocratic and-priestly domination how scandalous had been the misappropriation of their property. The strongholds of the nobles were shorn of their defences, and their materials employed in fortifying the Capitol; no man, whatever his birth, was permitted to bear arms, save in the defence of the state; and the widows and orphans of all those who fell in that cause were declared wards of the country, and pensioned, or provided for in the public service. National granaries were formed for the people, preventing all danger of famine; and the vast apostolic revenues, hitherto drawn by a non-resident pope, were confiscated to the use of the people, and applied to the relief of the indigent, and the maintenance of order. Rapine and murder were checked by the abolition of the law of sanctuary. The palaces of the nobility had hitherto been sacred from intrusion—thus affording secure asylums to malefactors in the train of their followers; Rienzi declared no distinction should exist between the dwelling of the baron and that of the artisan, and imposed the severest penalties on whoever should harbour or conceal a criminal. The barons had been in the habit of imposing arbitrary tolls, and of encouraging brigandage in consideration of receiving tribute from the spoil : Rienzi held the barons responsible for the safety of the highways, and visited with terrible justice any breach of the peace, or infraction of the law.

Well aware that to enact statutes without having the ability to enforce them would be folly, the Tribune simultaneously created a large military power, paid and equipped by the state, and equally distributed through the thirteen quarters of the city— while the coasts were guarded by a fleet of light gallies, and the country placed under the inspection of judicial officers. Always intent on sparing the religious prejudices of the age, Rienzi associated the Bishop of Orvieto in the government, which was carried on in the name of the people and the church. Having thus established his authority through the three branches of justice, finance, and arms, the Tribune summoned the nobility from their strongholds in the country, to swear allegiance to the GOOD ESTATE. Unwilling to come, but more fearful to refuse, the princes and barons returned to their palaces—without arms, without pomp, and, for once, without insolence. Side by side with the working man, they stood undistinguished before the tribunal of the people's magistrate ; and the faltering oath of fealty may have been qualified by a mental reservation, which devoted their plebeian conqueror to ultimate revenge.

Meanwhile Clement the Sixth, partly rejoiced at the fall of an aristocracy by which he had been enthralled—partly unable to resist the growing torrent of popular power—thought it wisest to glide with its waves, and gave his apostolic sanction to the political Reformer, The influence of the Tribune once secured, its beneficent effects were soon felt beyond the walls of Rome. Near Caprinica a poor man had been robbed of a mule and jar of oil, on the territory of the Orsini. The proud baron was forced to make good the loss, and pay a fine of four hundred florins for neglecting to assure the safety of the highway. Peter Agapet Colonna was arrested in the streets for debt and violence ; and Martin Orsini was publicly executed for having pillaged a shipwrecked vessel at the mouth of the Tiber. These terrible examples soon tamed the aristocracy : the blows fell thick and fast, but never undeserved, upon their loftiest houses—even on those terrible Colonna and Orsini, who had desolated Rome with their ambition and their feuds. The purple of a cardinal, and the coronet of a prince, could no longer screen a criminal. The guilty barons silently and quickly withdrew from the Roman states. Society was purged of its scum, and trade, commerce, and industry, began to flourish.. " In this time," to quote the words of the historian,

" the woods began to rejoice that they were no longer infested with robbers ; the oxen began to plough ; the pilgrims visited the sanctuaries ; the roads and inns were replenished with travellers ; trade, plenty, and good faith, were restored in the markets ; and a purse of gold might be exposed, without danger, in the midst of the highway." And what was the secret of this vast prosperity ?—ONE RIGHT, ONE LAW, FOR ALL.

The fame of the Tribune and the Good Estate now spread over Europe, and the kings of the earth began to wonder on their old thrones, at the strange and mighty power suddenly raised by an obscure plebeian, without drawing a sword or striking a blow, in the midst of an armed and fortified aristocracy. The wide extension of his influence is no less a matter of surprise, than its rapid and apparently inexplicable origin. Rome, dwindled into a small territory, its capital now containing but a fraction of its once mighty population, long sunk into national and, since the withdrawal of the popes, into ecclesiastical insignificance, suddenly soared like a meteor into the political horizon, and rose into disproportionate importance in the scale of empires. But Rienzi had embraced an idea that has often since recurred to the Italian mind, that circumstances have retarded in its developement, but that time will ere long bring to its realisation : *the nationality of Italy.* He wished to combine its different heads into one federative republic under the supremacy of Rome, and quick to execute as he was prompt to conceive, the Tribune summoned the various senates and princes of Italy to second the undertaking. No gaudy ambassadors announced the plan, but white-wanded messengers on foot, traversed the countries with his letters ; the populace poured forth to meet them, the blessings of the enthralled followed their footsteps, and, while public rumour heralded their approach, and thronging thousands welcomed their entrance into the cities of kings, mighty sovereigns were forced to receive them with respect, as representatives of that popular power which had began to feel its way among the dark ruins of empires. The republican states sympathised with Rienzi; and Venice, Florence, Sienna, Perugia, and many other cities gave in their adherence ; while the princes of Lombardy and Tuscany promised their friendship, and all sent their ambassadors and envoys to congratulate the 'Tribune, to seek his favour, and to assure their support. Even transalpine kings paid homage to his virtue. So great was his reputation for wisdom and impartial justice, that Lewis, king of Hungary, appealed to his decision, in his quarrel with Jane, queen of Naples, the wife and murderess of his brother. The cause was tried before Rienzi, the crowned heads pleading through their advocates, when the Tribune, after hearing either side, adjourned a cause, afterwards decided by the chance of war. But greater than the homage of crowned heads was that of Petrarca, who surrendered the friendship of the Colonna, and the favour of the pope, to sing the praises of the patriot.

The chief task of Rienzi now was to maintain his power at home, while he was spreading its influence abroad ; and this was no easy undertaking. He had a turbulent, benighted and brutal populace to control—without confidence in themselves, without respect for their equal. He had risen from their own order, he had once been treated with the familiarity of equality, and to gain and keep the requisite ascendancy, demanded more than ordinary wisdom.

It was therefore that he enshrouded himself in a mysterious halo, by insinuating a divine mission for the regeneration of Italy ; it was therefore he led the minds of the people back to the glories and associations of ancient Rome; it was therefore he directed their attention to an Italian federative union, as calculated to attach them to his government by leading them onward to anticipated triumphs—for half-enlightened people, like children, often slight the prize they have obtained, making it the wisdom of the statesman constantly to hold a distant goal before their view.

Hatred of the oppressor, physical suffering, and the novelty of the democratic doctrine, at first rallied the people under the guidance of Rienzi ; the incipient triumph past, ambitious plebeians might have questioned the self assumed authority of their equal, had he not dazzled their vision with his magnificent pageants and silenced the grumbling of envy by his lofty eloquence. In these circumstances we must seek for an explanation of those high sounding epithets of " NICHOLAS, SEVERE AND MERCIFUL," " DELIVERER OF ROME," " CHAMPION OF ITALY," " FRIEND OF MANKIND AND OF LIBERTY, PEACE AND JUSTICE," " TRIBUNE AUGUST," with which he awed, yet refined the vulgar ears, accustomed to the less noble titles of baron, duke, or prince. To these must be ascribed the magnificent pageantry of his public life ; and the historian who sees in these the exhibitions of a puerile vanity, or the drunkenness of overgorged ambition, shows himself alike ignorant of the character of his hero, and of the state of the people he was called to govern. A little reflection would have proved that every pageant of Rienzi had a lofty object; they were not the unmeaning pomps of inflated success. The great banner which was carried before him, a sun with a circle of stars, a dove with an olive branch—was emblematic of Rome's chieftaincy over the federative union he desired to found, and of the mission of peace on which he sent his ambassadors. Gifted with almost superhuman beauty, " the party-coloured robe of velvet or satin, lined with fur, and embroidered with gold; the rod of justice or sceptre of polished steel, crowned with a globe and a cross of gold, and enclosing a small fragment of the true and holy wood," his " white steed, the symbol of royalty," the " fifty guards, with halberts, attending his person," the "troop of horse preceding his march,· and their timbals and trumpets of massive silver," were but the necessary appliances to distance the familiarity of a people, incapable of appreciating simple greatness, and too benighted to distinguish a great principle from the man by whom it was propounded.

Again, in coveting the honour of knighthood, we are told that Rienzi "betrayed the meanness of his birth, and degraded the importance of his office." The historian forgets that knighthood was achieved by men of the humblest orders, that it was supposed to be the prerogative of merit, not of birth, and that the example of a Colonna and Orsini sanctioned the proceeding. Nor was this without a deeper object. Every day the Tribune may have felt (subsequent events prove that he must have done so) more and more the impatience of plebeian ambition, fretting and chafing at his authority. In his person democracy was enshrined, for he was the only democrat of Rome; with him it would (it afterwards did) fall; therefore, the more he could remove himself from the vortex of the mass, the longer might he hope to rule, and by his eloquence instil a nobler spirit in their hearts. And the historian should remember, that his deportment never exhibited either arrogance or levity—that while his foot was on the necks of princes he spoke of himself as but the humble servant of the people, and that while he scourged the great for their crimes, he never committed one act of cruelty or injustice.

THE POOR MAN'S LEGAL MANUAL.

IV. The Poor Laws.

Although we have headed this article with the title of the Poor Laws, it is not our intention to enter into an examination of the whole of the cumbrous, complicated, and imperfect system known by that name. We will, at all events, for the present, pass by the subjects of commissioners, poor rates, settlements, and removals, and treat merely of one branch, but that the most *practically* important and interesting—namely, the relief of the poor.

We will turn away from the political and general aspect presented by these laws; we will examine their immediate influence upon individuals, who, suffering from " the ills, that flesh is heir to," come within their operation.

Behold a picture so often presented to our view—a destitute family. An aged couple, it may be, who cannot work; who will not steal; and who are ashamed to beg. Children they may have, who are willing and able to labour, but cannot obtain employment. Whatever the cause, whether misfortune or imprudence, or both combined, they find themselves reduced to extreme poverty.

What are they to do?

Where, how, and from whom are they to seek relief?

Such are the questions which the legislation relating to pauperism professes to solve.

FIRST.—The poor have a claim on their own relations their own "flesh and blood"—for support, provided that those relations have the means. Thus, the old, blind, lame, or impotent, or those who are in any way unable to work, may enforce their right to assistance from relations by blood, but not by marriage, in the following degrees: father, mother, grandfather, grandmother, and children.

If a man marry a woman, who has a child at the time of marriage, whether legitimate or illegitimate, he must support it.

The mother of an illegitimate child, so long as she continue unmarried, must maintain such child until it attain the age of sixteen; but if she can prove who is the father of the child, he may be charged for its support.

Every person able to support his family by work or other means, and wilfully refusing to do so, or running away from them, whereby they become chargeable to the parish, shall be deemed a rogue and vagabond, and be liable to imprisonment.

SECONDLY.—The aid of relations failing them, the poor must look to the parish.

1. We will first consider, who, in such case, is to give relief. The power of doing so is vested in the guardians of the poor (subject to the control of the commissioners), or in a select vestry, and overseers are not allowed to give other or further relief than is ordered by the guardians, or by the select vestry, except in the following instances.

1. In case of sudden and urgent necessity, when they are to give it, whether the party applying be settled in the parish or not. If the overseers refuse, a magistrate may in such case, order relief to be given

and if they disobey such order, they are liable to a penalty of £5.

2. Any magistrate may give a similar order for medical relief, when sudden and dangerous illness requires it, and overseers are liable to the same penalty, as above, for disobeying it.

2. As to the mode by which relief may be given. This may be by a loan to a poor person, where it is deemed advisable. Guardians are also empowered to let land in small allotments. But the most usual mode of relief is by supplying food and other necessaries; this may be either within or without the workhouse.

1. As to relief within the workhouse. No person shall be admitted into the workhouse but by

1. An order of the Board of Guardians signed by their clerk.

2. Or one signed by the relieving officer or overseer of the poor.

3. The consent of the master of the workhouse (or during his absence or inability to act, by that of the matron), without any order, in case of sudden or urgent necessity.

The following is the classification of paupers in the workhouse :—

Class 1. Men infirm through age or other cause.

2. Able-bodied men and youths above the age of fifteen.

3. Boys above the age of seven and under fifteen.

4. Women infirm.

5. Able-bodied women and girls above the age of fifteen.

6. Girls above the age of seven and under fifteen.

7. Children under seven.

These classes are kept separate and distinct. Thus, husband, wife, and children are separated from each other. But parents may have an interview, once a day, with their children under seven years of age; and by a very late Act of Parliament, a married couple of the age of sixty are not to be " put asunder."

The following observations are offered with a view to inform persons who are reduced to this condition, as to the rights which they still are allowed to possess.

The medical officer may direct an addition to or change in the diet.

A pauper may require the master to weigh, in the presence of two other persons, the allowance of provisions served out at any meal.

He may quit on giving reasonable notice, but his family are to be sent with him, unless the guardians otherwise direct.

Any person may visit any pauper by permission of the master and in his presence.

Any licensed minister of religion may attend at the request of an inmate of the same persuasion, and no inmate is bound to attend service celebrated in a mode contrary to his religious principles.

The guardians may prescribe a task of work to be done by any person relieved, but may not detain him against his will, for the performance of such task, longer than four hours from the hour of breakfast in the morning succeeding his admission.

No corporal punishment may be inflicted on an adult person, nor may he be confined for more than twenty-four hours, or such further time as is necessary to have him brought before a magistrate; nor is he, if of sane mind, to be chained.

2. With regard to relief out of the workhouse.

Two justices may order it to be so given to any adult person, who, from old age or bodily infirmity, is wholly unable to work.

Guardians and overseers *may* also order it to be so given, subject to any rules of the Poor Law Commissioners, and these rules have limited the power to such cases as urgent necessity, sickness, accident, burial, and the like.

We propose in another paper to review the law relating to the settlement and removal of paupers, and then to offer some general observations upon the whole system.

THE BARD'S LAMENT.

BY ERNEST JONES.

Spirit! Why hast thou fled? Etherial thought!
  Thou camest once like gush of ready flame,
Wrapt on the currents that wild fancy fraught,
Strong in a mighty melody untaught—
  Thou thing of fire! say, why so still and tame?

Is this poor heart, thy whilome tenement,
  So worn, that thou despisest there to stay ?
Has sorrow seamed my house with many a rent,
Through which the world's cold storms their chill
    have sent,
  And scared my heavenly visitant away ?

Oh ! still at times thy hovering form I trace,
  Thin wavering ghost at fancy's fading feast :
Re-cross the threshold of my dwelling-place,
Where once thou camest, uninvited grace !
  And yet most welcome when expected least.

Come back 1 I'll deck thy home with dainty pride—
  Its open doors thy fitful stay invite :
Alas ! 'tis but the ruin's portals wide,
Through which the storms their dripping steeds may
    ride,
  But whose black arches scare the blest sunlight.

In vain ! Thy cold and dewy fingers play
  Across my heartstrings, yet they wake no sigh !
The chords are broken and the charm's away ;
Harp out of tune—and Bard without a lay—
  The music's lost—then, lost musician, die !

RACE versus NATION.

A change is rapidly approaching over continental Europe; not a mere governmental, but an elementary change. In the early ages, the savage spirit of conquest impelled race against race ; the confines of either were alternately broken down, and an amalgamation of discordant masses was the result. In the middle-ages, individual ambition, seconded by the progress in the art of war, broke these empires of races into nations, and the conflict of nations perpetuated and increased the confusion of races. Thus, most of the kingdoms of Europe are put together of incongruous parts, annexed by invasion, held by force, and perpetuated by diplomacy. Centuries have in some instances elapsed since these forcible annexations ;—one would have expected them to have given the stamp of perpetual nationalities to their various constructions; they have brought national associations, national histories, national traditions, and national monuments; they have created and fostered national prejudices and animosities; and, despite all, the old sympathies of RACE appear and appear again, even under circumstances and in places where least to be expected. We purpose illustrating this hereafter. At present, we will look into the causes of this apparent anomaly.

A distinguishing type has been preserved by the hand of nature. The Scandinavian, the Sclavonic, the Teuton, the Italian, the Frank, and the Celtic races, differ from each other in their physical appearance, and their mental constitution. Of course, by the word "race," we are not alluding to those broader distinctions, typified in the Caucasian, the African, the Malayan, etc.—but to those minor differences which have stamped an individual characteristic on different members of the European family. It is in this sense in which we have ventured to speak of an "Italian race;"—for, in the amalgam of which the Italians consist, we find, although broken into separate nationalities, one pervading and distinctive mental and physical characteristic.

This in them, as in others, has manifested itself in social customs, language and literature; and it is to these causes that the wonderful sympathy of "race," still existent after the lapse of so many ages in the breasts of otherwise conflicting nations, is to be attributed.

To this active cause, the remodelling of the European system will be indebted for its origin. It is one great lever in the hands of modern democracy. It is one great aid to the realisation of that noble principle, ALL MEN ARE BRETHREN. The splits in the human family, induced by the ambition of kings and conquerors, are about to be partially healed by the extension of the feeling of fraternity from the narrow limits of a kingdom to the boundary of a race. Verily, KINGDOMS are changing into KINDOMS.

Thus we find the Italians struggling, not for the independence of Naples from Rome, or Rome from Austria, but for that of Italy from the German. "*All Italians are brethren !*"

Thus we find even the most discordant national animosities smothered, and he Russian and the Pole struggling for one Sclavonic republic ! Thus the conspiracy of Pestel,

Bustazeff, and Ryleyeff was intended to amalgamate both nations under one free government—and thus Nicholas endeavours to use this very circumstance 'for tyrannical purposes, in trying, and with some effect, to impress the Poles with the belief, that his mission is to gather all the scattered wrecks of the Sclavonic race into one great union. The latter part of his object will be realised by the people, but the tyranny will be frustrated, for here too it is democracy that raises the cry : " *All Sclavonians are brethren!*"

Thus we find that Sweden, Norway, Denmark and Finland,* are drawing nearer to each other. Here, too, the national animosities engendered by kings are being rapidly forgotten. The *crowns,* not the people, of Denmark, Sweden and Norway fought with hostile interests. Norway and Sweden *are* united; and when the present king of Denmark dies, a union between the Danes and Swedes is more than probable. The people on either side the water desire it, and the weak barrier of a debauched and imbecile prince will hardly be insurmountable. The Finns, too, are looking back with affection to the time of their union with Sweden; and looking forward with impatience to the renewal of that union. There, too, in those northern lands, the cry is being raised: "*All Scandinavians are brethren!*"

Thus we find that Germany is endeavouring to reconstruct her lopped members into one great body. In Germany, as well, feelings of national hostility are being smothered. Long wars and rivalries taught the Prussian and the Austrian to hate each other; and kingly ambition made Prussia disliked by the minor states. Now, mark the change! Now, what is the cry? "One father-land! One Germany!" "*All Germans are brethren!*"

Even in our own country, the same spirit of "race" is apparent. It is a striking feature of the times, that the "Celt" is speaking of the "Saxon" as a foreigner, and that the Saxon, after the lapse of eight hundred years, speaks of the domiciled "Norman" as an invader, and points to the scions of our aristocracy, descended from a Norman stock, as conquerors and aliens in the land! The distinctive features of race and their requirements are becoming daily more apparent.

Scotland, indeed, possesses her Scottish kirk and Scottish law; but in Ireland the cry is raised of " Ireland for the

---

* The Finns may, indeed, trace a difference of race from the Swedes —but the difference is still greater between them and the Russians; therefore, an alliance with the Swedes would be an approximation on their part to the principle of the sovereignty of races.

Irish." It is a cry of "race," under the guise of a shout of nationality. Yet the link of friendship is not wanting between the sister countries, and through this little island-world of ours, this cry, as well, is raised: *"Saxon and Celt are brethren!"*

This is an approximation to that greater principle of "ALL MEN ARE BRETHREN." A principle propounded by the society of Fraternal Democrats in England, and echoed—loudly echoed—on the Continent. But we must walk before we can run. Much will be achieved if each distinctive race can be gathered into a separate family bond—it will pave the way for general fraternity, since democracy is at work throughout the world. A glance at the state of Europe will show that the present system cannot last; that the present thrones will crumble, and the present limits of kingdoms shrink or spread. Then, out of the deluge of convulsive change that will, ere long, agitate the continent, we shall see it emerge under a new aspect. The present national boundaries will be swept away, and the dominions of races will be established in the Scandinavian, Sclavonic, Italian and Germanic unions. Nor, thanks to the spirit of freedom, will these be moulded under the grasp of monarchs; but, as the storm will be raised by democracy against despotism, so shall we trace the victory of the latter by the establishment of federal republics. Those national feelings, which, in some countries, might yet militate against this great result (and we are aware that the Pole and the Dane yet cling fondly to a restrictive nationality,) may be spared and harmonised, by these still retaining a separate individuality, a separate government, and yet forming a part of each great union of race, by joining each other in a federative system of republics. Thus, Poland may obtain an independent government, yet form one of the Sclavonic confederation. Thus, Ireland seeks a Repeal of the Union, and would yet remain the confederate ally of England.

These are the results to which the approaching crisis in Europe appears pointing. But this brotherhood of race will be extended in the lapse of time; and it may not be a mere dream of the visionary to contemplate the period in which these narrower limits will be widened into Caucasian, Malayan, African republics, spreading thus the circle of human sympathy, until indeed the words are realised: "ALL MEN ARE BRETHREN."

THE ROMANCE OF A PEOPLE.

A HISTORICAL TALE

OF THE NINETENTH CENTURY.

(Continued from page 82.)

CHAPTER V.

There was a change in the farm-house of Sandomir,—lonely no more—for there were gatherings of men in the neighbourhood, as, quicker than the fiery-cross, the glad tidings of Warsaw's liberation spread trumpet-like athwart the country. The farm-house was full, but every moment some new face appeared at the door-way, and was greeted by a smile of glad welcome from those already there. Without, too, there were many—but these were the *peasants*—within it was a meeting of *nobles*, deliberating as to the organisation of the province. The old farmer and his wife, however, played the host and hostess. The shutters and doors were closed and fastened; while the wind howled without, the beams and rafters creaked around them, the wine-cup circled freely, as though the body thirsted with its burning thoughts, as the quickened blood beat faster with anticipated triumph.

Even the farmer smiled a melancholy smile, shadowed by the thought: how would the absent have exulted now! Among that gallant company he missed the noblest form;—while the father would be marching to liberty, the son might be plodding on through exile to a grave.

The mother, woman-like, indulged in brighter dreams, of how, when Russia was cast prostrate at their feet, the exiles and the captives would be restored, and long years of happiness atone for transient misery. Oh, weakness of woman—that is her strength! Oh, folly—that is wisdom! Oh, shadows—that outweigh our sad realities!

Of all that company, one only smiled not. That ill-fated scarf would not progress in the hands of Zaleska. It had been intended to deck the breast of a soldier on the day of his first battle. The hour was nigh, but the soldier was far, and the unfinished work was a memorial of his absence.

Thus they sat—while louder grew their mirth every moment, prouder their challenge of the Russian, deeper their reliance on their own strength—when a low wailing voice was heard at the door. The noisy converse within would have prevented their heeding the cry, had not the girl, whom abstraction from the present scene made sensitive to every sound from without, directed their notice to the circumstance.

"For the love of the mother of mercy, open the door! I am fainting, dying," said the piteous voice.

The door was unbarred. On the threshhold cowered an abject thing, shaking as with palsy, its wiry fingers clenching the lintel, and its thin white hair falling in long flakes over its sepulchral temples. A dim gleam flickered in the sunken sockets of its eyes, and the gaunt bones rattled beneath their fibrous covering, as, with a side-long, shuffling motion, this wreck of humanity came moving through the room.

"Good heaven! Whom have we here? Whence come you?"

"*From the Belvedere!*" gasped the wretch, in a hoarse, half-extinguished voice; and the sound of that dreaded name sunk like ice on every spirit.

With feverish eagerness he drained to the last drop the proffered drink, and crawled so near the fire, under the deadly chill that had struck into his heart, that those present were forced to draw him back.

By degrees, however, the triumph of the mind over the material became developed. A spiritual expression began to beautify that distorted countenance; and, at the electric touch of the rekindling soul, despite grey hairs, decrepitude, and furrows, all present recognised the youth of the wretched being before them.

When he heard the daring plans of the nobles, his face assumed an expression of admiring pity, whether it was that the spark of courage had been trodden out of his heart by the heel of the oppressor, or that he more fully knew, from sad experience, the resources and determination of the government, whose anger they had provoked.

"You are strong to do, and ready to dare—but oh! mother of mercy, think of the power you are braving!—think that the voice of that icy man, sent from his distant throne, can shrivel you up like parchment, and set the racks twirling and groaning throughout his mighty hemisphere."

"What! would you have us shrink?"

"No! onward! but beware how you march. Go not in the old path. New times, new measures."

Questioned as to his advice,—for in him, too, they recognised a noble,—and as to his history, the stranger, with fitful pauses of exhaustion, pain, and memory, gave the following picture of the past, and warning for the future; aptly timed, when Poland's fate was hanging in the balance:—

I am the only son of Count Tyssen. At an early age I was sent to the college of Vilno, and there participated in the glorious and ennobling doctrines of Zan, Lelewel, and Sniadecki. Here still seemed a rallying point of liberty, one spot where Poland might yet be said to live, till at length even from here the spirit was expelled, and driven from the seat of learning to the woods and wilds. And this was the occasion: Michael Plater, a child only ten years of age, wrote the following words on one of the school-slates :—"Long live the constitution of May the third ! ' Who shall restore it to us ?"

Novosilzoff, immediately appearing at Vilno, based upon this trifling groundwork the pretended discovery of a conspiracy, and imprisoned twelve hundred students in eight of the surrounding convents. Here they were subjected to torture, though some of them were mere children.* My father bribed Novosilzoff with thirty thousand ducats to restore me to his hands ; and, suffering more from unutterable indignation, than from the wounds and maltreatment I had received, I returned once more to my home. Being their only son, you may imagine how my aged parents tried to shield me from the fate of so many—exile and conscription : for, like many others, we had lost in the continual wars our patent of nobility; and not being able to produce it, were declared *serfs*. My father was constrained to repurchase his rank at a cost of one hundred thousand ducats ! Reduced in fortune by the continued extortions of the tyrant, we lived in strict retirement, and closed our doors against the world, save when forced to open them for the admittance of Russian spies into the sanctuary of home. How I burned to rush forth at the head of our retainers, when, from the turret-windows of the castle of Tyssen, I beheld detachments of Russians marching across the plain, dragging with them hundreds of manacled conscripts, on their way to reinforce the far Asiatic regiments of the tyrant !

Once, when little in expectation of such visitors, a body of Russian soldiers marched up to the gate, and demanded admittance. It was admitting so many robbers and murderers, but we durst not refuse. Accordingly, the castle was soon filled with the riotous and insolent soldiery. They entered every chamber, searched every nook, and polluted even the room to which my mother had retired, with their defiling presence. My father, cowed by long years of captivity and torture, broken-spirited, unlike his former self, pale and trembling, looked on in silence. Ah! there was a time when he would have levelled the defiler to the earth, and buried himself beneath the ruins of his house, ere it should have been stained by the presence of such miscreants. But he had been a captive in the Belvedere ! For many years he had vanished, as it were, from the face of the earth, and no one knew what had become of him. At last he had been liberated, upon a dreadful oath never to reveal the secrets of the prison-house. When hope had almost vanished, he suddenly re-appeared among his family—none knew

---

* The knout, and salt herrings for food, without drink, were some of the mildest modes of torture resorted to.

whence. But how altered was that once noble form! how lightless that once flashing eye!—it was piteous to behold. He spoke not; he recognised scarcely any one. His countenance bore the marks of intense suffering; his body was covered with scars he had never gained in battle! When questioned, he only replied, " Peace, peace! Oh! let me be at rest!" That once glorious spirit was broken.

He now cowered abjectly in a corner of the apartment, though the sword his ancestor had drawn for Sobieski was slung at his side. I burned with unutterable indignation. Oh, it was an agony! But—I was silent.

" I believe we have a relative of yours in our keeping," said the officer in command, leaning, already half-intoxicated, across the dinner-table to my father. " The Starost Lawenski."

My father turned pale, but said nothing.

" Is he *here* ?" I asked.

" Yes," replied the Muscovite. " Ha, ha! he is visiting his relations !"

As I spoke, my father started with terror, and cast towards me an appealing look. He knew that one rash word would seal my fate. I have often marvelled that I controlled myself so long, listening to the brutal jests of our tormentor. I now marvel whence the spirit came that prompted me to brave him. O God! it is trodden out—out!—oh! they can tame the strongest!

Before I could answer, a piercing shriek rang without, and a young girl, flying from a licentious and drunken Muscovite, entered the room.

" Save me, save me !" she cried, rushing to my father, and, falling at his feet, she clasped his knees in supplication.

" Ha, ha !" laughed the brutal Muscovite, " does the frightened dove fly to the ark ? Come here, my pretty one! Here is a place for you by my side !" and he added coarse and brutal jests.

I looked at my father. I saw him stand irresolute, in utter silence.

" You are a kinsman of our house, Count Tyssen !" cried the girl, " save me, save me !"

He said not a word, but gently attempted to raise her from the ground.

" Surely you would not see your kindred dishonoured in your own house !" she exclaimed, as indignantly she started to her feet, and stood gazing at my father.

The words seemed to revive his fears, and he turned with a weak, appealing look towards the Russian officer. He, once so brave, the soul of chivalry under Napoleon—he, who had trampled under his horse's feet the platoons of the Muscovite, quailed in his own castle before the glances of a slave !

" Surely, sir," I said to the officer, still controlling my passion, " you would not insult the honour of a lady, or of an old man, who have done nothing to provoke such an outrage, and are unable to resent it."

"Silence! mouthpiece of mutiny," cried the insolent official, heated with intemperance. "Bring that fiery dove to my side," he added, addressing one of his escort who attended in the room; "and whoever questions my intentions or my power, has his answer *here!*" And he swung his double-thonged Cossack-whip with insolent brutality over the table, till the lights blenched, and a hoarse laugh echoed from the attendant Russians, whose iron faces had relaxed into a wolfish smile.

My father started from his seat, with an impulse of former days, and laid his hand upon his sword; but scarcely had he done so, before he quailed under those looks, sunk back in his chair, and buried his face in his hands.

My first thought was one of sudden vengeance,—but fortunately I controlled myself, and affecting not to have noticed what had passed, entered into conversation with a Russian beside me. When I thought I had ceased to be an object of attention to the rest, I quietly rose from my seat, and left the room unobserved.

As I re-entered, the scene of riot and insolence was at its height. My father sat like a palsy-shaken image at the head of his board, the young Polish girl cowered trembling by the side of the Russian officer, whose looks and words left no doubt as to his intentions, while the rafters rung with the ribald jests of the licentious revellers.

I advanced towards the chair of the Muscovite leader; and bending over it, gently raised the pale girl by the hand, and led her towards an inner door. Her large, speaking eyes were fixed on mine with a look of grateful pity, which plainly seemed to say, you but destroy yourself in vain; let me perish, and I shall not blame you!

Up started the Russian, commanding in a voice of thunder her instant return, and staggering after us with vollied threats and imprecations; but I turned upon him with a calmness which seemed to awe even him for the moment, and demanded to see his instructions.

"Here they are!" he roared, shaking his whip; and then, turning to his escort, commanded them to bind me and drag me away.

"Stay!" I replied; and, as I spoke, the doors of the apartment opened, and admitted the retainers of my father, whom I had armed and assembled during my short absence, and found well ready to second me in any design against the Russian.

In a double line they marched up either side of the table, and effectually held our enemies at their mercy.

"Rebellion!" cried the leader of the latter. "You shall pay for this!"

"Your instructions," I quietly replied.

He handed them to me.

"I¡ find here stated, that you are to arrest the Starost Lawenski, and conduct him a prisoner to Warsaw. No mention of his daughter—nor authority to intrude into this house."

' He answered not a word.

"You have disobeyed your instructions, Sir! The lady remains with us—no word! at your peril! Now, bring your prisoner here."

They durst not disobey, and the captive was brought before me, in chains!

"Unlock those fetters! you were to arrest a nobleman, not to drag a criminal to punishment."

The fetters fell, while deep silence reigned among our terrified oppressors.

"Starost!" I said, "it shall never be told that our honoured kinsman came to our house, and partook not of its hospitality. I pledge you in a goblet. God grant you liberty and life."

He drained the draught—he took a cheerful leave of one and all, but a tear glistened in the eyes of that venerable man as he embraced his daughter.

"She is safe with us; our home is hers."

"Bless you for that! Now, farewell! I am ready," He turned to the guard, and with a firm step, though every one brought him nearer to those dreadful dungeons, from which so few return—with a firm step and a placid smile he left our presence.

"Now, Sir!" I said, addressing the officer, "you quit Tyssen this instant. Untouched and unpunished—as such best beseems our honour;" and with muttered imprecations the trembling wretch fled from our house.

During this scene my father had stood an inactive spectator. When I confronted the Russian the ancient spirit seemed to be rekindled in his breast, and I believe, if an actual conflict had taken place, he would have displayed again the valour of his early days. But as he stood passive at the head of his serfs, dreadful recollections appeared to overcome him, he turned deadly pale, and his sword-arm sunk by his side. Yet there was not one of his faithful followers who would not have stood by him as truly as when he lead them on in the pride of courage and chivalry. They honoured him not less than of old; they loved him not less; they never accused him of cowardice or treachery when he delivered them up to the tyranny of Russia, for they knew from what accursed hand the blow had come, that had killed the spirit, though it spared the life.

When silence and order were again restored in the castle, we joined in a mutual thanksgiving to heaven for our deliverance, and the success of the effort that had achieved it; but my father, who knew, better than I did, the dreadful consequences that might result, was sad and dejected.

"Thekla is safe," he said, "but this may cost us our lives! Oh! Theodore! Theodore! I see death darkening the walls!"

"We must be prompt," I replied, "let us hasten to Warsaw this instant. Blood has not been shed, the Muscovite has evidently transgressed his orders. I will represent this, and gold will do the rest."

My father accompanied me to Warsaw. I pass over our interview with Novosiloff. At the cost of an enormous bribe, that left us scarcely a wreck of our ruined fortunes, we were permitted to escape with life and liberty, but not one word was uttered by the Russian, or dared be breathed by us, of justice on the vile satellite of government.

Fortunate in having escaped so well, we returned to our lonesome home, and for a short time I was permitted to taste of that melancholy happiness we feel, when knowing that the time is nearing rapidly in which the dear blessings we still enjoy may be torn from us for ever.

It was now spring, that came in its beauty and its glory. The forests around the walls of Tyssen again put forth their broad, green leaves, and the birds sang their blithe carols of liberty. Spring is the time of love, and that was mine. I now seldom left the castle, for we were almost prisoners on our estates ; but my captivity became less irksome, since it contained a being whose presence turned the gloomy mansion into a paradise. It was Thekla. Never did the deep sorrow leave her heart, never did the flash of joy steal over her pale but tranquil face, yet never did a word of plaint escape her lips. That was a happy time—and even balanced by my sufferings, I feel that I have had my share of earthly bliss.

Thekla was a true daughter of Poland—fair and gentle, but brave and highminded. I could see the fire ascend from the depth of her heart into her large, pensive eyes, and flash forth whenever a fresh tale of oppression and wrong was borne to our solitude ; and she it was who soothed my father's declining age and prolonged his life, like a soft, sunny gleam at the end of a stormy day.

Circumstances, in themselves trifling, often shew the heart more than great events. The songs of ancient Poland were forbidden.

I had given Thekla a canary, that one evening I had found fluttering alone before my window. It seemed like a little spirit, its wings still dyed with the golden glories of heaven, that had thus escaped from captivity and fled to us. Thekla had taught it to warble the tune of an almost forgotten national air of Poland, and loved to hear the little bird sing the forbidden melody. We both cherished it with an almost superstitious fondness. It would fly around Thekla and nestle in her bosom, nor think of escaping. I mention this circumstance, trivial as it may seem to you, in reference to a subsequent event.

The summer came and passed. Autumn deepened the hue of field and forest. The strength of Thekla appeared to wane, every day, but a flush began to steal over her cheek. I often watched her with an intensity of pain. Could that be the forerunner of death? Could that rosy hue be the dawn of the eternal day gliding on the night of earthly life? She became more weak and dejected the nearer winter approached, and myself partook of her sadness, whether it was but a reflection of her own, or a foreboding of the future.

At length the winter came with unusual severity, casting an additional gloom over our desolate home.

In the mean time the condition of Poland had been rapidly changing for the worse. The tyranny of our rulers grew more and more insupportable. No house—no sanctuary was safe. The old faithful serfs had been banished from the country, and the menials in most families became spies in the pay of Russia. To such an extent was this carried, that men conversed by signs, or in some foreign language, in their own houses, and often the traitors invented falsehoods of the master whose bread they ate, and brought destruction on the time-honoured head of the venerable warrior, who had perchance escaped the dangers of many a campaign. So great was this evil, that many families lived in perpetual dread of their servants, and ventured not to rebuke them for neglect or insolence, lest they should gratify their revenge by perjury, and turn informers. In many instances commissaries of police were invited by noblemen to reside in their mansions, that no opportunity for falsification might be offered; in some cases they were forced upon those particularly obnoxious and suspected, and thus a particular inquisitor and tyrant was admitted into the inmost recesses of the house.

Thus it was with us. As may be supposed, we were marked and doomed by the government; but, as long as we had gold to give, we could buy a temporary safety. Even that resource soon ceased. Ruined in fortune, and broken in spirit, the Lord of Tyssen had no hope but in the mercy of the tormentor. With the winter came the last blow to our ruined house. One day a commissary of police, attended by a number of officials, demanded admittance, and produced an order authorising him to reside with us, as suspected of rebellion and discontent. My foreboding at once traced the devilish conspiracy laid against us, when I beheld in our hateful guest the very officer I had before ignominiously expelled from the house.

He affected the most studious politeness, but triumphant malice burnt in his eyes. He soon threw off the mask, and the insolent official behaved in such a manner, that I have often almost cursed myself for having brooked his conduct. Nothing but Thekla withheld me. I bore it all for her sake—as I felt that I was her only protector, and that it would delight the Muscovite to remove me from the spot. My poor father seemed once more paralysed; the dungeons of the Belvedere evidently again floated before his sight.

But friends, would you believe it? The Russian spy dared

aspire to the hand of Thekla, and torment her with his odious suit. For a time I knew it not. She concealed it from me, lest my anger should lead me to any rash, imprudent act. But at length, when I questioned her one day more earnestly than ever, as to the cause of her still increasing dejection of spirit, she burst into a flood of tears, and confessed it all, after having extorted a pledge from me that I would not compromise my liberty by punishing the insolent slave. However, as *that* was not in my promise, I immediately sought him, and calmly but sternly forbade his aspiring to one so infinitely above him in every sense. At the same time, the conduct of Thekla ought to have convinced him that no earthly power could force her to yield to his wishes.

"Be mine," said the spy to her, "and your family shall not be molested again. Refuse——and dread my vengeance!"

He spoke in vain. Never shall I forget his fiendish look, when he found that even his threat proved unavailing. From that moment his conduct became insupportable. Everything that malice could invent to torture and aggravate, did he resort to—and, shortly afterwards, we were ordered to find permanent quarters for a detachment of police under his command.

The health of my beautiful Thekla declined daily more and more beneath her sufferings; but I believe even *they* were as nothing, compared to the agony *I* endured, in seeing this, and not being able to save or avenge!

For her sake I bore every indignity as long as the human heart could brook it, but I well knew the time must come when the fatal collision would take place, and I augured truly.

One day I was sitting by the side of Thekla, enjoying a moment's tranquil converse—a boon but rarely granted, since the eyes of our tormentor were on every spot. She had freed the canary I had given her from its cage, and it flew around her and nestled in her bosom, singing the melody of that sweet and stirring Polish air it had been taught by her, when suddenly the brutal Russian burst into the chamber.

"Ha! What is this I hear?" he cried. "This nursery of sedition baffles our efforts. Say, vile trickstress! who taught the bird that air? I warrant it shall never sing again!"

So saying, he snatched at the affrighted bird, that had taken refuge in Thekla's bosom. I rose, unable any longer to restrain my anger, but ere I could speak, Thekla had sunk on her knees before the monster.

"Pardon! pardon!" she cried. "Spare *that* ——!"

He answered but by a brutal laugh, and tore the little warbler from her bosom. She folded her white arms over its fluttering wings, but he dashed her violently aside, and, before any one could prevent it, the poor bird was cast dead at her feet.

"Even these are made the instruments of sedition!"—he exclaimed.

Scarcely was the deed accomplished, ere I felled him to the ground, and would have destroyed him on the spot, had I not been suddenly seized and disarmed by a couple of his Muscovite officials, who rushed into the room.

"Ha!" said the spy, rising with a livid frown; "I have waited long for this. Seize that girl and her paramour. Bind them, and let them await further orders. Before to-morrow night we will be at the Belvedere."

His words were instantly obeyed, despite my frantic efforts to free myself and seize a weapon; and they were obeyed with brutality. The cords were strained around Thekla's tender limbs, till they were reddened with her blood. She uttered not a groan, but kept her speaking eyes fixed despairingly on mine.

At length, the order to march came, and accordingly our fetters were partially loosened, and, surrounded by a guard, we were brought into the court of the castle.

The troops were marshalled, and the spoiler appeared.

His brutal jests fell on unheeding ears; the chibouque-men took their places; and he even dared to lift his arm and strike—ay! strike—the tender form of my beautiful Thekla!

It was December, and the day was intensely severe. The snow fell fast and thick, and the bitter wind froze to the core. Thekla had nothing to protect her from the cold but a thin robe and a shawl, which the piercing blast lifted every moment from around her, exposing her snowy bosom to the icy chill of death! But even of that slight fence she was deprived by a brutal Russian, who tore it from her with the words—"A vile rebel, like you, must not be covered, while we are freezing."

Thus we commenced our way over the wild and desolate plains.

I contrived, whether from the heedlessness of the guard, or from a feeling of pity on their part, to reach the side of Thekla.

I took her hand—it was icy cold; the snow flakes melted not as they fell on her bosom. She could not speak—but she smiled on me as I approached. I pressed her slender form to my breast: it was cold—cold as death! She moved with difficulty, but still that celestial smile played around her angelic face, as though the joy of heaven was stealing over her fleeting spirit.

"Thekla!" I breathed, "farewell!—Die! die! my Thekla! —there is no peace for you on this earth! Oh! one more smile!—one more, on this side the grave! And, now— farewell!"

As I spoke, her form grew rigid, and felt heavier and heavier: her beaming eyes were still fixed on mine—the spirit of death came over her—her smile became more unearthly, and she glided from my powerless arms.

I paused a moment, and beheld a little white mound gathered where she lay, as the snow fell over her, like a shroud folded by the invisible hand of God—pure and stainless, it well became her pained and spotless spirit. The outline of her form might still be traced beneath, as though a marble statue reclined there.

(To be continued.)

THE LAW AND THE LAND.

The assailants of the National Land Company have, among other numerous assertions, declared that it, or its promoters, have violated 'the statute' relating to joint-stock companies. We have thought that a few pages devoted to this subject may not be unacceptable to our readers. To begin at the beginning, it is necessary to state that, previously to 1844, joint-stock companies or associations were formed under various instruments, viz. 1. By act of parliament. 2. By royal charter. 3. By letters patent. 4. By deeds of settlement. 5. By articles of provisional agreement. And even now companies may be established by any of the first three instruments above mentioned, as the act passed in 1844 does not apply to such cases.

In that year a statute was passed (7 and 8 Vic. c. 110), for "the registration, incorporation, and regulation of joint-stock companies." The object of this statute, amongst others, was to prevent the formation of fraudulent companies, and to obtain a registry or account of all companies. It expressly excepts from its operation "friendly" or "benefit" societies. The requirements of this act may briefly be stated to be, that companies coming within it should be formed by deed, should be first provisionally registered, and then completely registered. There is no time fixed for complete registration to take place, but if certain acts are done before such registration, penalties will be incurred by the promoters of the company.

The legal charge against the Land Company is thus stated by "One who has whistled at the plough;" and it is a great pity he ever was taken from it. He must have been the plough-boy "who whistled as he went *for want* of thought."

He certainly s not cut out for a lawyer. We give his own words :—

"The Society," he says,'" is not yet registered. It never will be registered. It cannot now be done. . . . S. 23 of the Joint-stock Company's Act, enacted for the protection of the public from fraudulent schemes, provides that it shall not be lawful for a company, until completely registered, ' to make calls, nor to purchase, contract for, or hold lands,' &c. It provides penalties for the infringement of its clauses, the penalties varying from 5l. to 25l. each ; every one of which clauses the Chartist Land Company has already violated ; to every one of which penalties they are already liable, amounting in the aggregate to several thousand pounds. The penalties may be recovered as soon as they are registered, but not sooner, as it is not until then a company."

Now, in the above extract there are as many blunders as can possibly be stuffed into an equal number of words. The statements made are not only erroneous in law, but also in fact.

First—The society *is* registered. Not completely, but provisionally registered ; which the "Whistler " seems to think is no registration whatever, as he says, "it is not registered ;" and again, "until registered it is not a company." In this also he is wrong, if he means it is not a company until completely registered, for it became one on provisional registration. To show this it is only necessary to refer to their powers at such a stage, and to the 23rd section of 7th and 8th Vic., c. 110, whereby it is enacted, that "on the provisional registration of any company being certified, it shall be lawful for the promoters of any company so registered to act provisionally," while by section 25, on complete registration the company becomes incorporated. Probably the writer was not aware of the difference which prevails between a company and a corporation, and thus was led to mistake one for the other.

Secondly—He says that the society cannot now be registered. As we have said, it *is* registered provisionally. And we repeat, that a company may be completely registered at any time ; there is no limitation as to period whatever. We should like to see the reference to the act, and the section of it, that prevents a company from being completely registered at any time.

Thirdly—In this lawyer's opinion innumerable penalties have been incurred by the company, or its promoters, by their having purchased land before they were completely registered. In the very same article from which we have made an extract, he attacks Mr. O'Connor because he has purchased the land in his own name, and as if it were for himself. There is, therefore, a gross inconsistency on the face of the statement; first, the company is liable to penalties for having purchased the land; but presently it appears, on his own showing, that not the company, but Mr. O'Connor, has purchased it. How is this to be reconciled? We know not, but this we know; that with a due regard to the state of the law, and the difficulties that occurred to the company, the land has been bought in Mr. O'Connor's name, conveyed to him, and allotted by him. It is not held by the company, but by him or the allottees in their individual character. The fabric raised by this imaginative writer, therefore, falls to the ground. No penalties whatever have been incurred, nor can any, therefore, be recovered. On complete registration the land may be conveyed to the company. We are not aware of any law prohibiting the purchase of land by an individual, as such, at any period, or under any circumstances, or the allotment of land by him to any number of persons that he may think proper. If it were otherwise, all landowners who have bought their estates, or who have let them out to tenants, or allotted them in small or large parcels, would have violated the law. The joint-stock company's act was never intended to apply, nor does it apply, to such cases.

We would refer this writer, for his information in other cases, to a late statute, which appears to have escaped his notice, the 10th and 11th Vic., c. 78, which repeals many of the penalties which are imposed by the statute, 7th and 8th Vic. c. 110, in those cases where companies, as companies, have infringed its enactments.

In the same article from which we have quoted, it is suggested that Mr. O'Connor might devise the land to the company if it were completely registered; but if he did not devise it the land would go to his next of kin, or if he devised it to the company not completely registered, he must devise it separately, perhaps, to about 50,000 shareholders. Now the first part of this suggestion admits that he may convey or devise the land to the company when completely registered, which is something for an opponent to admit, though presently we shall see he states that the original owners of the property, from whom it was purchased, may resume it,

and all contracts now made relating to it will be void, even
if the company be completely registered !

In the latter branches of the above proposition this writer
has conveniently overlooked very important facts. First,
that the land purchased *is* conveyed to the allottees, as so
many individuals, as soon as possible after it has been purchased; and, therefore, that Mr O'Connor is then divested of
all property and title in it. Secondly, that it may be
devised to one trustee for numerous parties. And thirdly,
that in any event equity would enforce the trust reposed in
Mr. O'Connor, and see that the parties beneficially entitled
to the land became possessed of it. If I am employed as
a land agent by five hundred persons, or any number, and
am entrusted with their funds to purchase land for them,
and do so purchase it, in equity it is their and not my property.

It is next alleged by this writer, that on complete registration of the company " all contracts become illegal and
lapse. (What is the meaning of a contract lapsing ?) The
original owners of the estates may resume ownership, as if
they had not been sold, and penalties to the amount of
nearly 4,000*l.* may be enforced."

" The contracts will become illegal" by doing what ?
By pursuing the act of parliament and completely register-
ing the company ! If they are legal now, it seems strange
that illegality should be imparted to them by doing what
the act requires. This is new law. It will also be observed,
that throughout this passage the writer assumes that the
company, as such, have purchased the land, although he
had before asserted that Mr O'Connor alone had done so.
We have already said that the company do not purchase
the land ; but, even if it were otherwise, the above conclusion by no means follows. Supposing, for the argument, that
the promoters had infringed the statute ; the only result
would be that they might be liable for penalties, but their
contracts would not be void. The original owners could
not recover the property. It is well established in law that,
even under an illegal contract, where money has been paid
or land conveyed, it cannot be recovered again.

The law will not assist parties to an illegal contract,
either to enforce or rescind it. Although if an action be
brought to carry into effect an unexecuted contract, the
illegality thereof is a defence ; yet, after it is once executed,
a party to the contract and the illegality of it cannot on
that ground render it null. No party would be allowed to

avoid his own deed by stating that he had been a party to the violation of a statute, that he had received the purchase money for so doing, but that now he would like to have the land also, as a reward for his own wrong.

What is to be said of one who sets up for a public writer and teacher, and thus blunders in every assertion which he makes ? Who can depend either upon the facts or the law (heaven save the mark!) which he publishes for the mystification of his unhappy readers ? However, we have done with him for the present, and his effusions.

We will now proceed to lay before our readers a statement relating to the Land Company, regarded in its legal aspect.

When the Land Plan was first projected, its promoters were anxious to avoid every unnecessary expense, and to render it as simple and as economical as was consistent with a due regard to the protection of the interests of the subscribers. For this purpose they submitted the rules to counsel, who were not in any way connected with the project. The rules were settled by these counsel, who advised that the company should be enrolled as a friendly or benefit society. Mr. Tidd Pratt, who is the gentleman officially appointed for the purpose of enrolling such societies, decided that this association—so novel in its principle, and so extensive in its contemplated operations—did not come within the intention, or provisions, of the statutes relating to friendly societies. His own individual opinion was in favour of its enrolment; but he stated that a learned judge had recently held, that a more limited construction was to be put upon these statutes than he himself had thought requisite, and, of course, he was bound by the judicial holding. The rules were again laid before counsel for revision and alteration, so that they might be rendered conformable to the statutes, provided that could be done without sacrificing the essential principle of the association. They were remodelled, and again laid before Mr. Tidd Pratt, who still, however, refused to enrol them, much as he regretted what he considered his duty, on account of the judgment above mentioned. Consultations were held with him, but all to no purpose. What, then, was to be done ? A bill was actually prepared, and was brought into parliament by Mr. Duncombe, to amend the Friendly Societies' Acts, so as to include the Land Company within them. This, of itself, shows how strenuous were the efforts made to give the members of the company the benefits, privileges, and protection, of a friendly society. The bill passed, but so altered and limited in its provisions, by amendments proposed by Sir James Graham, and adopted by the House—with a view, it is believed, to exclude the Land Company—that still it was not supposed to come under the denomination of a friendly society.

Counsel were again consulted, and then it was resolved, as the most proper step to be taken, to make the association a joint-stock company, and to bring it within the provisions of the Act 7 and 8 Vic., c. 110.

The deed was prepared as soon as possible; the company were provisionally registered; Mr. Duncombe was registered as the trustee; and, in the meantime, purchases were made, under legal advice, in the name of one individual.

Thus, the only law in existence of which the company were permitted to avail itself, was brought to bear upon it; but, for want of proper machinery, under the statute, to conduct so huge an affair as the Land Company—from the magnitude of its constitution and operations—from the vast number of members, and the distances at which they reside from each other—delay and difficulty in the complete registration of the company have unavoidably occurred. As one instance, among many, it may be sufficient to state, that the deed must be signed by at least one-fourth of the subscribers, before a certificate of complete registration can be obtained—that the first deed required the signatures of between 8,000 and 9,000 persons, scattered throughout the country! Notwithstanding, however, all these obstacles, the deed has now received almost every signature that is required; and, in a few weeks, the company will be completely registered, and an application be made to the Board of Trade, under the statute, to enable the company to hold lands in the names of their trustees. Such is our *legal* statement of the matter, so far as it comes within the scope of the present article.

In concluding these remarks we would observe, that, for the purpose of preventing fraudulent schemes, and bubble speculations, as far as they can be prevented by acts of parliament, it is a great mistake to suppose that complete registration is the material point. *Provisional* registration of companies is the most important part. It was so intended to be by the statute (7 and 8 Vic., c. 110), and it is well known that railway companies, seldom, if ever, register, except provisionally. It is the provisional registration that gives the public information as to the nature

and purpose of the company—as to the names of 'the promoters and committee—their occupation,' and places of
residence—their agreement to take shares in the undertak-,
ing—the names and residences of the officers, and the like.
All this is required on provisional registration, by section.
5 of the Joint-stock Companies' Act. It was to give this
publicity, and to impose the consequent responsibility, that
the act was chiefly passed. This purpose is answered by
provisional registration alone. Whoever will turn to the
act of parliament may satisfy himself on these points.

MONTHLY REVIEW.

In the ever-shifting scenes of the great drama of politics, fresh changes, and some of them important ones,
have occurred since last we addressed our readers.
The recent measure affecting the Currency in ENGLAND,
is one of those startling acts, forced on the legislature
by the cumbrous and complicated machinery of government, showing the badness of its original construction,
and requiring sudden and violent remedies to keep it,
for a short time longer, in apparent order. It is a symptom of "the beginning of the end." Look where we
will, we find fresh signs of dilapidation and insecurity
in the old legislative structure : the elements of disorganisation are indeed at work. The middle class has raised its
hand against the aristocracy, and either are bidding for
the people. The aristocracy cry : "Give up the Charter in
its entirety, and we will aid you in our feudal charity."
The middle classes say : "We are for the Charter, only
you must give up 'THE NAME!' You must not talk
and make a noise; you must, in short, give up agitation
and leave the whole matter in our hands, and you shall
have the Charter—when you can get it!"
They must, indeed, be devoted adherents of the Charter,
when they already shrink at the mere name ! They must
be ready to give us the substance, when they won't even
tolerate the shadow. We are not to speak, not to meet, not
to act, not to agitate; what then are we to do? We are

to trust in them! Why not in ourselves? They must
show us in what way they are more able to obtain the
Charter for us, than we ourselves. Are they, the middle
class, so much stronger than the people? Why—they
could not even defeat the aristocracy without us! They
could not carry free trade without us! And now they find
they cannot escape pecuniary ruin without us. Now they
find home trade is the only thing that can save them from
bankruptcy, and that the working-classes are the only
source to which they can look for replenishing their coffers.
Then, after all, the middle-classes, despite their vote, are
nothing, can do nothing, without the people!—can only
live, act and govern through the people; yet they want
the people to give up agitating for themselves, and dele-
gate their cause to the keeping of a secondary power!
But the people are wise enough to know that they must
work for themselves, if they wish their work to be done.
This the people are doing—Land and Charter bear witness. Then the middle-class steps forth again, and tries
to blight the buds of political promise. The essentially
middle-class papers must attack the Land scheme, sneer at
the Charter, and enter into an infamous conspiracy against
Mr. O'Connor. In the leader they wish to crush the
movement—and, as they cannot attack his public, they
seek to damage his private character; thinking, trusting,
hoping, that as most men have something they wish to
conceal—though they know their accusations to be false—
there may be something or other, nobody has ever heard
of, he may fear to have brought to light, and thus shrink
from refuting the false, out of dread lest they should discover something not yet found out. Happily for the cause
of progression, Mr. O'Connor has *courted*, not shrunk
from investigation. He has nothing to conceal. He
lays the whole course of his life bare before the people,
discloses all his public and private transactions, gives
name and address of all with whom he has stood in business or family relations, and then, turning the tables
on his enemies, proves them to have been guilty of
the very things, and worse, of which they dared to accuse
him. This attack and defence will be a memorable page
in the history of our times; and every honest man
must reprobate the base cowards who paid a spy for nine
months to pry into another man's family affairs, and then
let out their bottled venom at a time when its object was
on the Continent—trusting some weeks would elapse before
he could reply—that the poison would have had sufficient

time to circulate with fatal effect—that the procrastinated answer would come too late to efface the impression—and when made, that they could confuse and bewilder the public by a Babel of figures, accusations, charges, and misinterpretations of laws, from all sides at once ;—bringing such a torrent of attack, such hosts of figures and legal quibbles, that it would be out of the power of man to answer them *all*, while the omission of one would seem to substantiate each. But they miscalculated their own strength, and that of their opponent. They forgot, too, that the confidence of the people was not so easily shaken by the vague howl of untried advocates, who vouch for their honesty in words alone, and have no long career of active usefulness and devotion to the people's cause, to point back to as their voucher. They were mistaken, we say. Scarcely was their first arrow launched before Mr. O'Connor hurried back to England, and scattered their vile accusations to thin air. Never has the Land Plan been so prosperous—never has the Charter showed more real and healthy vigour.

Meanwhile, the Cabinet are at their wit's end, if ever, they had any " wit." The speedy meeting of Parliament, convoked for the 18th, shows their perplexity—and how fearful they are of taking responsibility on their own shoulders. That responsibility, however, they will have to bear.

The House of Commons has been a congregation of tails—the Peel tail, the Bentinck tail, the O'Connell tail, the Cobden tail. Parliament has been the representation of four great *personalities*. And, if the government are at last fearful of such personal responsibility, the only way of relieving themselves of it is to admit the People to a just share in the representation.

Abroad, ITALY, MEXICO, and SPAIN afford materials for much comment, which the limits of this article preclude. Sanguinary battles, sacked cities, horrible slaughter, revolting atrocities—outrages at which humanity blushes for the name of man—have failed as yet to destroy the Mexican, while the following paragraph well shows how the American people will have to suffer for their victories :—

" The receipts into the Treasury of the United States duaing the last three months amounted to 20,405,000*dol.* of which 8,130,000*dol.* was the produce of the revenue and land sales, and 12,240,000*dol.* of loans. The amount of Treasury Notes outstanding on the 2nd instant was 14,274,000*dol.* Notwithstanding the large amount of receipts from loans, the expenditure during the same period exceeded the receipts by 2,000,000*dol.*—the whole amount of expenditure being 22,475,000*dol.* The greater part of this immense expenditure is applied to carrying on the war with Mexico."

What are the people doing in SPAIN? Narvaez has returned, like the courier of Christina, who follows, a worthless courtesan, with her titled paramour. The gold jingles, the bayonet glitters, and the wicked old man of the Tuileries laughs, while poor Queen Isabella is made the fool of faction, and the people suffer for her weakness. Let this shew the people the necessity of struggling for themselves, instead of trusting in princes : had they taken their liberties into their own keeping, a palace intrigue could never have subverted them.

In ITALY, the treachery of the King of Naples is so gross, that it will act as its own antidote :—the people, driven to desperation, will fly to arms—and then——events will prove whether they are capable of making a good use of victory.

Pope Pius has paused in his career of reform—he is resting on his laurels. We warn him not to sacrifice the liberty of other countries (Ireland for instance) for the good of Rome—but to remember that it is only the growing spirit of liberty in other countries, that can interpose between him and the barbarism of Austria and Russia.

LITERARY REVIEW.

EBENEZER JONES.

There is decidedly a democratic tendency beginning to pervade our literature. It has first stolen into the pages of poetry. Byron, and Southey (in his earlier works) first impressed them with this feature, and since then they have had copious and unequal imitators. Simultaneously with having taken this direction, poetry began to rise in feeling and power—and it is a significant fact, that not one modern poet has written a work, poetically good, upon a slavish theme. Is not this a proof how poesy and truth are one—how poesy is the exponent of the living spirit of the age? We know of no exception to this rule. Elizabeth Barrett (now Mrs. Robert Browning) embraces the side of democracy in her "Lady Geraldine," in her touching cry of the factory children; the spirit of freedom pervades even her chivalrous "Flight of the Duchess May." Even the court poet, Tennyson, has chided the pride of "Lady Clara Vere de Vere." Browning himself has illustrated the dignity of man in his magnificent play of "Colombe's Birthday." Knowles, in one of his best productions, where he finds the true nobility (that of nature,) in the breast of a serf—and again where he makes a peasant his hero, in "The Rose of Arragon." Mackay has attuned his admirable lyrics to themes of liberty—even Bulwer emits some scintillations of its light through his elaborate and metaphysical productions. There are hosts of others; but we are now alluding only to those who are not professedly democratic authors, and whose associations and general themes appear to point to the reverse tendency. But, while there is much to applaud in modern poets, both in the beneficial direction and vigour of their writings, there is also much to regret. Even those among them who avowedly write for the people, write in a language utterly unintelligible to the general, and, indeed, in some instances to any, reader. Others affect a forced simplicity, that has something irresistibly comic. Thus, imitating the worst features of a bad school, we have:—

> " The cloudy impulse of his surcharged soul,
> Wrought in the alembic of his teeming thought,
> Forced the full rivers of his life to deluge,
> Swamping the frail shell of ideal cares."

Proh Jupiter! What an extraordinary being he must have been! Or: " The air was cool, heavy and thick. Snowflakes flew about; they fell here; they fell there; they fell also upon Olof's hat, as he went down the street." Why, of course they did, always supposing Olof had a hat on; but what moral or sentiment is conveyed in the fact that the snowflakes fell on Olof's hat, any more than on his coat or boots, or buttons, we are at a loss to discover. The (almost questionable) pathos of the passage in Tennyson's poem, where the lover buries his face in the grass of his bride's grave, and cries, " Speak a little, Ellen Adair!" is out-heroded here.

Canning ably lashed this style of writing, when he sang,

> " By thé side of a murmuring stream
> An'elderly gentleman sat;
> On the top of his head was his wig;
> On the top of his wig was his hat."

It is into both these faults that the author, whose name is prefixed to this notice, has fallen. We are ready to give him credit for great power at intervals, great originality at times, and for the production of a few little pieces which are among the sweetest gems we have for some time met. But most of the subjects—a grave fault—are unhappily chosen : at times he degenerates into unintelligible obscurity, is fond of transposing words, neglectful of the harmonies of rhythm, and partial to placing his heroes and heroines in the most preposterous and extraordinary situations. These are grave charges against him as a poet, but there are others, still more serious, which we shall make against the tendency of his writings. We notice this author in our magazine, since he aims at being a democratic poet, and it is necessary that democratic poets should, in their pages, *elevate* and not endanger the dignity of the democratic character. In the work before us, to recur to our primary objections, (a work entitled, quaintly enough, " Studies of Sensation and Event,") there is a poem, entitled, " The Crisis." A young gentleman goes to " propose " to a young lady. The lady is in a meadow. As he approaches :

> " She lifts her head; against the tree behind,
> She plants its crown ; her feet move slightly back;
> Up outwardly she boldly lifts her form ;
> Like a ship-sail, windcurved from the mast,
> She roundeth out ! "

But the gentleman surpasses even this. After indescribable grimaces—hesitating whether he shall not trip up her heels—he tears, " with a cry," a " talisman " from his breast, and runs away. On the talisman words are written, ending thus :—

> " Witnessing love she loves not, uncurtained :—
> Then, beautiful girl ! though one could love thee so ;
> His passions in tumultuous armies waiting,
> Worshippingly to convoy thee down time ;
> He wills not love exultingly shall go ;
> His passions past thee, loudly jubilating
> Towards life's fit ways, so crowdedly sublime."

We would ask one of our fair friends, if they received a love letter like that, what would they think of the author? The end of the poem does not redeem, but, on the contrary, seals its condemnation.

Again: we have the son of a Lord Apswern, whom his father (who, it appears, had been a sort of Duke of Wellington, and "lashed" the world with his armies and his statemanship,) desires, by his will, to go every day naked into a naked room, reared above the roof of the house, and there wrestle nakedly with himself. We rather think Lord Douro would not much like his father to make such a will, and have some doubts as to the sanity of the maker. And what is the moral of this poem, (replete with intense imagery and great descriptive powers)? Absolutely none.

Besides these faults, there is one, however, far more grave, which we lay at the author's door: it is that of indelicacy. We would warn him that freedom is not license, and that poetry is not to be profaned, in glossing over those obscenities which, in plain prose, would subject the writer to contempt and disgust. We cannot illustrate these remarks with quotations, since their nature precludes the possibility, but we could instance "Zingalee," "The Crisis," and very many others. Having expressed our opinion of his faults, it would be unjust were we not to illustrate his beauties, which we purpose doing by extracting the following little poem, the refined beauty of which needs no comment.

REPOSE IN LOVE.

"I flew to thee, love, I flew to thee, love,
   From a world where all's deceit;
The river rushing to the sea, love,
   Speeds not so wildly fleet:
And now while basked beneath thine eyes,
   Where truth so calmly glows;
Than the saint's first rest in paradise,
   I know more sweet repose.

In former time beside thee glowing,
   I've seen all life grow bright;
Kindness o'er hardest faces flowing;
   O'er falsehood new truth-light:

And then I thought it matchless bliss,
 To see the stars twice shine,
All baseness from the earth to miss,
 Because I felt me thine.

But now I know joy deeper far
 Attends our love's career;
It now no more veils life's vile war,
 But lifts me past life's sphere;
And no joy may with this compare,
 I see life's base design,
Yet know no fear, no pain, no care,
 Because I feel me thine.

We may also allude favourably to "A Slave's Triumph," "Inactivity," and many descriptive passages dispersed throughout this author's poems, and trust that he will shew more judgment in the direction of his talents than he has hitherto displayed.

We shall recur, from time to time, to this discrepancy existing between the talent of the author and the direction it assumes, since we believe, in few ages has England been able to boast of so great an amount of literary genius, as in the present—and in no age has that genius been turned to so bad an account. It falls still-born from the press, because it is not tuned to the popular key, and the works of an author, to descend to future times must ever be the faithful exponent of his own. In France, Germany, and Italy, we have names eminent and idolised in the world of letters, yet belonging to men no greater than we can boast of, simply because they have paid due regard to this truism, and because they have not cloaked their thoughts under an affected and ridiculous obscurity of diction. We are far from wishing our authors to become *imitators;* genius, to be true and brilliant, must be original; yet, without imitation, much may be learned from foreign literature. We therefore purpose, in ensuing numbers, to give a digest of the most popular works of continental authors. We shall begin with the poets, since poetry is the graceful peristyle through which we enter into the temple of thought.

It is the first language of civilisation—a nation's history, a nation's literature, begins with it; and it puts the seal upon its records and its glory. "Let me write the ballads of a country, and who will may make its laws,' was, indeed, a true sentiment—attesting alike the antiquity, the power, and the perpetuity of poetry in the moral government of man. It will, therefore, be well to contemplate the phases of differing nationalities on the Continent through the medium of their literature; and we intend commencing our series with the authors of Poland and Russia, since these are, we believe, least known to the English public. The prose works of these two countries are, indeed, very defective, which may be accounted for from the relative situations of either people. The Pole has been led through centuries of discord to feel more than to think; through subsequent heroic struggles, when thought was called into action, it has been imbued with an impassioned sorrow, which we find apparent in almost every specimen of Polish literature. The Russian, on the other hand, has been cramped and confined by despotism : his practical energies were allowed to develope themselves only in works of statistics, geography, &c. Still in their hearts were the secret aspirations after freedom, which could only find vent in the covered allegory, the dreamy abstraction, or the obscure lament. These, again, required to be carefully veiled from the critical eye of the censor, and thence the frequent discrepancy between the commencement of a poem and its conclusion. Thus, for instance, we shall find a poem beginning with an impassioned call to liberty and arms, and concluding with deprecating the same, since it might be all very well for other countries, but needless under the beneficent rule of the august Czar. The poet was wise, the poet was sly; since the language of liberty is the same all over the world, and praise given to the undeserving is the most cutting of satirical condemnations. We think we may safely promise our readers some amusement and instruction from the series of articles we intend giving on this subject, and we would recommend our poet-friends to study some of the models of foreign composition, both in prose and verse, and not in an imitative spirit, but since new lights and new views, will open to them as they read—and since the intercourse of minds, like the confluence of streams, deepens the tide of thought, feeling, and imagination, and is more likely to produce the great, than isolated brooding over individual fancies. As a proof of this, the literature of isolated countries has ever been the poorest—need we point to Iceland, Finland, Siberia, Tatary, China, and Japan.

THE LABOURER

THE AGE OF PEACE.

BY ERNEST JONES.

Men! exult with one another,
   See how wrong and bloodshed cease!
Man in man beholds a brother—
   'Tis—oh! 'tis the age of peace!

Peace! ha! ha! be wind and vapour,
   Foolish thought of feeble soul,
Keep alight thy twinkling taper,
   While the whirlwind seeks its goal!

Hark! from distant eastern waters,
   To the farthest western wave,
Comes the voice of many slaughters,
   O'er the earth's unclosing grave.

Hark! in seas of China booming,
   How the loud artillery roars;
And a thousand masts are looming
   On La Plata's battered shores.

Hark! the Caffir groans unheeded,
   Scourged by strong invader's hand;
And the Indian lance is needed
   To defend the Affghan's land.

Hark! along the wide Zahara,
   Rings the volley—flames the steel;
From Morocco to Boccara,
   Columns march and squadrons wheel.

Hark! by Otaheite's garden,
   Threats and flames the French corvette;
And the blackened bodies harden,
   Where the west its wigwam set.

Hark ! to slaughter's ruddy riot,
   Where New Zealand's mountains soar ;
And the gathering storm's unquiet,
   Over Madagascar's shore.

Hark ! between the Grecian islands,
   Speeds the fleet with captive crqwds ;
Hark ! along Albanian highlands,
   Lie the dead in bloody shrouds.

Hark ! beneath Circassia's mountains,
   Moloch sports with human right,
Veins are torrents, hearts are fountains,
   For the streams of freedom's fight.

Then ! exult with one another.
   See, how wrong and bloodshed cease !
Man in man beholds a brother—
   'Tis—oh ! 'tis the age of Peace !

Peace !   The lightning-shaft must shatter
   Chains, the sunshine cannot part.
Peace with all your canting clatter !
   Sword in hand ! and hope in heart !

" Oh ! but this is all the ravage
   Of untamed barbarian life !"
Not so—European savage !
   It is you who brought the strife.

Go to each enlightened nation .
   Little need afar to roam—
Bid your mild civilisation
   Look at home—ay ! look at home !

Hark ! In plains of Poland blighted,
   Murdered men in myriads fall ;
And the fires of faith are lighted
   In the Minsk confessional.

Hark ! the Austrians in Ferrara,
   And the Goth has passed the Po,
And the Pontiff's peace-tiara
   Is a helm to fight the foe !

Hark ! there's murder in Messina ;
  Treachery rules in Naples' bay,
Where Sicilia's crowned hyæna
  Reigns to trample, lives to slay.

Hark ! In Spain the armies gather,
  Myriads fell where myriads fall !
In the Asturias stormy weather,
  Treason in the capital.

Hark ! Oporto's lines are tinted
  Red with sally and assault ;
And the fields of fight are stinted
  But to fill the prison-vault.

Hark ! the Swiss to battle sounding !
  Clans on clans defying call ;
'Mid the bayonets all-surrounding
  Of the Austrian and the Gaul.

Hark ! the mason's horrid clangour
  Piles the fort round Paris' streets,
To defy a nation's anger
  At a crowned impostor's cheats.

All thy cannon will be wanted
  When thy withered pulses cease,
For thy death-bed will be haunted,
  Thou Napoleon of Peace !

Hark ! 'mid Mexico's surrender,
  Comes a challenge ill repressed.
Where's thy honour ? poor pretender !
  Shame ! Republic of the West.

Talk no more of freedom's glory,
  Manhood's truth and people's right
Thy "*stripes*" on slavery's back are gory,
  Thy " stars " shine truly, but in night.

Mourn to mark thy institutions,
  Vice's kingly semblance take !
Mighty child of revolutions,
  Young America, awake !

Hark to bleeding Ireland's sorrow !,
  Tyrants, take your fill to-night ;
'Tis the people's turn to-morrow—
  Wait awhile. 'Twill soon be light !

Hark to England's voice of wailing !
  Not alone the People rue;
Commerce tarries—banks are failing,
  And the smiter's smitten too.

Baffled League and palsied faction,
  Lords of land and lords of trade,
Stagger 'neath the vast reaction
  Of the ruin they have made.

Hark ! the poor are starving daily ;
  Gold is jingling, bayonets clank ;
Hark ! the great are living gaily,
  And corruption's smelling rank.

But the sands of time are running ;
  Ever hope, and never fear !
Oh ! the people's hour is coming '
  Oh ! the people's hour is near !

Then ! exult with one another,
  Then shall wrong and bloodshed cease ;
Man in man respect a brother,
  And the world be won for peace !

THE INSURRECTIONS

OF

THE WORKING CLASSES.

(Continued from page 208.)

CHAPTER VIII.

The Revolt of Rienzi, 1341—1357.

The ceremony of Rienzi's knighthood has been transmitted, with various comments, by the annalist. A vast procession followed the Tribune from the Capitol to the Lateran ; magnificent arches and pageants enlivened the way ; the guilds, and ecclesiastic, civil and military bodies moved under their banners in separate detachments, the Roman matrons attended the Tribune's wife, and the ambassadors of Italy accompanied the chief magistrate of Rome. When they had reached the Lateran, Rienzi dismissed the assembly, and the ceremony of installation commenced. The purification of the bath was performed in the porphyry vase in which Pope Sylvester was fabled to have healed Constantine of his leprosy ; and when the court of Avignon reproved him for this desecration, and subsequently mentioned it in the papal anathema, he wittily replied, that " a vase which had been used by a pagan, would not be profaned by a good christian." He held his night-watch in the baptistry, but, as he ascended his state bed, it broke under him, and his attendants shrunk at this omen of his approaching downfall ; a venerable knight invested him with the order of the Holy Ghost ; and at the earliest hour of worship impatient crowds were dazzled by the scene of solemn splendour in the church, and the majesty of Rienzi, who, advancing before the congregation, summoned the sacred college of cardinals, and pope Clement, and commanded him to reside in his diocese of Rome ; who designated the rival emperors, Lewis of Bavaria and Charles of Bohemia, as pretenders ; and challenged the Electors of Germany to shew him on what pretence they had usurped the inalienable right of the Roman people, the antient and lawful sovereigns of the empire. The historian may pity or admire the spirit which prompted these words, but he must remember that they were based on the strictest truth ; that the Tribune had at this time received the most solemn assurances of aid from lying princes and fickle republics ; that the chief of the federative union of Italy might well dictate to the kings of mediæval Europe ; that crowned heads had already appealed to his justice ; and that a summons as startling and as bold had already succeeded in establishing the Good Estate. Those words have rung on the ear of nations. They compelled in a later day the popes and college of cardinals to return to Rome, and they are now, under altered phases, hurling the ardour of Italy on the cold diplomacy of the north. A gorgeous banquet closed the ritual of the day. The courts and halls of the Lateran were spread with innumerable tables, the nostrils of Constantine's brazen horse ran wine ; countless multitudes were feasted, yet, such was the discipline and order established by Rienzi, that no act of licence, no breach of peace, marred the festivities of the day. The Tribune was subsequently crowned by seven of the leading clergy with seven circlets of different metals, emblematic of the seven gifts of the Holy Ghost, while the barons of Rome, stood humble and tamed, with bare heads and downcast looks, in the presence of their plebeian master.

Bitter was the vengeance they vowed for their humiliation, and to effect their purpose, the long continued feud of the

Colonna and Orsini was suspended, but they dared not openly avow their enmity. The blow, which they themselves feared to strike, was confided to an assassin. But the vigilant power of the Tribune seized the criminal, who confessed the names of his employers and the extent of the conspiracy. The prompt decision of Rienzi prevented the escape of his enemies. As soon as the culprit had been seized he was questioned and confessed, and as the names of the guilty nobles fell from his lips, a messenger was despatched to each, inviting him in courteous terms to the Capitol. They came, unknowing whether their emissary had yet attempted the crime, and believing they were summoned to a banquet or a council. They were soon undeceived, when, surrounded by tribunal guards, the gates were closed in their rear, and the great bell of the Capitol began to summon the people.

They were led into the presence of the multitude ; formally arraigned and convicted; not a voice, not a hand, was raised in their defence ; and one sound of execration dismissed them to their prisons.

Five of the Orsini and three of the Colonna, with the heads of many other noble families, were in the Tribune's power. They passed the night in separate cells, the venerable Stephen Colonna frequently dashing his head against the bars, and calling on his guards to save him by a sudden death from the disgrace of captivity and punishment. In that night they might curse the slaves they had oppressed, and the man who had avenged their tyranny, but they could not urge one just reproach against the people or their leader ; they, who had plundered on the highway when in power ; who had pillaged the wrecked vessels on the coast ; who had outraged the honour of the Roman matrons, and trampled the rights of the Roman men, had not lost one piece of gold or one precious treasure from their palaces, at a time when all Rome was in the people's power, and the lives and the fortunes of the barons in the people's hands. They had still their rights as citizens and their riches as nobles. Why, then, did they conspire—why did they once more deluge Rome with blood ? Because aristocracy never did and never will, permit the only source and guarantee of national prosperity : *One Right—One Law for All.*

In the morning the presence of a confessor announced the sentence of death—the bell tolled—and the prisoners were led to the great hall of the Capitol. The red and white hangings on the walls, the stern countenance of Rienzi, the bare swords of the executioners, and the solemn silence of the gathered people, denoted the hour of death. Martial music drowned their attempts at speech ; till Rienzi, rising from the judgment-seat, astonished his hearers, who expected the signal for the executioners, with a speech in which the mild doctrines of brotherly love were dwelt on with impassioned eloquence, and the mighty Tribune, humbly turning to the assembled populace, implored them, as his masters, to forgive their enemies as he now forgave his, and having shewn how futile it was to conspire against the Good Estate, besought them to spare the lives and liberties of their prisoners.

The captives and the people were alike astonished at the godlike clemency of Rienzi, who, turning to the former, said: " If you are spared by the mercy of the Romans, will you henceforth swear to live as good citizens of the Good Estate ?"

The guilty barons, overwhelmed with this unexpected clemency, perhaps touched with the generous conduct of their victor, renewed with real or apparent sincerity their oath of allegiance. A priest, in the name of the people, pronounced their absolution, and to render their obligation more solemn, they partook of the communion with the Tribune.

Dismissed to their homes with gifts and favours, the recollection of their danger restrained for a time the hostility of these unscrupulous men. But their implacable spirits could not brook their humiliation. The chiefs of the Colonna and Orsini secretly left the city,—rallied their retainers in the country, who, lawless as themselves, unwillingly bore the restraint of peace and order—concentrated their forces at Marino, and fortified its castle. From all parts the punished outlaws flocked to their standard—and the entire country was laid waste up to the gates of Rome. Famine began to be felt in the city, and the inconstant people clamoured loudly against Rienzi. Their disobedience prevented his checking the evil in time. He had difficulty in raising troops—the barons gained leisure to fortify their castles and increase their force, and when he issued from Rome at the head of twenty thousand men, the enemy were well prepared to receive him. Retiring behind the strong ramparts of Marino, the barons laughed at the unskilled efforts of the Roman citizens, who returned with discomfiture and loss from the expedition. This failure encouraged the rebels and lowered the Tribune in the estimation of the people, who were, however, skilfully beguiled from the contemplation of defeat by questionable emblems of an ideal victory.

The barons, invited by their secret supporters, now resumed the offensive, and attempted to surprise or storm the Capitol with 4,000 foot and 1,600 horse. The first was prevented by Rienzi's vigilance. They found some of the gates strictly guarded, others thrown wide and without a defender. This seeming negligence alarmed them more than the preparation apparent in other quarters, and two divisions of their army marched past the walls ; but the third, commanded in person by the principal nobles, carried away by martial ardour, made the attempt to enter. They were met by Rienzi and his citizens—who had been inspired by the fiery eloquence of their leader. The brilliant valour of the nobles achieved a first success, but the masses of the Roman people bore them down, —they were defeated and massacred without quarter. Six members of the Colonna, the illustrious Stephen (the younger) among the number, perished on that day; and the Tribune, issuing forthwith from the city, fell on the retiring divisions of the baronial army, and completed his victory by their destruction. Returning to the Capitol, Rienzi offered his crown and sceptre at the shrine of its saint, boasted "he had cut off an ear neither pope nor emperor had been able to amputate," and knighted his son on the spot where the barons had fallen. His threatened intention to expose the bodies of the slain with those of common malefactors, was prevented by the affectionate sisters of the Colonna. The cardinals of the family had founded and endowed the convent of St. Sylvester, for the express use of those among the daughters of their house who should assume the veil. They were now twelve in number, and in the dead of night the noble virgins drew the bodies of their kinsmen from amongst the heaps of slain, and interred them in secret.

Their grief, and the indisputable gallantry of the slain, wrought on the feelings of the people, which had grown estranged since the first open rising of the barons, and the scarcity attendant on their ravages. A moment's reflection must have taught them that this was not attributable to Rienzi; but it is surprising, when once the good understanding between a people and their leader is disturbed, how difficult it is to re-establish the former friendship. The treachery of the barons, their horrible ingratitude, and the wavering attachment of those Romans, for whom he had done so much, may also have soured the spirit of the Tribune, and tinged his conduct with a severity, signally impolitic at such a juncture. All the adherents of the old cause now rallied their strength, and soon increased their numbers. An opposition was organised, and when the Tribune proposed, in the national council, to impose a new tax and regulations touching the government of Perugia, for the first time he found himself publicly opposed, and thirty-nine members voted against his measure.

The populace, at first indignant at this defection of the middle classes, for it was these who first deserted the cause of Rienzi, were gradually reconciled by the sophism of the deserters, and the scarcity entailed on the city by the raids of the neighbouring barons. The ground having been thus prepared, the secret motor of the conspiracy stepped into the foreground. The church had never trusted Rienzi, despite his avowed adherence to its tenets. It beheld in him the avowed champion of liberal opinions, and as such it feared him, but it availed itself of his power. It had used Rienzi to crush the barons by whom it was oppressed; it now used the barons to crush Rienzi by whom it was endangered. The feeling created in the heart of Rome opened its gates to the arms of the barons, and at the critical moment a cardinal legate was sent to Rome, and a bull of excommunication hurled at the head of the Tribune. In this instrument the latter is accused of heresy, sacrilege, and rebellion, and, as a type of the accusation, the crime of having bathed in the porphyry vase of Constantine is especially recorded.

Rienzi bided the storm unmoved. He saw he had lost command of the vessel, but, like a good captain, refused to quit the deck. The terror of his name was still so great, the barons feared to accept the invitation of the citizens—and, none other daring the venture, a condemned criminal, Pepin, count of Minorbino,* was released from prison, and entering Rome at the head of one hundred and fifty men, fortified himself in the quarter of the Colonna. Desperate as the undertaking seemed, he found Rienzi powerless—the alarm bell rung incessantly, but no Romans gathered at its summons, and the rude adventurer scared the majestic shadow from the Capitol. In his act of abdication the Tribune reproached the people with their ingratitude, and the triumvirate of the Cardinal Legate, a Colonna and an Orsini, who succeeded, in 1347, to his power, abolished the Good Estate and set a price upon his head. Rienzi scorned to fly, and, though denuded of authority and deprived of friends, remained for more than a month in the castle of St. Angelo, awaiting the assault of his enemies, or the repentance of his friends. So great was the fear of the former and the treachery of the latter, that he was neither molested nor succoured, and at last withdrew in the guise of a pilgrim from the scene of his glory and his fall. It is amusing to record that the accusation of cowardice has been brought against a man, who thus braved savage and exultant enemies, and struck such terror to their hearts, that three days elapsed after his abdication before the warlike barons ventured to return to their palaces.

Their long repressed hatred now burst with fearful retaliation on the heads of the ungrateful citizens, and in addition to their old despotism, a court of four cardinals was established to maintain the power of the holy see, and constitute the supreme head of the republic. Once again the palaces of the nobility were fortified. Once again a lawless banditti, in the shape of retainers, infested the streets; once again robbers lurked along the highways—extortion, rapine, and murder were the order of the day, and the ferocious barons, untamed by disaster and untaught by experience, renewed their former feuds, and like wild beasts, unable to live in peace, side by side, within the barriers of civilisation, deluged the capital with kindred blood.

Then a dream of their old power recurred to the Romans—

---

* It is a curious circumstance that Petrarca, the friend of Rienzi, should have solicited the liberation of Count Pepin.

and a recollection of the Good Estate. A brotherhood of the Virgin Mary was formed; again the citizens gathered at the sound of the alarm bell; again the armed barons quailed before the unarmed people—Colonna escaped through the window of a palace, and Orsini was killed' at the altar of a church. The office of tribune was restored, and the choice fell on a citizen named Cerroni. But the people needed more a man able to curb themselves than to control their enemies, and the mild magistrate retired from the seat of justice. He was succeeded by Baroncelli, a fierce determined spirit, whose suspicion sacrificed his best friends, and whose ambition aped the tyranny of the nobles. He perished beneath the indignation of the citizens.

Seven years had elapsed since the departure of Rienzi; sufficient time to forget hostility and remember gratitude; while the varying fortunes of the exile, and his constant attachment to his country, kept his name before the eyes of Rome. On his departure from the castle of St. Angelo, he sought successively the protection of the sovereigns of Hungary and Naples, whose want of sympathy was manifested in unmeaning courtesy or exposed by cold denial—contrasting strangely with those hours of prosperity when crowned suitors pleaded at the justice seat of the citizen. Indignant at the sufferings of his country, Rienzi next endeavoured to enlist a band of armed adventurers in his cause, but the bull of excommunication clung around him like a pest, and the superstitious *condottieri* feared to risk their fortunes under the condemned of heaven. Yearning for his native land, and desirous of testing the hearts of his former friends, he entered Rome with the pilgrims of the jubilee—but oppression had not yet done its work; he returned disheartened, and wandered, a proscribed fugitive among the gorges of the Apennines. Outlawed, friendless, and shelterless, he dragged a miserable existence through the cities of Italy, Germany, and Bohemia; while his name still struck terror to his crowned oppressors, and his identity was unrecognised in the person of the wretched outcast. But what was the astonishment of the emperor Charles IV. and his court, when a way-worn stranger one day entered the magnificent assembly, and boldly announcing himself as Rienzi, the banished Roman, poured into the startled ears of his imperial audience, one of those glorious bursts of eloquence, in which he predicted the downfall of tyranny and the restoration of the people's rights. If Rienzi had measured his enemies by the standard of his own soul, he was deceived. The pardoner of the Colonna and Orsini was made a captive by the emperor, and delivered by him into the hands of the pope. Securely guarded in the tedious journey from Prague to Avignon, though yet unjudged, he was dragged through the streets like a convicted criminal, plunged into a dungeon and chained by the leg, because he had given thousands their liberty. A tribunal of four cardinals.

was appointed to investigate the charges of heresy and rebellion ; but the majesty of the captive was greater than the courage of his gaoler ; broken in health, shattered in body, alone in the capital of spiritual Europe, surrounded by racks, inquisitors, and troops :—his congregated enemies dared not raise the question of his wrongs and their authority ; dared not hold the majestic ruin of the Capitol before the eyes of earth. His trial was postponed *sine die* — the accusations melted into air, the accusers shrunk from his prison, and Pope Clement, touched by his courage, his sufferings, and his wrongs, exchanged his dungeon for an easier prison, and his solitude for the fellowship of men and books.

The anarchy of Rome, the tyranny of Baroncelli, and the accession of Pope Innocent, were the signals for a new era in the life of Rienzi. The papal authority was wholly unrecognised in its Italian states, and none were willing or able to restore its lost supremacy. Baroncelli spurned the envoys of the pontiff, and defied the feeling of the people ; and in this emergency the eyes of Innocent fell on his captive as the only man capable of re-establishing the influence of the church. Decked with the title of senator, Rienzi, after swearing fealty to the holy see, was set at liberty and sent to Rome. Before his arrival Baroncelli had perished—his mission appeared superseded ; the great enemy of the church was no more, and the legate, Cardinal Albornoz, reluctantly permitted the prosecution of the enterprise, but withdrew all succour of men, arms, and money from the returning exile. Alone, Rienzi appeared at the gates of Rome. His reception was a triumph, his entrance a victory—the Good Estate was re-established, and the mere presence of Rienzi sufficed to banish the turbulent, awe the discontented, and protect the peaceful. But the legate Albornoz never intended Rome to regain her liberty. He used Rienzi as the means of papal aggrandisement—he crushed him as the agent of republican power. The first torrent of enthusiasm having ebbed, the people were taught to see in their senator, not the elected tribune, but the imposed master. Again, the character of Rienzi may have been changed by experience and chilled by disaster. Distrust may have been taught by treason, and severity by suffering. He was the wreck of his former self, and the legate, intent upon his ruin, threw in his way all the obstacles ingenuity could devise. The man had fulfilled his mission—the object was accomplished, the instrument a burden. The revenue of the impoverished state was no longer adequate for its government—disorders broke forth—men and arms were wanted to repress them, and there was no money for either. Steadfastly Albornoz refused all succour—Rienzi the senator dared no longer act like Rienzi the tribune. Appointed by the Pope, he could not now appropriate the papal revenue, and the imposition of a tax increased his unpopularity and sealed his fate. His authority began to be contested, his laws to be in fringed ; the Chevalier Montreal, who first introduced free lances into Italy, ravaged the Roman states with impunity, and when at last taken and executed by the senator, his death, though just at the hands of the magistrate, was unmerited at those of the friend, since it was Montreal who had often aided and shielded the fugitive Tribune with his money and his arms.

Once more the barons rebelled—the senator failed to kindle the enthusiasm of the citizens—his mercenaries either betrayed him or were beaten. A civil war raged for a while, with varying success, until the people, either suborned by their enemies, or disappointed in their friend, swelled the phalanx of rebellion, and nothing remained to Rienzi but a ruined fortress and a doubtful garrison.

He had governed but four months when a fresh impulse was given to public hostility by the machinations of the barons. One by one the defenders of Rienzi deserted, and he was left almost alone in the Capitol, when a raging populace beset its gates, thirsting for his blood. Waving the republican flag, the fallen hero appeared on a balcony, and endeavoured to address the multitude ; but his words were interrupted by a volley of stones, and drowned by the loud yells of his infuriated audience. An arrow having pierced his head, he retired to an inner chamber. The assault was prolonged till evening, and the gates having at last been destroyed, he was let down from a window, and, just as his assailants were rushing in, endeavoured to escape through the crowd in the disguise of an artisan.

Discovered, he was dragged by the malice of his enemies to that very platform where he had so often sat in judgment, and silent, motionless and bleeding, he stood for the space of an hour, the object of their wonder, their pity, or their hate. A silence sunk upon the crowd—old recollections haunted them—words of former eloquence yet thrilled in their ears, and fallen greatness challenged admiration. He might still have been saved, had not an assassin, more brutal than the rest, struck him through the heart. He fell lifeless. Like famished tigers the mob closed in upon him—and, torn limb from limb, trodden under foot, his mangled remains were consigned to the flames, the dogs, and the Jews. Anarchy and oppression wrote his epitaph.

The life and death of Rienzi read a deep lesson to the nations. The people were unconquered while true to themselves. The plan of despots is, either to set one section against another, or to estrange the masses from their leaders. Thus, in Rome, the people were used against the people, that liberty might be crushed—and when they struck at their own heart in Rienzi, then, and not till then, Church and Aristocracy annulled the GOOD ESTATE, Rome lost her hope, Petrarca mourned a friend.

THE MORALITY OF COMMERCE.

" The mean rapacity, and monopolising spirit of merchants and manufacturers, who neither are, nor ought to be, the rulers of mankind, though it cannot perhaps be corrected, may very easily be prevented from disturbing the tranquillity of anybody but themselves."— ADAM SMITH, *Wealth of Nations, Book* 4, *Chap.* 3.

I do not conceive for a moment that commerce or barter is of itself ungenerous, mean, or rapacious; to do so would be to argue that the first advances in civilisation and improvement were not conducive to the best interests of mankind. The employments of commerce are not in themselves unfit for man, or unworthy of the exercise of his nature; but, in the present state of society, when the acquisition of a fortune is the main object of life, it is not to be wondered at that a dereliction from moral duty is common among men. In any case, where the means are mistaken for the end, blunders and evils are inevitable— and in the mercantile world this is too generally the case. The object of life, and therefore the acquisition of property as a means to an end, should be a cultivation of the heroism of nature. The greater and nobler objects of existence being happiness and virtue, and not grandeur and luxury, it must ever be a national and individual loss to acquire wealth at the cost of man ; to erect mills, fill granaries, build ships, at the cost of fair dealing and honourable reciprocity. Such a course must destroy the nobler aspirations of youth, turning generous emotions to sordid and ignoble ends, and be especially injurious in a country like this, where so much depends on trade; where the sons of merchants and farmers are educated for the counting-house; where almost every aspiring artisan desires to become a trader—a merchant—or, if his means do not admit of carrying his wishes to their summit, sits down to reason on the profits of keeping a huckster's shop, or briefly builds a fortune from the trading in old clothes, becomes a broker in rags, buying cheap from the degraded poor and selling as dear as possible to the unfortunate purchaser. Thus, fair and honourable dealing falls a sacrifice to a love of gain; and, in too many instances, the rich merchant on 'change, the horse-dealer at the country fair, and the dealer of old clothes in your filthy lanes, wynds, and alleys, have but one motto : " Everything is fair in trade." I think a brief inquiry into the, doings of the past—a few thoughts on our commercial, morality and general state of mental and moral elevation—is opportune ; the more so, as the public attention has been awakened by the fraud and imposture of corn-dealers, who have mixed bran with meal to fill the stomachs of the starving poor. And here I beg to remark that nothing short of an extraordinary exposure commands public attention. White must be flogged to death before there is an outcry against flogging in the army. Bannantyne must be tried, convicted, and sent to prison, before that sleeping dor- mouse, the public mind, will awaken into living action— nothing short of extremes will be heard by the ear of England. Are we then so moral and good that these evils are of rare occurrence ? Are our morals like those of a peaceful village, where men, women, and children run to their doors to look with astonishment on a monkey, grotesquely dressed in cap and feathers ? Do we live so secluded from imposture, that a single instance should alarm the city, and make us gape with astonishment, and almost burst with indignation ? Let us pause and inquire. We every day hear of our country's greatness—her manu- facturing greatness—and now and again our public orators indulge in glowing rhetoric about our national grandeur, and our commercial power. But by what means have we arrived at our present pinnacle ? Is the evil of the system but of yesterday, or is it of many years standing ? Is the corn-ulcer a disease in a single limb, or is it one of the many sores, which, like spots on the leopard's skin, cover the body ? Perhaps the following statements may help the reader to come to a conclusion, gathered as they are from men of all political parties, and extending over a series of years, and all bearing to one result :—

Mr. R. Gordon.—" It appears, that overseers of parishes, in London, are in the habit of contracting with the manufacturers of the north for the disposal of their children ; and these manufacturers agree to take one idiot for every nineteen sane children. In this manner waggon loads of these little creatures are sent down to be at the perfect disposal of their new masters." (*April* 3, 1816.)

The late Sir Robert Peel.—" About fifteen years ago, I brought in a bill for the regulation of apprentices in cotton manufactories. At that time they were the description of persons most employed in these manufactories. I myself had a thousand of them, and I felt the necessity of some regulation with respect to them. * * * It was notorious, that children of a very tender age were dragged from their beds some hours before daylight, and confined in the factories not less than fifteen hours; and it is also, notoriously, the opinion of the faculty, that no children of eight or nine years of age can bear the degree of hardship with impunity to their health and constitution."

"Little children of very tender age are employed with grown persons at machinery, and these poor little creatures, torn from their beds, are compelled to work, even at the age of six years, from early morn till late at night—a space of perhaps fifteen or sixteen hours a day.—(*April* 3, 1816.)

MR. HOBHOUSE.—"In the *best regulated* mills the children are at present compelled to work twelve hours and a half a day, and for three or four days in the week are not allowed to go out of the mills to get their meals, which they are obliged to take off the floor of the mills, mingled with the dust and down of the cotton. In *other mills* they are obliged to work fifteen and sixteen hours a day. Now, *is it possible for children to live,* who are daily suffering under an atmosphere, the temperature of which is warmer than the warmest summer day? They scarcely bear any resemblance to their fellow creatures after being long subject to this torture. Their skins are literally the colour of parchment. My honourable friend says, that if the bill passes (to limit the hours of labour), ' *we shall lose two millions and a half of productive revenue.*' But ought we to allow a portion of our fellow subjects to be rendered miserable for such a consideration? No; it would be better to give up the cotton trade altogether, than to draw such a sum out of the blood, and bones, and sinews of these unfortunate children."—-(*House of Commons, May* 16, 1825.)

MR. W. SMITH.—"This act (late Sir R. Peel's, to limit hours of labour in factories), has been evaded in the most shameless, barefaced, and inhuman manner."—(*May* 16, 1825.)

" No one can reprobate the system of slavery more than I do, but the labour performed by the negroes in the West

Indies is actually less than is exacted from those poor children at Manchester, and is far less detrimental to health."—(*May* 21, 1825.)

MR. HUSKISSON.—"I have seen, and many other gentlemen no doubt have seen, in a Macclesfield newspaper of the 19th of February, 1825, the following advertisement. 'To overseers, guardians of the poor, and families desirous of settling in Macclesfield—Wanted immediately from 4,000 to 5,000 persons.' (Hear, hear.) The house may well express their surprise, and I beseech their attention to the description of persons required by this advertisement—'from seven to twenty years of age;' so that the manufacturers were content to receive children of the tender age of only seven years, 'to be employed in the throwing and manufacturing of silk; the great increase of the trade having caused a great scarcity of workmen. It is suggested that this is a most favourable opportunity for persons with large families, and overseers who wish to put out children—children of seven years of age—as apprentices to ensure them a comfortable livelihood. Applications to be made, if by letter, post-paid, to the 'printer of this paper.' "—(*Feb.* 26, 1826.)

MR. M. T. SADLER.—"Children of very tender years work for twelve, thirteen, fifteen, and sixteen hours a day, and often for thirty-five hours, without intermission, save only a few minutes for meals."—(*Feb.* 1, 1832.)

"They are kept at labour," to use their own phrase, "seven or eight days a week." * * * In many instances they are employed on the Sabbath."—(*Feb.*7,1832.)

"Mr. Wood (a large and highly respectable manufacturer at Bradford) says, 'children have been confined in the factory from six in the morning to eight at night—fourteen hours continually—without any time being allowed for meals, rest, or recreation; the meals to be taken while attending the machines, and this the practice of years.' * * * This is the practice at Bradford. * * * The children there occasionally work twenty-four hours every other day, out of which they are allowed three hours only for meals, &c. *When trade is particularly* BRISK (!!!) the elder children work from six in the morning till seven in the evening, two hours allowed for meals, &c., *and every other night, all night;* which is a still more severe case. For this additional night labour they receive fivepence. There is another lamentable circumstance attending the employment of these poor children, which is, that they are left the whole night alone, the sexes indiscriminately mixed together, consequently, you may imagine that the depravity of our work-people is indeed very great."

"Even at this moment, while I am thus speaking in behalf of these oppressed children, what numbers of them are still at their toil, confined in heated rooms, bathed in perspiration, stunned with the roar of the revolving wheels, poisoned with the noxious effluvia of grease and gas, till at last they turn out, weary and exhausted, almost naked—plunge into the open air, and creep, shivering, to beds from which a relay of their young work-fellows have just risen; and such is the fate of many of them, at the best, while in numberless instances, they are diseased, stunted, crippled, depraved, destroyed."—(*March* 16, 1832.)

"The degree of labour which is carried on by these infants is not to be endured. They are regarded as machines of no value. The employer makes his calculation, as to how many hours his machines are to work, to yield a certain profit; but as to what the human machine will bear, he makes no calculation."—(*June* 7, 1832.)

MR. HUNT.—"I can confirm many of the statements of the honourable member for Aldboro' (Sadler) *from my own observations.* The honourable member has very truly stated, that such a system as exists in civilised England could not be carried on in any part of India. I am convinced, that *not even the American savages—not even the cannibals, would suffer their children to be worked in this way.* Indeed, I will go further—the brute creation have too great a regard for their young to suffer them to meet with such treatment. * * * A blow from that instrument (the over-looker's scourge) is almost as bad as the infliction of the dreadful punishment of the knout, which is used to the criminals of Russia. A father, who would patiently suffer his daughter to be treated in this way, would prostitute her, and live upon the wages of her shame. * * * The whole of my constituents (of Preston) are in favour of this bill. They have instructed me to support it, but even if they had desired me to oppose it, I should have refused, as I would rather have resigned my seat in this House, than have done so."—(*March* 16, 1832.)

MR. STRICKLAND—(in reference to the foregoing.)—
"There does not exist in Scotland any freedom from the evils of England on this subject. Children are worked as long there as in England, and their health as surely suffers. These poor children are entirely unprotected. A great portion of them are apprentices, and I look upon that apprenticeship as a sort of qualified slavery, by which the child is placed beyond the means of redemption, at the control of the manufacturer."—(*June* 27, 1832.)

MR. COBBETT.—"The question amounts simply to this—Mammon or Mercy? After the eulogium which has been pronounced upon the house by the honourable member for Marylebone, I trust that Mercy will prevail over Mammon. At any rate, if we cannot be humane, we can be sincere, if we will. * * * I will be sincere, at any rate, and say, on the part of my constituents, that 300,000 of the most helpless creatures in the world hold up their hands to the noble lord opposite (Ashley) for mercy, for deliverance from the worst slavery ever endured in the world."—(*July* 5, 1833.)

MR. W. DUNCOMBE.—"To what does the evidence amount? It establishes the fact, beyond the possibility of a doubt, that a system of overworking children of very tender years does exist in this country; and that they are overworked and worn out by labour; that they are in the habit of being dragged from their beds to the mills at break of day; that they are often worked till human nature is exhausted and can bear no more; that they are frequently crippled for life; and that they not unfrequently sink into an untimely grave. These are the facts of the case—facts which cannot be contradicted."—(*July* 18, 1833.)

MR. JOHN FIELDEN.—"I know very well, that the large cotton mills, and it is the same with other mills, obtain information, beforehand, when gentlemen are coming down to inspect them, and I know that when these gentlemen see the mills, they are in a very different state from what they would be if they were taken unawares. I know that I have felt very fatigued and weary after a day's work in the cotton mill, and I had many advantages which other children had not, because I had a mother and father (to whom the mill belonged) to take care of me. I believe our mills were as well conducted as any. We employed from 1000 to 2000 people, and I believe they were all kindly treated, but I can bear testimony to the exhaustion of the children manifest before the time of leaving off arrives. * * * It is a notorious fact, that labour is carried on for thirteen, fourteen, and fifteen hours a day in *defiance* of the law. I think ten hours would be *profitable enough*, both for the employers and the employed. * * I will only add, that, thinking as I do, that the medical evidence on which the noble lord has grounded his bill *is borne out by my own experience*, &c. &c."—(*April* 3, 1833.)

" It is acknowledged on all hands, that the law on every side is grossly violated. * * The mill-owners say, 'if you do not keep up the twelve hours system, we cannot stand against foreign competition. * * If the noble lord (John Russell) wishes to enforce the Factory Act, *he must call in the military to do so at the point of the bayonet, it may then be observed, but not otherwise.*" — (*July* 20, 1838.)

I could multiply facts on the factory question to the thickness of a volume—remark would weaken these peaceful but powerful monitors on the morality of our trade; and though the advocates of protection to the victims of avarice and aggrandisement, have at last carried the Ten Hours Bill, at this hour hundreds of the producers of wealth are going idle in Manchester, Bradford, &c. and suffering distress incalculable; and, as an inevitable result, prostitutes crowd our streets and criminals fill our gaols. But I hasten to lay before the reader a few facts on the truck system, which, in my opinion, legitimately bear on this question—disclosing, as they do, a system of cunning that would disgrace an adept of the " light fingered " profession—the pickpocket department being closely allied to the pick-wages practice. And though I regret that men claiming the name of " respectable," and associating intelligence with wealth, should be guilty of such practices, justice demands a full statement of facts; and reason says, that he who robs commits a theft, and he who legally or illegally takes advantage of the dependant condition of workmen, for his aggrandisement and the workmen's disadvantage, is not honest.

Mr. R. King.— " A manufacturer generally keeps a shop of dry goods. The poor workman is paid in full at one counter, but he is obliged to go to the other (by a private understanding, that if he does not, he will not be employed), where he receives a shawl, or a gown-piece, or a coat, or something that is useless to him, and at one third more than he can buy it for with his money at another shop. What he receives he takes to the pawn-office immediately, and pledges for half the amount he is obliged to give for it, and most probably he never afterwards redeems it."—(*May* 3, 1830.)

Mr. Bright.—" Who would believe, were it not explicitly stated, that when labourers who are in want of subsistence apply to their masters for wages, they are paid in umbrellas, watches, and toys, which they can neither use themselves, nor convert into the means of subsistence ? * * By them (truck masters) the retail trader is grievously injured, for the labourer having no money is obliged to have recourse to his master's warehouse for everything ; and if he goes elsewhere to buy what he wants, he is turned out of employment. To keep up this system, the *masters combine in all the manufacturing districts, and reduce the men to slavery;* at least, I cannot call the man free, who cannot change his service, however ill he may be used, and who gets for his labour no other reward than what his master pleases." (*May* 3, 1830.)

Sir John Wrottesley—(presenting petitions against the truck system.)—" They next state, that if a workman seeks for redress, he is *immediately discharged.*' They complain that the masters resort to various expedients to *evade the law* (the law against truck) ; they delay to settle with the men sometimes for six weeks ; and when the latter, in want of sustenance, apply to the masters, they supply them with *goods* 30 *per cent. above the market price.*—(' *Cheap bread ! ! !*') Other masters pay their workmen in money in one counting-house, with which they are obliged to purchase goods, the property of their employers, in another. They state, that, as many months elapse before the masters pay the bills which the workmen are compelled to run up with the shopkeeper, the latter force the poor workmen to pay exorbitant prices."—(*Feb.* 18, 1830.)

Mr. Littleton—(on the truck system.)—" Tea is given out at a *profit* of from 2s. to 3s. per lb. ; butter from 3d. to 4d. per lb. ; tobacco at a profit of 25 per cent. Most articles sold by them are of an *inferior quality, particularly* meat, on which they get a profit from 2d. to 3d. per lb. (Reader, is this ' *cheap bread for the poor man ?*') Some time since, I myself saw a sample of flour sold to a poor mechanic, which resembled more the colour of chocolate than any thing else. I have seen workmen carrying about tongs and pokers, and such things, which they had received as their week's wages, to sell, in order to buy food. A man discharged for exposing beef that had been given to him for wages; was charged 5s. 10½d.—sold for 2s.; the man who bought it, after exhibiting it in the market-place at Hanley, gave it to the pigs.—Silk handkerchiefs given for 6s., worth 2s.; Irish linen, at 3s. per yard, worth 1s.; check, at 1s. 4d. per yard, worth 7d.; cheese at 7d. per. lb., worth 4½d., &c. For a month together only 2d. in money, and that to buy soap for his work. Workmen pay rents in flour, meat, groceries, &c. Cloth-dressers dress cloth for men who have taken it in truck at 50 per cent. more than its value, and who suffer a further loss on the sale." (The following given in evidence) :—" I do certify that I have been in the service of a truck-master, and in the agreement which I made with him, he inserted a clause that I should not, under any circumstances, take him before a magistrate; that my average wages were 15s. per week; and that, out of that sum, I had to take 8s. worth of truck per week, which truck consisted (in substance) as follows ;—flour at 3s. 4d. per stone, worth 2s. 8d.; bacon at 9d., worth 6d.; beef and mutton at 8d., market price 6d.' Overseers of poor of Stoke-upon-Trent certify, that the rates are increased; and the poor are grievously oppressed by being paid in truck at 100 to 200 per cent. above the market price. Wine taken at 4s. per bottle, and other things of inferior quality, and at extravagant prices. A man obliged to take a suit of clothes at 30s. which he sold to the tailor for 12s., who had supplied it to the master for 15s. Another case (says Littleton) I will mention, was one which came before the Court of King's Bench in 1823, and was the case of King v. Kaye, in which an inventory was put in of the articles a workman had been obliged to take in payment, and which could scarcely be matched in a pawnbroker's shop. I will read only a few of the articles : 29lb. of Dutch butter, at 1s. 5½d. per lb.; sundries, a sum of £1. 8s. 2d.; 14½ yards of calico, at 1s. 4½d. per yard; 3 yards of linen at 2s. 6d. per yard; half piece of ribbon; 4 yards of broad cloth, at 26s. per yard; 2 ditto, 25s. per yard; 1 dozen calico fronts; 5½ yards cord, 9s. 6d. per yard; a hat 10s. 6d.; an umbrella, £1. 10s.; 7 yards print, 2s. 3d. per yard; 22 yards dimity; ½ yard cambric; 10 silk handkerchiefs; 3 scarfs; a scarf; a parasol; 2 metal foreign watches; a tea chest; 25 yards linen; 2 bushels Dutch onions; 7 yards broad cloth; 2½ ditto; 8 yards cord; a brooch; 15 bags; an old rotten mourning pall, consisting of 10 yards velveteen, **valued at** 15s., &c. &c."—(*May* 17, 1830.)

So much for the truck system. Now for the combination laws.

MR. HUME : " For many years past the country has been burthened by a system of laws preventing the labouring classes of the community from combining together against their employers. Their employers, though few in number, are powerful in wealth : may combine against them, and may determine not to give more than a certain sum for their labour. The workmen cannot, however, consult together about the rate they ought to fix on that labour, without rendering themselves liable to fine and imprisonment, and a thousand other inconveniences, which the law has reserved for them. The masters, on the other hand, can combine against the men : they are comparatively few in number—possess every advantage of power and station, and can, at any time, agree among themselves what rate of wages they will allow."—(*Feb.* 12*th*, 1824.)

" In some cases the conduct of the masters is worse than that of the men, and I will give a few instances of it. The first act of combination in Glasgow, was the act of the masters. A few men in Mr. Dunlop's manufactory, in Glasgow, disagreeing with their master, I believe, on some point of wages, they declined to continue working for him. What was the consequence ? why, the masters immediately combined together ; for they called a meeting at which the subject was discussed, and which came to a resolution to make a stand against the men. This they effected in the following manner : They published a notice stating, ' that if the men in Mr. Dunlop's factory did not return to their work on, or before, Monday morning next, they (the masters) would discharge from their employ all the men, amounting in number to ten thousand, until the men who had quitted Mr. Dunlop returned to him.' The workmen who had gone away disclaimed acting in concert with any others, and said, ' Do not punish them for what we have done ;' but their disclaimer was not attended to, and all the men in Glasgow of the same trade were actually turned out of employment. Now, I would ask, whether the mere declining on the part of the men to work for their masters was to be put in comparison, for enormity, with that act of the masters. But that was not all. The property of the masters enabled them to get the better of the men, who were obliged at last to come in unconditionally. When they did so, the masters punished their resistance in a very decided manner; for they actually deducted the loss they had sustained by this cessation of labour, from the amount of the men's wages; the men being obliged to pay at the rate of ten per cent. per week, until the masters declared themselves satisfied.

" It was a regulation entered into by the masters of Scotland, that any person who quitted one factory should not be employed in another, and that object was effected by the masters sending round to each other lists of the men who, from any cause whatever, had quitted their employment, so that no man, who happened to differ with his master, could succeed in obtaining employment elsewhere. Was not this an odious combination ?"—(*March* 29, 1835.)

Mr. P. MOORE — (in debate on combination law.) —" I believe that nineteen twentieths of the poor rates are occasioned by the pinchings which the rich manufacturers inflict on the wages of their workmen."—(*May*, 27, 1823.)

Mr. COBBETT—(on distress of the hand-loom weavers.)— " After the description which has just been given to us, by the hon. member for Paisley (Sir D. K. Sandford), of the miseries of the industrious weavers of Paisley: after the description he has given us, of their deplorable situation, of their wretchedness, of their destitution—I hope we shall never again hear the Right Hon. President of the Board of Trade (Poulett Thompson), say in this House, that he prays God this country may become the great manufacturing shop of the world. It has been said, that if this House interpose in any way in matters of this description, it may drive certain branches of manufactures out of the kingdom. Drive them out of the country—drive them out of the world, and into the infernal regions, rather than that they should continue to produce such appalling distress. The hon. member for Middlesex seems to estimate the happiness of the people as nothing. All that he thinks of is, what the country is to gain, and he speaks of the people just as we talk of stock on a farm. ' You are working cattle ;' says he, ' I don't want to make you fat, because you won't pay. I want your labour, and you can give me your labour upon straw as well as upon hay. To be sure, hay would be better for you; but you see, it costs a good deal more; and, if I allow you to live upon such a luxury, I shall not be able to put so much money into my own pocket.

" Now, my views are of a totally different description. I am more anxious that the people should , be happy, than that the nation should grow rich, and therefore I do not wish England to become the great manufacturing shop of the world, seeing that her endeavours to become so have already produced such a plentiful harvest of misery and wretchedness. I do not care what becomes of certain branches of manufactures; if their being driven out of the country would remove this mass of misery and distress,- I say again, let them be driven out of the country—let them be driven out of the world—let them be driven into the infernal regions."—(*June* 11, 1834.)

How creditable, indeed, is the hearty denunciation of combined cruelty by the late Mr. Cobbett; and by the exertions of him and others, an alteration was effected in the combination laws, as also in the truck system. Yet the principle involved in the system of swindling and oppression remains · unaltered, and the numerous trials of the miners of the north of England remain an evidence that the oppression of the rich provokes a spirit of resentment on the part of the employed; and the numerous evasions of the truck act, by employing friends and relations to keep shops and supply goods, prove that the lust for gold has sharpened the senses of the keen money-getter, who makes no scruple to sacrifice conscience for gain, and builds for himself a fortune at the cost of morality and virtue.

So complete has become the system of deception and fraud—that it has found its way into every branch of manufacture and trade, and so multifarious and ingenious are the practices of its votaries, that the most acute are open to deception. Who knows that the razor he has just bought is not cast metal—seeing that the master cutler of Sheffield, but a few years ago, caused a large quantity of cutlery to be destroyed in the public market place, because made of spurious metal? But can all the deception of the hardware trade be detected by the master cutler? Decidedly not— and, in fact, deception is considered part of business. Remember, " everything is fair in trade." There lays on my table a knife, bought from a tradesman in one of the principal shops in Birmingham. I asked the seller if the handle was made of buckhorn—he confidently assured me it was a buckhorn handle, and I accordingly paid . him his demand. A workman at the trade has just informed me, that the handle is made of bone pressed in a die when warm, leaving marks similar to buckhorn, and regularly sold for buckhorn. The act of deception is constantly denied, and the principle constantly inculcated and made the practice, the habit of every hour. Our shopkeepers' assistants are trained to insinuate, to deceive, and entrap. Every dealer knows the truth of my statement, and every housewife has suffered from the practice. The manufacturers of the goods make no secret of their doings, and I cannot better illustrate my subject than by the following quotation from " A Letter to the Agriculturists of Salop, 1841," written by Mr. W. Whitmore, known to the public by his writings in favour of a repeal of the corn laws, and designated in the league circular " An enlightened, well informed and statesmanlike man, whose writings are prized as most admirable and valuable documents."

- " I cannot," says Mr. Whitmore, " explain this part of the subject better, than by inserting an extract from a letter I have received from a gentleman very largely employed in a branch of the cotton manufactures."

The following is the substance of the extract referred to :—

" I feel persuaded you will excuse the liberty which I now take in reminding you of one very important fact, which, in common with all other writers on the subject, you have omitted. * * * You are, perhaps, aware, that the manufacturer of cotton cloth is an extensive consumer of flour, or glutinous substance—flour, I believe, is invariably preferred—viz., for sizing the warp. * * * The amount, *annually* paid by our *concern* for wheat in various forms, as well as other agricultural products ; viz., flour, starch, calcined starch (ordinarily called British gum), and bran ; viz., from £4,500 to £5,000."

I regret Mr. Whitmore does not inform us the number of hands employed by the firm whose letter he publishes : we should then perceive whether the greater quantity of flour was consumed by the *workers* or the *dressers* — whether the staff of life was used to besmear flimsy and rotten calicoes—to deceive the customer by adding to the weight and appearance of body in the cloth, and every ounce of which will find its way to the wash-tub and dung-hill ; or, if the greater quantity of food for man was consumed by the producers ! Ignorant of the division, I will not venture a surmise, but leave the inquiry for the consideration of the reader. The woollen trade, too, has its full share of ingenious deceit: those familiar with Yorkshire, the seat of woollen manufactures in the north of England, have seen a machine called the " devil," and also a material called " devil's dust," or " shoddy," being, in fact, rags gathered from the rag shop and the dunghill—old clothes ground down to be made into new cloth; and so finished is the article, when completed, that the most experienced dealers in the fabric are often deceived, and cannot distinguish shoddy cloth from the genuine article; and our retail clothiers ticket the commodity with the words " cheap cloth." How much nearer the truth it would be, if the words "cheat cloth," were used to denote the true meaning, for the unlucky purchaser never fails to find that his trowsers of superfine cloth get threadbare in a month, whilst falling buttons, splitting, &c., &c., indicate that the " devil's dust" has been to him, indeed, a devil—robbing him of his money, and healing the sore with the consolatory expression of the retail shopkeeper, who says:—" I am sorry, indeed, the cloth you bought turned out so badly ; It looked so well—I am quite deceived in it, but I will try to do better for you next time." Which only means that the manufacturer deceived the retail tradesman—the retail dealer the customer—and the *moral* of the whole is the motto of the Jew : " Everything is fair in trade."

If the limits of this article allowed, I could quote the practices of fraud and deceit *ad infinitum*, including every branch of business, from the commissioners of the national debt and dealers of bullion, down to the travelling lottery and the dealer in nuts, whose customers shoot with a pea gun, or put down their farthings on a painted crown and anchor, awaiting their fate, as indicated on the so called " wheel of fortune." But, as corn is the great requisite of life, I will briefly call your attention to a transaction in Glasgow, between Alexander Bannatyne and the Highland Relief Committee, and content myself by quoting only part of the exculpatory evidence, which will be all-sufficient for my purpose. I quote the same from the Glasgow Saturday *Post* of October 2nd, 1847, premising that the case was tried before the Glasgow Autumn Circuit Courts on Wednesday, September 29th, and the prisoner, " Alexander Bannatyne, acting partner of the firm of Alexander Bannatyne & Co., grain merchants in Glasgow, was placed at the bar on the charge of falsehood, fraud, and wilful imposition, in so far as he having written, or caused to be written, and delivered to the Committee in Glasgow for the Relief of Highland Destitution, a letter dated 13th March, 1847," which letter offers meal to the relief committee at a fixed price, which offer was accepted, and in the words of the lord justice Clerk, when passing sentence on the prisoner:—

· "Alexander Bannatyne—You have been convicted on a charge of falsehood, fraud, and wilful imposition, with the exception of that part of the indictment which charged that you had mixed bran with the oatmeal. The offence of which you have been convicted does not consist in any charge resting upon a question of construction or legal form. The violation of any statutory rule, or any provision of law in regard to which it is possible for the integrity or honesty of a party to fail, is cognisable by law; and in your case, I must say, the offence is great, direct, manifest fraud—fraud committed in plain matter of fact, and persisted in, in your thus having undertaken to furnish the article of oatmeal, instead of which you did wickedly, feloniously, and fraudulently mix and adulterate that article with other articles and substances, barleymeal and thirds, fully intending to deceive the committee to whom the article was sold. And you did deceive the committee, in so far that your mixture being such that those who undertook to examine it passed the sample, understanding that they were receiving pure oatmeal. Therefore the fraud of which you have been convicted is, unhappily for you, one of plain direct dishonesty."

The sentence of the court was imprisonment for the period of four calendar months, and a fine of £300; failing in payment of the same in four months, the prisoner to suffer the punishment of an additional four months' imprisonment. ·

EXCULPATORY EVIDENCE.—"John Lamb, grain-merchant in Glasgow—Has dealt a great deal in buying and selling of meal. Knows that there is a practice in the trade of mixing oatmeal. Sometimes it was mixed with wheatmeal, also barleymeal, second flour and third, according to the quality required and the price agreed. The practice was known to every one acquainted to any extent with the trade in oatmeal. Lately saw some samples of oatmeal in the hands of Mr. Salmon the Fiscal. They were mixed. As a person accustomed to deal in the article he had no difficulty in discovering the mixture; he at once detected it. Some samples were better than others; but, upon the whole, it was a fair quality. He could not have been deceived as to the quality of the article in buying or selling it.

· "Cross-examined for the prosecution—The mixing is sometimes done at the mill. It was more generally done at the mill, but was done after it came from the mill in some instances too. Could not say that he himself had frequently done it after it came from the mill; but he did so when requested by his customers.

" By the Court—It is the practice of the trade, in supplying an order, to mix it with something else, according to the sample and the price; if he could not get a price he would be forced to do it. If he had got an order for oatmeal at 55s. and could not supply it pure at that price, he would send a mixed article without saying anything about it. To make a difference of 2s. per load, as between 57s. and 55s., would require one in five of barleymeal or thirds. There was no established rule of mixing; every man did it according to his own estimate of the price.

· " Alexander Isles—Is a grain dealer, and occasionally supplies small shopkeepers. Examined the samples of oatmeal in the house of Mr. Salmond yesterday. There was only one sample, No. 4, that appeared to him to be pure oatmeal.

" Being cross-examined by the Court in reference to the practice in the trade with respect to mixing, the witness said he did not think persons ought to be called on to criminate themselves. The Lord Justice Clerk said, he could have no protection there, but must answer the questions on his own responsibility.

" Examination resumed—It is the practice of the trade to mix the meal. Had never known it done to such an extent as in the period from September to May last.

- " —— Wilson, miller—Has known oatmeal to be mixed, especially last year. He should say it is known to be done in the trade. It is sometimes done in the mill, but not always—sometimes in the store.

" By the Court—It is understood to be done to a certain extent in the trade. It was done to a greater extent last year than was common."

Can any man read such evidence as that just quoted, without reflecting on the causes producing the results ? · It is to be remembered that the money paid for the adulterated meal was collected at our church-doors—it was a nation's alms to a starving people: but neither the nature of the object for which the money was collected, nor the prayers of our clergy, could protect it from being tinged with the slime of the golden serpent. Trade conducted on its present principles contaminates all that it touches. The famished highlander or emaciated pauper, weigh as nothing in the balance against the practices of trade; the morality of love and sympathy of natural feeeling must be laid aside, and man use deceit and practice imposture; he must lie, pilfer, and steal to support the glory of our country—to maintain the commercial dignity of England—and say to every onlooker, " See our commercial greatness! mark the wealth of our merchant princes!" If I were asked the question: " Would you prefer the present state of trade, if fixed for ever, to a return to savage life?" I would answer, " Perish the present system, let what may follow; better that man should roam in woods naked as when born, than forge a claim on virtue with the deed of vice! better that progression should emerge from the bud of its infancy and in its new developement run all hazards, than be fixed as with an iron grasp in the jaws of refined cruelty and rapacious falsehoods." Yet such is England in her greatness, that, in haughty self-esteem, she boasts of aiming at the civilisation of the world, and contains within her very heart the impure blood that stinks of the itch of gold; and when stripped of her robes of fine linen, presents a body covered with sores from the sole of the foot to the crown of the head—a huge moral ulcer filled with uncleanness and all vile things.

" The mean rapacity, and monopolising spirit of merchants and manufacturers, who neither are nor ought to be, the rulers of mankind," as written by Adam Smith, has become the very principle that governs all. It rules in St. Stephen's and regulates the Exchange; it preaches in the pulpit, and penetrates the sanctity of the domestic hearth; even life is as nothing in its balance. What matter if a hundred colliers be buried in a coal mine? Their mangled bodies and weeping wives, are as nothing to the saving of a few trap doors. Half the children born in Bradford die before they are seven years of age. What matter? There are plenty of work-people! We must have cheap woollens. In Manchester the annual duration of life of mechanics and their families amounts to seventeen years; that of gentry and their families to thirty-eight. But what matters the killing of half the work-people, if we have only cheap cottons? In Rutlandshire the average age reached by labourers and their families is thirty-eight years—by gentry and their families fifty-two. How foolish to regret the murder of one-fourth of our brethren, when balanced against the landlord's partridges, hares, rabbits and rent.

Reader! Do you say how true is all I have written ? But can you say you are free from the charge ? I fear we are all implicated. But must we remain so ? The question requires an answer—and it is for you to reply. Have you settled down in the school of ease, content with things as they are ? Have you agreed to move through life, sometimes bowing your head, to let the wave pass over, as a timid boy who bathes and cannot swim ? Are you to be a footman wearing livery, and kneeling at the door of custom, jerking round the corners to be out of sight, and playing at hide and seek for life, supple and humble to day for a shilling, honouring wealth with man's worship to a god, and wearing the old notions of men in mental sloth and worthless laziness ? If so, for you at least there is little hope ; you are in leading-strings, and cannot help yourself.

But though from you we may not even receive sympathy, yet there is much to be hoped for from the progression of man. Time is the great revolutionist, the rectifier of all, and the reign of évil will ye pass away for the empire of good. No branch of history, literature, or science, even now, is free from innovation. Carlyle has given history a new dress ; Lamartine has changed the garb of Robespierre ; Lyell has been át the falls of Niagara, and found for creation a new date ; Channing has made an old, creed the alembic for a new philosophy ; Hood has rendered the distresses of needle-women as immortal as the death of Hector ; and Mackie, with the foresight of poetic prophecy, has said truly, " There's a good time coming." No institution is safe from the new ideas in which the spirit of the age has clothed itself ; and, better known in the workshop than the study, instinct is at war with old books, and unfolds its influence every hour. The new thoughts are everywhere and reflect signs in our benefit-societies, sick-clubs, trades-unions, land societies, co-operative labour associations, &c. Instinct is begetting a consciousness of self-reliance, and a band of bold men preach non-conformity. These men will yet aid in changing the principles of our commerce, and destroy usury and gain for love and reciprocity. All the good tendencies will grow ; the old become formal ; ages may pass, but progression will remain young, and its influences leaven the whole mass ; man is a reformer, therefore " be a man."

Trade will yet be purged of its filth, and the mean rapacity and monopolising spirits of merchants and manufacturers will be both corrected and prevented from disturbing the tranquillity of the ; state and that, too, when labour learns its own powers, and man feels the true mission of life. Society cannot be changed as with the wand of a magician ; but the result is not less sure that the process seems slow, and the present condition of the masses unites the disease and the means for the remedy. Give, then, to the reformer your aid, and your labour will one day bring its reward. SAMUEL KYDD.

THE ROMANCE OF A PEOPLE.

A HISTORICAL TALE

OF THE NINETENTH CENTURY.

(Continued from page 226.)

CHAPTER V.

The marching escort drove me on. I started away—as awaking from a dream—and, roused to sudden vengeance, struck at the advancing Russian with the chain that was still wound round my arm. But the effort was transitory—my strength forsook me—and I fell senseless to the ground. I had wished to have struck one blow for revenge, and thus provoked them to kill me: but no ! it would have been too great mercy to have granted me death.

Intense, insufferable pain told me of returning life ; and as the torture of the body decreased, came the sting of memory. The whole past rushed over me with a leaden weight—but I was myself no more. Almost as incapable of thought as of action, I was living in a horrid dream : I scarcely discerned surrounding objects. A train of phantoms seemed flitting around me, and the earth appeared to my darkened sight like a vast unsubstantial shadow, sinking away beneath my feet. At length, after a wearying and dreadful march, the pain and tediousness of which were hardly perceived by my blunted senses, we arrived at Warsaw late on the following evening. I recollect seeing the long lines of the illumined streets, whose lamps seemed to race past me; the towering houses and palaces, with the gray-cloaked sentries, stalking like evil demons on the watch for innocence ; and the dark space of the park, stretching away like a boundless grave, as, winding round, we stopped at last before the palace of the Belvedere.

Through long, dark passages, lined with the fierce and statue-like soldiery, that glared on me, as I passed, with scorpion eyes, we descended to the dungeon-vaults, and faint cries stole on the ear from every side, as we proceeded. I, felt exhausted nature giving way—but those sounds roused me again to life; My heated fancy seemed to hear the voice of Thekla in every shriek, and anger, that infallible, though but temporary restorer of strength, dispelled the chill of death that was stealing over me, and consciousness of the present and the past returned. I knew I should soon be brought into the presence of Constantine, and I determined upon concealing from him, at least, the sinking of my spirit.

We stopped before a low, iron doorway, on passing which I beheld a sight that would have moved the sternest heart. I found myself in a damp, low-vaulted dungeon, crowded with a mass of victims awaiting torture. Some were half naked, and their ghastly wounds yawned through the rents of their torn apparel; some seemed scarcely able to rise from the ground—but, as I was thrust in among them, every livid, glassy eye was turned on me, the new victim, with a fixed, hideous stare, as it should say: " Welcome, new companion ! You may enter now haughty, and firm, and strong ! Ha ! ha ! soon like us ! soon like us ! " An uncertain and unholy light fell around, and deep silence reigned among the spectre-like group. Some I saw were young—very young—and, horrid to relate, there were several women among them ! One I recognised—I had known her in better days. She had been beautiful and glad of heart; now she was loathsome to behold. Filthy rags clung to her attenuated form, that had once floated buoyant in the joyous dance, the admired of every guest; a dull, spectre-like gleam broke from that once sunlike eye ! I, knew her well—but she recognised me not. Her past life, was blotted from her mind, and the smile of idiotcy flitted around her lips.

At sight of her I breathed a prayer of gratitude to heaven, that my poor Thekla had been, at least, spared this.

While I was watching this wretched group with half-averted eyes, I saw a sudden change pass over every countenance—a fierce wildness, unlike anything I had ever beheld—and turning round to discover the cause, I perceived that a large black curtain at one end of the vault had been drawn back, and an indistinct mass of machinery it had concealed was shifting and moving in silence amid the gloom. It was the rack ! while dim red lines looming forth, here and there, told that parts of it were heated !

They were led towards it, one by one ; the wretches gasped and moaned. I could not bear the sight, and closed my eyes, but as I heard those heart-breaking sounds and abject prayers, I felt a proud strength coursing through my veins, and I looked with a glance of edifying scorn upon the minions of tyranny waiting around me. They shall not wring one groan from me, I thought; I will shew them that my spirit, at least, is far beyond their power; would I were bound there now—and they shall see that man, if thus he chooses, cannot be conquered by man.

My turn came. I felt myself seized and hurried towards the engine. An involuntary tremor took away my breath, as I mounted the platform, and my limbs half refused their office, but I still bore up. All I remember is, rough hands grasping me—a pang, lost in a deadly sickening sensation—a reeling, dinning, stunning—and no more !

When consciousness returned, I found myself in the corner of a long passage, on the ground, chained, mangled, and bleeding; without strength, or power to move or speak. My tongue adhered to the roof of my mouth with raging thirsty fever ; my head had been compressed by the engine, and my eyes were starting from their sockets : I could not think on any one subject connectedly more than an instant—my resolution had vanished, my courage was gone—it is vain to deny it. I was cowed, abject, broken. What had been done to me I know not —but my sufferings must have been dreadful, though I remember them not ; for they had changed my heart, destroyed my very individuality. Good God ! Is the soul such a creature of the body, that it sinks with its wreck, like a mariner with his vessel !

A sudden commotion roused me from torpor. I looked up— there was a glare of torches shining on rich uniforms—a man stood over me—I heard him asking who I was ; his eye was like that of a wild animal, small, fierce, and restless ; his figure huge, square, and strong ; at every sound of his hoarse and stifled voice, a shudder ran through the paralysed wretches cowering around ; at every shade passing over his distorted features, that seemed a libel on the human face, each victim quailed in expectant terror ; for it was the Grand Duke Constantine, who towered above me, and never had nature more clearly stamped the character on the external form, than in the instance of this torturer of men.

He passed on. I dragged myself forward along the ground until I could stretch my neck round the corner of a buttress, and watch his course down the gallery.

As he proceeded, a still more deadly pallor than that with which the cold, clammy air of those infernal dungeons had literally coated the cheeks of his victims, came over their flaccid and imploring faces ; half naked they crawled from their corners, shewing their filthy rags and mortifying wounds, and in hoarse, unearthly voices whined for mercy ; some asked for but a sight of a green field or tree—but an hour's breathing in the sunshine, for the song of a bird, the perfume of a favourite flower, as their wild, sickly fancies clung with a morbid and almost childish love to some little wish or longing. Others, whom their fetters and remaining strength permitted so to do, rolled their bodies in his path, and howling frightful curses up towards him, tried to provoke an instantaneous death. In vain! He drunk the sounds with greedy ears, and an occasional stroke from the clotted whip he carried, sent them back yelling, and once more cowed with pain, like baffled beasts into their lairs. By the dim light of the torches, large, feverish, despairing eyes peered forth from every corner, and when out of sight, you might still tell the Grand Duke's progress through the distant passages, by the change of sounds that ran along his course, from the strong ravings of insanity, to the childish whining of broken-hearted age, or the repulsive gibbering of maudlin idiotcy.

At every sound denoting his progress, a convulsion shook the gaunt, shadowy limbs of those around, who listened with a strange and greedy eagerness to the infliction of that on others which they had endured themselves. Thus brutality can brutalise! and yet these had been the best of our country—the soldiers, statesmen, poets, teachers—the first of its sons, and the most lovely of its daughters.

At length a distant thundering of doors, and succeeding silence, told that the Grand Duke had completed his rounds, and nothing was heard but an occasional low moan, that never failed to elicit some sharp imprecation from those whom their neighbours' complainings roused from a lethargy, their only respite from despair.

Thus, often, the Grand Duke Constantine would hold his rounds, starting up from his table in the palace halls above, hot, mad and furious, when the unnatural longing for human blood came over him, and a ghastly desire for himself inflicting torture; while a fierce, demoniac kind of lust made him single out the women from that wretched crew, whom I have seen faint, and even die, beneath his hands.

This was the nature of a prince—one of those who are of the Lord's anointed, called special favourites of heaven, arrogating to themselves a heavenly mission for the governing of nations! Days—months—years passed. I was drafted from the dungeon on my way to the mine. The escort were passing near to Sandomire, when the voice of liberated Warsaw overtook them. Three wersts from here, they left me on the road—Behold me!

He ceased. He had commenced in low, tremulous tones, that died away in long intervals of exhaustion: but a wild, superhuman strength seemed to uphold him, and his voice was louder and clearer at the close, than when he began.

Scarcely had he ceased when the entire audience, whom eager sympathy had kept in silence, rose as with one impulse, and

loudly burst forth the cry of all, as with one voice; " Death to
the Russians ! " Liberty to Poland !" " Our cause is sacred !"
" Our arms shall be as strong as our cause !" and denunciations
of defiance and triumph, might soothe or sadden the failing spirit
of the captive.

" What are your arms ?" he asked, with a melancholy smile.

" Our wrongs !"

" In what rest your hopes ?"

" In ourselves !"

" And who form the rising ?"

" The nation !"

" Then you might dare a divided world," said the captive of
the Belvedere. " But oh ! *Does* the nation rise ? Who joins
your ranks ?"

" The noblemen of Poland, from the one end to the other !"

" Proceed ! you want more."

" The army—to a man !"

" Proceed—you want more."

" The church————."

" Proceed, you want more yet.—Oh ! does the *people* rise ?"

" We shall arm the *serfs*————."

" *You !* Not till the serfs arise and arm *themselves*, shall
Poland be regenerated. Your nobles, and your army, and
your church, are but as single waves in the mighty ocean ; they
may serve to toss a boat, that holds a king; but they can never
waft our fleets into the harbour. Oh ! listen to me, nobles !
patriots ! friends ! Give freedom and equal rights to all : array
the great body of the people for their country not for *yourselves* ;
let them be freemen before they are soldiers,—and there is a
chance of victory. But remember the words of a man, from
around whom suffering and approaching death have broken
down the pale of convention. Polish freemen will baffle
Russian slaves, but Polish serfs can never conquer Russian
soldiers."

There was an imploring earnestness in his tone, as he spoke
rapidly, leaning forward in his chair. He sunk back with the
effort, his head drooped slowly on his breast—and there was
silence, for his hours of trial were ended. The effort had
proved too much—the martyr was a saint.

" Poor Tyssen !" said prince Tsartima, " he had learned those
weak notions in the dungeons of the Belvedere."

" They say, truth is on the lips of the dying,"—exclaimed
the Palatine,—but the farmer knelt at the feet of the departed,
kissed his cold head, and murmured : " The words of a
prophecy !"

THE POOR MAN'S LEGAL MANUAL.

V. The Poor Laws.

SETTLEMENT AND REMOVAL.

In order to prevent the poor from suddenly flocking into the richest parishes, the law has ordained, that relief shall be given in and by that parish in which they have gained a settlement.

Paupers are said to be settled in a parish when they have fulfilled such conditions as entitle them to relief therein.

Settlements may be obtained by various modes; some are original—as apprenticeship, renting a tenement, paying taxes, &c.; others are derivative—viz. by marriage and by birth.

I.—*Settlement by birth.*

1. *Of legitimate children.*

The place of birth of a legitimate child is presumed to be his place of settlement; but if the settlement of his father be proved, then that, and not the place of birth, shall be deemed the child's settlement.

If the father have no settlement, and the mother's maiden settlement be proved, that shall be deemed the place of the child's settlement.

2. *Of illegitimate children.*

An illegitimate child follows the settlement of its mother until such child attain the age of sixteen; or shall acquire a settlement in its own right.

II.—*Settlement by marriage.*

By marriage, the wife immediately acquires the settlement of the husband, if he has one; if he has not, the wife retains her maiden settlement; but in the latter case she cannot be removed to the place of her maiden settlement, so as to separate her from her husband without his consent. Her settlement, during marriage, in such case is said to be suspended, but on the death of her husband it will revive.

A decision on this last point has been turned into a catch, which is thus given in *Sir James Burrow's Reports*, (p. 124.)

> " A woman having a settlement
> Married a man with none :
> The question was—He being dead,
> If that she had was gone ?
> Quoth Sir John Pratt.* ' Her settlement
> Suspended did remain
> Living the husband ; but him dead,
> It doth revive again.'" '
> *Chorus of Puisne† Judges.*
> " Living the husband ; but him dead,
> It doth revive again."

III.—*Settlement by hiring and service.*

By statute 4 and 5 W. 4, cap. 76, s. 64, it is enacted, that from and after the 14th of August, 1834, no settlement shall be acquired by hiring and service, or by residence under the same. We therefore think it unnecessary to consider this part of the subject, which was formerly both extensive and complicated.

IV.—*Settlement by apprenticeship.*

Any person bound an apprentice by indenture, and inhabiting any parish, will thereby gain a settlement.

V.—*Settlement by renting a tenement.*

By 4 and 5 Wm. 4, c. 76, s. 66, this settlement shall not be acquired after the 14th of August, 1834, unless the person occupying the tenement (that is house or land) shall have been assessed to the poor rate, and shall have paid the same in respect of such tenement for one year. The rent of the tenement must amount at least to £10. and must be paid by the person hiring the same, who must occupy for at least one year.

VI.—*Settlement by estate.*

A man who has an estate in land in a parish, however small its value, and whether freehold, copyhold, or for a term of years, and who resides forty days in the parish while he has the estate there, thereby gains a settlement. By 4 and 5 Wm. 4, c. 76, s. 68, it is enacted, that no

---

* Then chief justice.   † That is, judges inferior to the chief justice.

person shall retain such settlement for any longer time than he shall reside within ten miles of the parish.

VII.—*Settlement by payment of parochial taxes.*

By 6 Geo. 4, c. 57, s. 2, it is enacted, that no person shall acquire a settlement in any parish, by reason of paying rates or taxes for any tenement not being his or her own property, unless such tenement shall consist of a separate building or land rented at the sum of £10. a year, for the term of one year, and be occupied for that term and such rent be paid.

VIII.—*Settlement by serving an office* is abolished by 4 and 5 Wm. 4, c. 76, s. 64, after 14th Aug. 1834

We now come to the question of removal of the poor, by which means, as soon as they become chargeable to a parish in which they have not gained a settlement, they may in general be removed, or taken to their place of settlement. Before a pauper can be removed, he and other witnesses must be examined before two justices of the peace as to his settlement, &c., and by such justices the order for removal is to be made.

Scotch and Irish paupers may be removed or passed to their respective countries. Very recent and important alterations have been made in the law of removal, and more extensive changes are anticipated. It was a great hardship that a poor man should be taken away from a parish, where he had resided for a long period, and where he had made friends, who might in time be able to employ him again, and that he should suddenly be taken to a place where, perhaps, he was born, but to which he had been a stranger ever since his birth. This was not only breaking asunder every association of place and person which might have been formed during his life, but also, by throwing him among persons who cared not for him, deprived him of the opportunity of leaving the workhouse for employment again. In part to remedy this, the statute 9 and 10 Vic. c. 66, was passed in 1846. By that act no person is to be removed from any parish in which he or she shall have resided for five years next before the application for the removal. The time during which a person shall be a prisoner or soldier, or sailor, or shall receive relief, shall be excluded in the computation of this period.

No widow shall be removed for twelve months after the death of her husband (s. 2.)

No child under the age of sixteen, whether legitimate or illegitimate, shall be removed in any case where its father, mother, step-father, step-mother, or reputed father, with whom it is residing, may not be removed from the parish (s. 3.)

No person who has become chargeable by sickness, or accident, shall be removed, unless the justices state in their warrant for the removal, that they are satisfied the sickness, or accident, will produce permanent disability (s. 4.)

Any officer unlawfully procuring the removal of poor persons, shall, on conviction thereof before any justice, forfeit any sum not exceeding £5 nor less than 40s. (s. 6.)

This statute has been amended by 10 and 11 Vic. c. 110, (passed in July, 1847) but only as to the expenditure incurred under it.

One of the latest acts relating to the poor generally, is 10 and 11 Vic. c. 109, which is a proof that the legislature are at length yielding, on this subject, to the pressure from without. Among other provisions, it is enacted by it, that certain members of the government shall from their very office be Poor Law Commissioners, so that they may be responsible both in and out of parliament. By another of its sections (s. 23.) married persons, above sixty years of age, shall not be separated in a workhouse.

NATIONAL LITERATURE.

As we announced in the preceding number, we purpose editing, under the above title, a series of articles illustrative of the national literature of continental Europe. The plan we intend to observe in illustration of this object, is not to give a dry *resumé* or digest of the collective productions of a nation, but to take, as specimens of the whole, some of its leading works, in the different walks of literature, from which the reader will be best able to judge of the characteristics of the people; since, as a general rule, those works only obtain a lasting popularity, which are a reflex of the popular mind and feeling. We also intend to advert principally to the authors of modern times, as most congenial to our present purpose, and will commence our illustrations with—

I.—POLAND.

In perusing the works of Polish authors, the reader must recollect the peculiar circumstances under which they were written; either in the confusion of civil war, under the weight of slavery, or amid the sorrow of exile. We therefore find much of a melancholy spirit pervading the emanations of the Polish muse; a leaning to dreamy abstractions skilfully blended with harsh realities; and, as the undercurrent but controlling influence of all, a religious mysticism guiding or perverting the moral of the work. This is often the concomitant of slavery. The fettered will, the curbed aspiration after freedom tries to find a vent in the shadowy dreamland, beyond the reach of earthly tyrants; cherishes a devout hope of, at least, spiritual liberation, and indemnifies itself in a transmundane future, for the earthly sufferings of a perishable present. Thus we find religious traditions lingering among enslaved nations, of some distant but still certain time, in which a divine liberator should appear, to lead the captives back to peace and independence. Thus the Negro, the Zingara, and the Jew look to the Messiah of their varying creeds. Thus even the slaves of Christendom long for their anticipated millenium; thus the Pole believes his subjection to the Moscovite, to be only a period of infliction and probation entailed by the past transgressions of his people; sees in the Czar only an instrument of divine punishment, and confidently awaits the hour when, the phial of wrath being turned, he shall once more enjoy in peace and independence the heritage of his fathers. Falsely has it been said that man is prone to despond. Hope is the elastic spring that ever keeps pushing him up beyond the gulf of misery, and, bounding even from the grave, lifts the withering atom into the paradise of a god.

The superstitious feeling of mingled hope and resignation to which we have alluded, is, though a pervading, not, we trust, an universal feeling of the Polish people. We believe that the majority are beginning to read the lesson of suffering in its true character; namely, that the people are being punished for their blind subjection to priests, kings, and nobles—the childish love of rotten institutions—and that they have learned, the time in which they shall recover their liberty, is that in which they have arrived at a knowledge of its true use in the abolition of class distinctions, and the equality of all.

The besetting failing of religious enthusiasm and melancholy is, however, apparent in the works of most Polish authors—a leaning to the spirit world, as the patriot, disheartened with the real, seeks in the ideal his comfort or his triumph. It is this pervading thought which gives a tone to the writings of

COUNT KRASINSKI

with whose "*Infernal Comedy*" we will endeavour to make our readers acquainted. This work is considered to be one of the finest, if not the finest, in the Polish language. It is a prophecy. It supposes the state of the world about the year 2,000, and imagines all mankind to be divided into two parties—that of the new-men, at war with the old. The Communists and Pantheists struggling with the men of the old faith, the old customs and old institutions. Traditionary glory and democratic innovation are at war; they have striven long; the latter has been in the ascendency, and now the last stand is to be made, the last battle fought between democracy and chivalry.

Truly, a great theme for a poet—but a difficult one. If he were a patriot, partiality might lead him to paint the champion of feudalism in colours of too dark a die; if he were an aristocrat, he might be tempted to depict aristocracy in too fair a light. Count Krasinski was both, yet he did neither. It was obvious that, in order to render justice to his theme, he must make the leaders of either party equally great, equally well-intentioned, equally heroic: he must place chivalry and democracy side by side—give them a fair start, and allow his reader to be the umpire of the race. This last the poet has not done. He judges the cause himself—he attempts to force his judgment on the reader, and arrives at a conclusion, perhaps unrivalled for poetical grandeur—but defective in its practical and philosophic truth, as bearing on the subject matter of the drama. When we assert that Krasinski has dealt impartially between democracy and chivalry, we think that the very nature of his plot goes far to bias the reader in favour of the aristocratic hero; the domestic sympathies are raised more around him, than around his opponent; the gentler feelings are enlisted most in his behalf—but the poet has nicely drawn the distinction between the individual and the cause, and while he slightly inclines you towards one of the rival leaders, deals, at least, fairly with the rival principles. Indeed, Krasinski appears to look down on the contending parties, and to see in the triumph of neither cause the end of human misery. The author stands aloof, and with a feeling of scornful pity watches the struggle. We wonder how a man, tossed in the political convulsions of his country, can thus keep clear of the vortex of party. The solution is given in the personal history of the poet. Belonging to one of the noblest families of Poland, his democratic feelings led him to espouse the cause of progression, and dissevered him from his aristocratic associates. But in the ranks of democracy he was met with the same coldness he exhibited towards his peers. His crime was being the son of a man hated by the people. His father, Vincent Krasinski, famous as a soldier under Napoleon — whose Polish lancers he had commanded—when a senator of the kingdom of Poland, was the only member who, against the otherwise unanimous acquittal of the senate, voted for the condemnation of the Polish conspirators in the insurrection of Pestel and Troubetskoi. Detested by his countrymen, the stigma attaching to his name descended to his son, who was repulsed by the Polish patriots, and hated by the Polish nobility. Weaned from all personal sympathy with either party, he was thus abstracted from party feeling, and enabled to produce a drama, which conquered prejudice, and won a reception that had been denied its author.

The " Infernal Comedy" (the very name of which shews the bitter satire lurking in the author's mind), represents the world as on the brink of a crowning change. The men of the old forms, the upholders of past institutions, are, as a class, exhausted; they are the worn out representatives of a worn out system—the priest is a tame reciter of cold formulæ—the soldier a military machine; and priest and soldier are the two last chief agents of the aristocratic drama. One man alone represents the brilliancy, the energy, and the intellect of the poet—that man is Count Henry, the last of the nobles. On the other hand, the men of the new world—the communists and democrats — are fierce, strong, active and triumphant; but these are blind instruments in the hands of a mighty leader named Pancrates, from πας and κρατια, the " all-strong." Thus we have, after all, two *personalities* arranged against each other—each, it is true, embracing and typifying a sovereign idea; but, we warn our author that he has here made a grand mistake in the design of his work—since an idea, forced by the will of one man on blind millions, will be very different in its results, from that same idea conceived, and therefore appreciated, by enlightened nations. Here Krasinski has been a false prophet; since we do believe, that men will no longer follow the blind instruments of individual intellect, but, on the contrary, reason and act for themselves. The author has made the universal insurrection merely the ebullition of brute force, the cry of hunger for bread, of suffering for revenge. We confidently anticipate that mind will be the immediate agent of the future movement; that the desire after rights withheld will be greater than the mere physical craving; that the people's energies will take a nobler turn, and that, as they desire " right to all," so they will inflict wrong on none.

Again, the author has made his democratic hero inaccessible to all the the feelings of humanity; a cold, mighty intellect, removed from human sympathy; whereas the strength, the promise and the pride of modern democracy is in the triumph of the *humane;* the vindication of domestic rights against the harsh calculating policy of political economists; and the claim of the man to individual happiness in antithesis to that system which seeks national aggrandisement at the cost of internal prosperity. The scene of the drama has been aptly and patriotically laid by the author in Poland; thus, the theatre of the greatest suffering has been made that in which the dramatist supposes the final triumph to be enacted.

Resident in his hereditary castle, the descendant of illustrious sires, Count Henry still maintains the old magnificence of the Sarmatian noble. With a fiery spirit and proud aspirations, he stands, a thing of fire, amid the withered forms of the old world. Unhappy in marriage, he has allied himself with a being—quiet, good, amiable; but in his eyes tame, dull, prosaic. The placid partner is not appreciated by the restless, *un*domestic spirit of the count. She has no thrilling response to his words : " Thou shall now be the living song of my life ! " Placidly she answers : " I will always be to thee a faithful and submissive wife." Years fly—and home becomes unbearable; not because the husband is bad or the wife in fault, but because the count falls into that pitiable, but frequent error of gifted men—that domestic duties and domestic happiness are incompatible with public life or poetic inspirations. The secret is thus solved : the count is creative of intellect, and not of feeling.

Beautifully is the character of the countess developed : the meek, placid wife endeavouring to render herself a worthy companion of her gifted husband—her blind husband—who, in this very effort, ought to have seen the due appreciation of his greatness, and bowed in homage before the ennobling affection of her heart; the fond mother, striving to instil the elements of genius in their child, that his father might love him! Ah! genius is a dangerous companion! They tried to draw the lightning from heaven, and it killed them!

The christening scene gathers the various fragments of old customs and old society before us; and powerfully is its cold, worn-out, formal state depicted in the priest, who brings no fervour, no life, into that only part of a decaying system, which could still prolong its withering vitality—superstition, which has made religion the handmaiden of tyranny. The wife, however, prays with fervour: "I bless thee, oh my child! may the angel of poesy watch over thee, and inspire thee, that so thy father may love thee!"

The vain effort to rise beyond her nature, bewilders the brain of the poor wife, and one day, on Count Henry's return to his home, he finds that the countess has been taken to a madhouse! The gentle, placid wife—intense image of woman's love! The conscience-stricken husband hurries after her, and, as the domestic portion of the tragedy is gradually coming to a close, with admirable skill the poet has made the political storm sound upon us from the distance. The representatives of society, in its state of disorganisation, are gathered in the madhouse. The religious and political prejudices find their organs in the tongues of the maniacs:—

" *Voice from the right :* You have dared to bind your creator—to crucify Jesus Christ.

" *Voice from the left :* To the guillotine! *à la lanterne,* hang up all kings and nobles!

" *Voice from the right :* Kneel! kneel! I am your legitimate sovereign!"

We must here admire the skill with which the poet has gradually introduced, and closely interwoven, the political with the domestic part of his tragedy; and, indeed, the reader may behold a satirical truism in the fact, that all these cries are made to come alike from *maniacs!*

The count endeavours to draw his wife away from this scene :—*

* The extracts from the original given here are transcribed, with but trifling variations, from a very able translation of the same by a popular writer.

" *The Count :* Come, take my hand, and let us leave this place.

" *The Wife :* Oh no ! I cannot; my soul has left my body; I feel it all concentrated in my brain.

" *The Count :* Come, the carriage waits us.

" *The Wife :* No, leave me ; I shall be worthy of thee, by and by.

" *The Count :* What do you mean ?

" *The Wife :* Since I have lost thee, a change has come over me : I have cried to the Lord—I have offered a taper on the altar of the Lady of the Purification, and on the third day I awakened the creative intellect of genius. Now thou wilt no longer slight me ; thou wilt not leave me to night, is it not so ?

" *The Count :* Neither by night nor day.

" *The Wife :* See, am I not now thy equal in power ? It is given me to understand all things—to find inspiration ; and I can burst forth in words and songs of triumph. I will sing of the seas, of the thunder, of the firmament, of the stars, and of the storms. But there is a strange word troubles me —————— the struggle ! Oh, let me see—lead me where I may witness the struggle !

" *The Count :* Come, will you not see your child ?

" *The Wife :* Oh ! my child is not here—it has flown away ; I gave it wings—I have sent it through the universe to imbue itself with all that is beautiful, and great, and terrible ; and when it returns, it will understand thee."

(*The voices of the patients without intrude again.*)

" *Voice from the left :* I have slain their monarchs : ten are left, and that may not be ————— there are some hundred priests, too, remaining ; I hear them at their mass.

" *The Wife :* Ah ! what a wicked game !

" *The Count :* True.

" *The Wife :* What would happen if God should become mad too ? Each worm would cry out, I am God, and one after another perish in its pride. . . Then even the Saviour could no longer save. Behold him take into his hands the Cross and cast it into the abyss. Hearest thou that cross, the hope of the wretched ? Hark ! how it crashes, as it bounds from star to star, and scatters through the universe, the fragments of its wreck ! There is but the Holy Virgin, who still prays ————— but she, too, will go whither the whole universe is going.

" *The Count :* You suffer ?

"*The Wife:* Oh yes! I feel as if an oscillating lamp were suspended in my brain—'tis insupportable."

We know of few things more truthful in description or more sad than this scene. The delineation of the bewildered brain is perfect—first, if we may use the expression, the consistent continuity of the one thought—then the wavering, the losing the thread, depicted in the words: "But there is a strange word troubles me—*the struggle!*"—the tremendous conception "if God should grow mad!"—and, thrilling through all, the undying fountain of a mother's love, while even the puerile superstitions of the bigot receive nobility from the suffering and affection of the woman.

One after another, the bonds of domestic happiness wither around Count Henry. The mother has, indeed, kindled the fire of inspiration in the child, but the body wanes before the spirit.

Was ever anything of the kind more beautiful than the following description ?—

"Child, why neglect thy toys and dolls? King of the flies and butterflies, the intimate of Pulchinello, what mean thy blue eyes so downcast, yet so bright and pensive, though thou hast only seen the flowers of so few springs? Already dost thou bow thy young brow down, and lean it on thy hand as if in reverie, and thy little head seems filled with thoughts as a flower with morning dew.

"When shaking thy fair curls aside, thou lookest up to heaven, tell me what seest thou there, and with whom dost thou converse? for then thy little brow seems clouded. Thy mother weeps and deems thou dost not love her; thy little cousins, and thy friends are hurt that thou neglectest them; thy father alone says nothing, he looks on gloomily, and silently, till his eyes fill with tears, which he suppresses and turns back into his soul. * * * *.

"And yet thou growest and becomest fair, though without youth's freshness; without the delicate whiteness of milk; the blush of the red strawberry. Thy beauty is the beauty of mysterious thought, which breathes upon thy brow, like the shadow of a world invisible; and though the lustre of thine eye is sometimes dimmed, though thy cheek is sometimes pale, thy little bosom oppressed—still all who meet thee pause, and observe, "How beautiful a child!"

"If a flower, when it begins to fade, had a sparkling soul, a breath of Heaven to animate it; if on each of its petals earthwards borne, there weighed, instead of a drop of dew, an angelic thought, then such a flower would resemble thee, fair child ! "

The mother dies in her husband's arms, and the father leads his child to pray on her grave. Here the first symptoms of insanity become apparent in the boy, who, instead of the touching prayer of the "Ave Maria," diverges into a beautifully graceful form of adoration to the "Queen of the Spring and of the Flowers!" The father interrupts the wild, but touching prayer—while a strange link of mysterious sympathy is hinted at in the supposition, that the child sees its mother, whom living it had never known, in its slumbers, and in repeating her fancied words, recites almost the very same she had used of her child, when living and struck with insanity.

"Can it be," exclaims the father, "that the last thoughts of the dying follow them into eternity ? Are there blest spirits—for assuredly she is blest—are there, then, blest spirits tainted with earthly madness ? "

The poor child is subsequently struck with madness, and in the consultation scene with the doctor, we are appalled by the father endeavouring to scrutinise the wisdom of providence, and by the physician coldly and professionally examining the child's eyes, admiring their formation, and pedantically explaining the origin and nature of the malady. Amid this abstraction of the father, this heartlessness of the attendant, we are refreshed by a gush of genuine feeling and emanation of the humane on the part of a humble, neglected and uneducated servant girl, who prays to the Holy Virgin that she will take out *her* eyes, and give them to the poor blind child. Gloriously, in this slight touch of feeling, has the poet vindicated human nature in the person of the lovely and the oppressed.

A few pages suffice to narrate all this; but, by this brief and masterly sketch—this tragedy within his tragedy—the poet has awakened a personal and domestic interest in the characters of his drama, and we can now sympathise with them, amidst the colder elements of political change by which they are surrounded.

The storm now bursts over Europe, and its deluging waters come sweeping onward from the West, destroying the stereotyped forms of society, with all their old institutions, till at length all has vanished before its fury—the old world is at an end, save that its last wreck is concentrated within the town and castle of Count Henry. Here, princes, nobles, merchants, bankers—all the feelings, all the relics of the past are gathered under the guidance of this widowed father of a blind and maniac boy. He is the last pillar left standing of a mighty ruin. The affections of the past have withered around him,—its cold forms still cling to his banner,—and in his heart he harbours the vain · desire to impress the stamp of the old world and the old faith upon the changed and the new. He believes in the eternity of the past, and stands there as the antithesis of Pancrates, opposing, in his person, all the good of the old to all the great of the new. With what effect, and with what truth, remains to be seen.

The world, all but this spot, has been conquered by the democratic leader. Millions of men in arms have deluged earth with blood—every thing is prostrate, everything is levelled before them, save this one spot, and now they have come in their countless myriads, besieging it on every side. The incarnations of either party are played at once before the reader. The count is alone, pacing the great hall of his castle, hung with banners, trophies, and portraits of his ancestors through far-back generations, when a servant announces an expected visitor; it is PANCRATES, the people's leader, who, like Charles the Twelfth, at Dresden, ventures alone into the stronghold of his foe and rival, to admonish him before the hour of the last great struggle.

(*To be concluded in our next.*)

END OF VOLUME THE SECOND.

Lightning Source UK Ltd.
Milton Keynes UK
UKOW06f0755260117
292875UK00001B/67/P